BEHIND THE SCENES AT THE MUSEUM OF BAKED BEANS

BEHIND THE SCENES AT THE MUSEUM OF BAKED BEANS

MY SEARCH FOR BRITAIN'S MADDEST MUSEUMS

HUNTER DAVIES

ISIS
LARGE PRINT
Oxford

Copyright © Hunter Davies, 2010

First published in Great Britain 2010
by
Virgin Books
An imprint of Ebury Publishing

Published in Large Print 2011 by ISIS Publishing Ltd.,
7 Centremead, Osney Mead, Oxford OX2 0ES
by arrangement with
Ebury Publishing
A Random House Group Company

Hunter Davies has asserted his right to be identified
as the author of this work

British Library Cataloguing in Publication Data
Davies, Hunter, 1936–
    Behind the scenes at the Museum of Baked Beans.
    1. Museums - - Great Britain.
    2. Museum curators - - Great Britain.
    3. Eccentrics and eccentricities - - Great Britain.
    4. Curiosities and wonders - - Great Britain.
    5. Large type books.
    I. Title
    069'.0941–dc22

02/16   ISBN 978–0–7531–5279–9 (hb)
         ISBN 978–0–7531–5280–5 (pb)

Printed and bound in Great Britain by
T. J. International Ltd., Padstow, Cornwall

For Amarisse and Sienna, who will be starting off on their own travels soon . . .

Contents

Introduction

I've often had this fantasy of opening a museum. All collectors, big and small, old and new, rich and poor, have been struck at some time in the night or the half-awake day or after a particularly long lunch by this mad notion. It's a human weakness, a natural desire, to share or display one's pleasures.

Some collectors fall so in love with their own collections, spend so much time and energy and thought on them, that one day they think, I know, why not reveal my private passion to the outside world? Wouldn't the world be very pleased? Why be selfish? Let others enjoy what I have enjoyed.

It can of course disguise other, baser motives. Such as the desire to show off. Look at the treasures I have collected, clever old me. I have created something unique and wonderful, and spent a fortune in the process, oh yes, it hasn't been cheap, and now the world will see what a cultured and knowledgeable and wealthy person I am and, if I create my own museum, with of course my name on it, the world will be bound to admire me, for ever.

This is what oft happens at the top end, with mega-plutocrats from America to Russia, with dictators and presidents, but it can also creep into the mind of the more ordinary, humble, everyday collector. You've got to the stage when your collection seems to be taking over your life, your house, spilling out of every crevice, drawer and wall, of your home and of your brain. You are getting fed up with all this stuff, though not as much as your loved ones are. What can you do with it? Where is it all going? What is the point? You've probably by now accumulated enough rubbish to open your own museum; heh, that's an idea, never thought of that before.

Should this notion ever enter your head, for whatever reason, then it is obvious what any sensible, rational person should do — ignore it. Well, it is mad — isn't it? Who would want to turn a part-time amusement into a full-time occupation? We might love our own little bits and pieces, but deep down, most of us are aware they are puny, piddling, loads of people must be bound to have much better examples, so who on earth would want to come and look at our stuff, even for free, even if we paid them?

Collectors know, only too well, that on the whole we are alone, the vast majority of people in our day-to-day lives seem to be totally disinterested if not actively antagonistic to the things that we find so fascinating. This always comes as a sad realisation but it has to be admitted and faced — if only to spur us on, damn it, what do they know? What do they care? I'll show them.

On the other hand, there are loads of us out there, doing similar things, thinking similar thoughts. I'm always surprised by how many people are collectors, who have themselves got little collections tucked away, or just things they have not yet thrown out. It's estimated that a third of the population in the UK are collectors — and in North America and Europe, for collectors tend to be thickest in the developed world, for obvious reasons. Hard to find money to buy a penny black if your daily struggle is to afford a penny loaf.

That means that some twenty million people in the UK must be collectors, of some sort. The popularity of the *Antiques Roadshow*, of eBay, or car-boot sales, does suggest that there are millions of us.

This apparent contradiction — that there are millions of other collectors, we are in fact not alone, yet people seem not to be interested in my stuff — can be seen as a challenge. Obsessive collectors do tend to be interested mostly in what they themselves collect, in fact they have to be single-minded to carry on, but surely the majority of people tuning in to *Antiques Roadshow* are willing to be interested in anything that is, er, interesting. However you define it. I know I am. I honestly do love other people's collections, almost as much as my own, regardless of the subject, amount or value.

Collecting used to be the preserve of the rich and powerful, of emperors and popes, kings and lordlings, who acquired gold and silver, precious objects, statues and ornaments, paintings and pottery, holy relics, or what are often referred to simply as antiquities, often by stealing, then putting them on display to show how rich and powerful they were.

By around the seventeenth century, well-off gentlemen had started to arrange their more modest collections in their own homes, creating what they called a "cabinet of curiosities". Natural history collections became very popular amongst ordinary folks as well as scientists and geologists, with people collecting fossils, shells, birds' eggs, plants, insects.

In the nineteenth century, with the urban wealth created by the Industrial Revolution, large-scale exhibitions were mounted such as the Great Exhibition of 1851, which inspired collectors big and small, and was followed by the creation of many of our famous provincial museums in major metropolitan centres, such as Liverpool in 1851, Nottingham in 1878. In London, the British Museum was established in 1753, the National Gallery in 1824 and the V&A in 1852.

We now appear to be in something of a postmodern period. Collecting has become open, democratic, eclectic. You don't have to follow what has gone before, you can create your own, unique collection — or what you think is unique but it usually turns out that someone somewhere has thought of the same thing, whether it's airline sick bags, mobile phones or baked beans, which you thought were really off-the-wall, mad ideas, till you find there's already an airline sick bag society and a mobile phone group, each with their own meetings, magazines, committees and rows — for once collectors gather together, clashes appear.

Take baked beans, for example. I like to think that on my journey I am going to visit the world's first collector of baked beans, with his very own museum, but I know the moment I have written that sentence, which I just have, see it burning bright in 10 point Galliard, that someone will be jumping and saying, I was first, I was miles ahead, baked beans, that was my idea, come and visit me instead.

There are no rules any more. You can collect anything you like and, if you are daft enough, open your own museum to celebrate your own individual passion.

And this is what is happening more and more often in Britain today. Our big national and municipal museums and galleries are world-famous, brilliant, amazing, awesome, how can any individual mortal compete? Yet all the time, ordinary people are having a go in their own ordinary, eccentric modest ways. And this is one of the reasons why I still find myself thinking, despite myself, that if they can do it, why can't I? Why keep all my collections to myself?

I collected as a child — the usual things, stamps, marbles, comics, cigarette packets, swapping and scavenging, rather than actually paying money, though relations might buy me a packet of assorted stamps and a cheap album from Woolies at Christmas time. I loved the collecting process, seeing how many I could get, and I also loved looking at them. When I had asthma and was lying in bed wheezing, I found that turning over the pages of my stamp album, thinking of all the countries I had scarcely heard of and never expected to visit, took my mind off my ailments when all medications had failed. Half an hour later, I would get up, my breathing back to normal. Oh, there is a lot to be said for the therapeutic properties of collecting. And perhaps even looking at other people's collections, as we shall discover.

I gave it up as a teenager, went on to other more exciting things, like life, work, family, home, but then suddenly in my forties I found myself returning to collecting. I became a born-again collector, which I now know is a fairly well-observed phenomenon, and started madly, wildly, excitedly, on a collecting odyssey, which so far has not left me.

During those fallow years, when I had not apparently been a collector — not apparent anyway to myself — I had in fact still been an accumulator, never knowingly going out and collecting but never knowingly or willingly throwing anything out. So when I came back to collecting, I found I had squirrelled away various things, such as letters from prime ministers I had interviewed in the course of my work, which I then decided to expand, to go out to seek and find other examples, at car-boots, stalls, auctions, fairs.

The result today is that I have twenty or so different collections, on different topics, though along the way I have dumped a few things which I grew sick of, or furious with, or disappointed by, for various reasons. Which we might come to.

I used to dream of being rich enough to buy a house with twenty rooms so I would have a different room for each of my twenty collections. Or perhaps a second house, and keep that purely for my collections. Beatrix Potter did something similar with Hill Top. She kept that as a sort of museum, using it from time to time, while doing her actual living with her husband in another house nearby, Castle Cottage.

I do have two houses, as we divide each year in half, between London and the Lake District, working away in each place, and my room in each is filled with my stuff, and the hall, and the bathroom wall, and any other spaces I can get away with, but I still have too much stuff stuffed away that I never look at and no one else sees. I am sure they would like to, so I still think, when that daft old fantasy rears itself once again — is it too late? Is it really a nonsense?

I am fascinated by all the people who have created their own museums, turning their daft dreams into reality. How did they do it and why? Was it just to share their passion or are they driven by other complicated motives that I can't yet imagine?

So I decided to set off round Great Britain in search of Mad Museums. I use the term "mad" because that is so often how others see such people, as eccentric, obsessive, weird, and their collections as potty, pathetic, pointless — viewpoints I would never express and attitudes I certainly don't share, for I understand too well the strange compulsion to collect.

I wondered, as I set off, if I would learn more about myself and my own passions by talking to them. If there would be patterns, common denominators, or would they turn out to be a random bunch, who just happened to have ended up running museums?

By Mad Museum, I mean something specific — a museum devoted to just one subject, one single topic. That is the vital distinction. Otherwise it's a gallery of assorted items, a collection of collections, which is how most museums have traditionally been organised. There are loads and loads of them, all over the world, in every little town. A Mad Museum must be more or less unique. OK, I know a thing is either unique or it's not — most of the museums I plan to visit most definitely are.

My other object is to seek out, where possible, the person who is, or was, the original creator of this Mad Museum, the guiding spirit. I am hoping that in as many Mad Museums as possible I will find the only creator still there, still running it, so I will get the benefit of their enthusiasm, experience, knowledge. I will want to know as much about his or her life, and associated madnesses, as about their museum's contents.

I plan to avoid the famous ones, the national museums and galleries we all know and are so proud of, which attract millions of visitors every year. We do have some of the best, most magnificent on the planet, with the British Museum attracting six million visitors in a year.

I also aim to miss out the big municipal museums, as they tend on the whole to cover a variety of topics. In many cases, they were indeed begun by an individual collector, many decades ago, but have been added to by donations, gifts and acquisitions. Inside many of these local museums there are mad exhibitions, dopey little collections, many of them fascinating, but I am looking for single-issue, stand-alone museums, devoted to just one thing.

I certainly am not looking for visitor experiences, for audio-visual excitements, for technological wonders, for interactive displays and amusements. Dear God, I'll run a mile from all those. I don't want state-of-the-art but dusty, old, real objects and, if possible, to be able to touch and smell them.

Nor do I want corporate exhibitions, even if they are free, PR exercises put on by dodgy industries to show us how caring they are. And I'll be avoiding exhibitions that are purely commercial, created to bring in paying punters, that are little more than theme parks, or part of some bigger franchise or entertainment conglomerate.

The museums I am looking for must be amateur, modest, low-tech affairs, many of which will probably turn out to be hidden away in back rooms, holes in walls, converted shops and warehouses, rarely ever professionally designed museum spaces. In these sorts of places I don't expect queues, bossy attendants ordering you to move around in a certain order at a certain time. I am sure I will be mostly left to my own devices, to wander round, to ponder and wonder, not always being able to find the madman — I mean inspiration — behind it all. Mad Museums represent a very quirky way of life — very British I was about to say, but America and Europe also have their share of the daft, the eccentric, the obsessive.

I expect among the museum creators and curators to find kindred spirits — or will I? Will they be as different as their collections, as different as their own differing life stories and motivations? They might be a dreadful warning to me. Or perhaps they will prove an inspiration and that old fantasy about opening my own museum will pop into my head again. Oh yes, it's still there. But will my journey round the Mad Museums be the end of it?

CHAPTER ONE

The Fan Museum, Greenwich

I'm not sure why I decided to begin with fans. I know nothing at all about them, have never had any interest in them. Perhaps that was part of the attraction. If you think you know something about a subject, even just a little, or have some similar stuff yourself, then you have a tendency to go round saying oh I've seen that, I've got this, huh, thought they would have had that.

I like to think I can understand and appreciate why anyone collects anything, without knowing much about the object itself, but this would be a test, to see if something I am totally ignorant about can engage and stimulate and fascinate. Anyway, everyone knows what a fan looks like, don't they? It's fan-shaped. Isn't it?

It also sounded a classic one-subject museum, devoted to one finite topic, not mixed up with other similar subjects. It was begun by the person who is still running it, so that was an extra, vital plus.

And it did seem sensible to start in London, before fanning out, around the country. And I fancied going to Greenwich again. Quite an adventure, for someone living in North London who normally never goes south of the river, if it is south of the river. I never gets the bends right once the Thames starts messing around, doubling back on itself.

It did feel quite exotic, as if I had arrived abroad, especially coming on the Docklands Light Railway, a wonderful relief after the horrors of the Northern Line. It was a sunny summer's day with lots of tourists around for Greenwich is a tourist-trap, with the Maritime Museum and the Park and all that, yet it somehow didn't feel touristy or honeypot-ish. Greenwich is not Blackpool or Brighton. It is too classy to lower its skirts, wiggle its hips, give unnecessary come-hither winks and nudges. It has also attracted some grand, classy people over the years.

I was last here, let me think, forty years ago, when I came to interview Cecil Day Lewis, who was then the Poet Laureate, married to the actress Jill Balcon. Their son Daniel Day Lewis must have been about twelve or thirteen the day I went to their house, but I don't remember him.

I do remember their grand Georgian house was in Crooms Hill, perhaps the best address in all Greenwich. Which is where the fan museum happens to be situated. Another reason for wanting to see it.

Helene Alexander herself came to the front door of the museum, which I could see was in fact two Georgian gems, a matching pair, formed into one even grander piece of architectural jewellery.

She herself is rather grand, not tall but very stately, artistocratic even, and sometimes talks of herself as "one", with a slightly foreign accent which I couldn't place at first, one of those European ladies of a certain age and era, well travelled, highly cultured, used to staff, telling others what to do, but with great courtesy and politeness.

She was on the reception desk, as her other member of staff that day had gone for lunch, selling the tickets, answering the phone. "Fan Muse-ee-um," she said, enunciating every letter. She didn't give her name, or reveal that she was the director, that it was her museum, containing four thousand fans, so the museum leaflet states, many of which she herself has collected, the only dedicated fan museum in the world. How did she begin? How does anybody begin collecting anything?

The idea of four thousand of them, though, that was a bit difficult to take in, or even believe. Different fans? Surely not. Surely there are only, let me see, a few hundred actually different ones in the whole world, but even while still half-thinking this silly thought I corrected myself. As a collector, I know you can have as many items in your collection as you can collect.

I wandered round on my own while she attended to members of the public who arrived in dribs and drabs. They mainly seemed to be single women in their forties, who stood in reverence before each case. There was a hush and seriousness to the fan museum, a feeling of academia, not the amateur, scruffy, hobbyishness of my own dear collections.

Then a cockney family, couple and teenage daughter, arrived, paid their money and stood looking, wondering where to begin. The mother and her daughter went over together to a glass case, ooh-ing and aah-ing at a caseful of fans while the father remained at the doorway.

"Too girly for you, is it?" said the mother, smiling sideways at her daughter.

"Whatjamean?" replied the man.

"I mean are you not coming in?"

"I'm reading this," he said, pointing to a long introductory notice in the doorway. "As you're supposed to."

He was right and she was right. In theory, in most museums, there is an order, picture storyboards perhaps, which explain the background and introduce you to what you are about to see, or just some blunt arrows, bossing you the correct way, directing you from case to case, room to room. If of course you can see them. Usually, I find myself, like the women, going to the first thing that looks interesting, only later realising there has been a plan, a carefully worked-out arrangement, which afterwards I might go back and follow. Or not.

I was waiting for Mrs Alexander. When her assistant had relieved her, she led me into a lift — that was a surprise, you don't expect lifts in a Georgian gem — to her office, where she called another member of her staff to make some tea, if he could be so kind, which then appeared in perfect little china cups.

Helene was born in Alexandria in Egypt in 1932, one of four daughters of a wealthy Jewish-Egyptian landowner and gentleman farmer, Victor Adda. They had an English nanny and lots of staff. Every summer, her mother and father would set sail for three months in Europe, taking their grandmother, aunts, plus all the daughters and nanny.

"It was really a caravanserai, when we set off, with so many people, so much luggage. We would go to Venice, where Mummy bought her table linen. We'd go to Florence where Mummy always got her underwear. In Paris, Granny bought her hats. In London, we bought children's clothes, and my father would go to see his chums at the British Museum. I remember a Mr Baldwin, whose relations, I think, are still connected with the numismatic department."

Helene's father was a world-renowned collector of coins, specialising in the Roman and Ptolemaic periods. He also collected paintings, as did several other members of his family, but coins were his first love. As a little girl, Helene did collect, but just dolls. She had a large doll's house and filled it with dolls of all the nations, brought back by relations or acquired when she herself was on her Grand Tour with her papa.

She was eventually sent to the French Lycée in Alexandria, where she learned fluent French (having already learned Italian), then in the early 1950s she came to London to learn theatre design at the Central School of Arts and Crafts, going on to study for a degree in art history at the University of London.

"My money ran out during my studies so I had to complete my degree at night classes. I did some work as a teacher, helping young ladies to get finished by teaching them about art. In London, during the Suez

15

Crisis, as an Egyptian I was looked upon as an alien, despite being Jewish, which wasn't very pleasant."

In 1958 she was married to A V Alexander-Dickie, whom she had first met on a family holiday in Scotland. He had gone off from Cambridge to do his national service and then become a successful insurance broker in the City.

"I knew him all my life. Growing up, I used to met him in Cairo as his father was an international lawyer who worked in Cairo for a while. It was a coincidence, I suppose, always meeting him — and of course even more so that he was called Alexander, the name of the place where I was born. It must have been meant."

They lost two children as babies, one after the other, which was a terrible tragedy, but then later they had a daughter Suzannah.

Helene took a job, unpaid, as a volunteer at the V&A, where she worked for thirteen years in the textile department, eventually as assistant to the keeper of textiles, picking up a knowledge of the history of dress and of accessories. "From my studies of the history of art I had always been interested in dress and design, so I knew quite a lot about it anyway. I was particularly interested in underclothes and corsets — and in fans."

She didn't at first collect fans, though she had been stage-struck with her grandmother, who used them. "She had been a lady-in-waiting to a sultana. She had a big black ostrich-feather fan, for she was in semi-mourning most of her life.

"It was only about 1963 that I started properly studying and collecting fans. My husband always used to say that the fans were my escape from thinking about my lost daughters, a distraction from the tragedy. I don't know. I wasn't aware of it. But I suppose it could have been some sort of sublimation.

"I was never an obsessive collector. I'm still not. It never took over my whole life. It was just an interest. What I was interested in was learning about the whole history of fans, so of course I collected them, because I wanted to study them. But even then, I would have to say it was only an occasional pastime, not every day."

Her husband Dickie encouraged her, pleased to see her interested and occupied. He himself was not a collector, though he had a few rather rare eighteenth-century seals — the sort that artistocrats used to seal their letters.

"When I first decided to start collecting fans, I told my father about it and I remember him giving me one piece of advice. 'Whatever you collect, you must try to be more knowledgeable than the expert.' It was good wisdom, for he knew more about the coins he collected than anyone else. From the beginning, I always made it my business to learn everything I could about fans."

She says she didn't spend a great deal of money on her fans, as she and her husband were not really wealthy, but she did begin to attend all the West End auction houses whenever there were fans being sold.

"Often I would buy a job lot for £30, an assortment of different fans, perhaps ten, one or two of which I wanted, as I had viewed them beforehand. The ones I didn't want I would put back into another sale.

17

"Of course at that time I would never buy anything blind, just from a catalogue. How unwise that would have been."

Hmm. When I became a born-again collector and decided to get back into stamps, I did that all the time, bidding for lots without looking or even understanding what was in them. I enjoyed the surprise, opening mystery packets I had forgotten about, even when I ended up with doubles, with stuff I didn't want, or total rubbish, which of course was very very stupid.

I asked her if she began to meet and make friends with other fan collectors once she started going to sales, which is what often happened to me.

"Not really. Collectors are very private, secretive, suspicious people. Some see other collectors as rivals."

That's not been my experience, I said, at least not at my humble level. Once I've displayed some minimum knowledge, I've always found other collectors more than keen to share their expertise and show off their own treasures.

"Perhaps it's just fan collectors — they of course are the ones I know. We really are very private people. We seldom reveal what we have. We're not as bad as dollies — collectors of dolls. They can be really vicious. Oh, I shouldn't have said that. Let's just say some of them can be sometimes."

When she started going for better-class fans, at places like Christie's and Sotheby's, she began to use a rep to do her bidding, telling her what price to go up to, and not beyond, having personally inspected the fans to be sure of their authenticity. "This started a very productive relationship with a most clever person who became a true friend."

But wouldn't her presence, once she had been spotted at the auction as a known collector, have put off other bidders, who might have given up and she would have got a better price?

"On the contrary. My presence would have alerted them to something unusual and valuable and I do not enjoy competition. I was becoming a world expert on fans, so they would have kept bidding longer than they might have done otherwise."

"To capture an overlooked treasure — or just to outdo you?"

"Both," she replied. "But I suppose the main reason was that I wanted to remain private, which many fan collectors do.

"Today, here in the museum, I often have members of the public coming in who bring a fan with them. They ask me about it, all rather hesitant and nervous, saying it has got broken, wanting to know how it can be mended. While I'm looking at it, I ask them about themselves. Very often they make several visits, and it's only then I discover that they have their own collection, sometimes very good ones. They have not told me about it because they have wanted to keep it a secret."

All the same, she did make friends with another fan collector who happened to live not far from herself and her husband in Blackheath. "This man said that he and others wanted to start a Fan Circle, for fan collectors, and they asked me to become the first president.

"I then contributed some of my fans to an exhibition which was being held at Preston art gallery. I'm not sure how that came about, but they had been left a collection of fans which belonged to the Countess of Rosse — Lord Snowdon's mother — which were also on show.

"Collecting fans began in the late nineteenth cenury, at least in Britain, and it was popular amongst many aristocratic ladies. When they died, their collections were usually handed over to some museum or gallery, as the next generation were not really interested. That's why both the British Museum and the V&A have some very important fan collections — not that you would know, as they are not on show."

The idea for a museum in which to display her own collection did not come to her till 1984, and it was sparked off by the fact that her late father's coin collection was to be sold at Christie's.

"I knew that my sisters and I would each be getting some money, and I did wonder what I might do with any inheritance. One idea was that my husband and I would buy a little country cottage somewhere and I could use one room to display my fans. My husband said no, you must do it properly, or not do it at all. You must create a proper museum, and it must be in London."

The search for the right location took several years and lots of missed opportunities in various parts of London. She had decided she wanted it to be near a major national museum — but not one that covered fans, so as not to be in competition, more in association.

She eventually picked Grèenwich, for its Maritime Museum, and because it was an area she knew, living in Blackheath. She heard about two adjoining Georgian houses coming up for auction in Crooms Hill, but they were in very bad condition. They had been council-owned, run as a nurses' home, but for many years had lain derelict. On her first visit, pigeons flew out of the front door and all she could see was a dark hole.

She didn't go to the auction herself, in December 1985, as she couldn't bare to lose the properties, having set her heart on them. She sent her husband, who bid successfully, but had to pay more then they had agreed.

The official owner of the building became the Victor Adda Foundation, the trust established by her father, which then handed the premises over on a 999-year lease to the fan museum, which she set up as an independent educational charity.

How much did you have to pay, I asked, for two wrecked Georgian gems back in 1985?

"Maybe it was £330,000. Yes, that was it. My memory is not what it was for those sorts of financial facts."

But she does remember that they spent over £1 million making the houses safe, then converting them for use as a museum. The work took seven years, far longer than they had expected, what with building problems, planning permissions and opposition from various local residents. "It still goes on, whenever we want to do anything. You would think a fan museum must be encouraging drunks and hooligans and all-night parties from the way some people are always complaining and objecting."

They vastly overran the budget, which the Foundation had agreed, though they never got into debt, but had to apply to various bodies, like the National Lottery, and City institutions, helped by her husband's contacts.

One of her sponsors is Canon, the Japanese camera company. "When you go out into the back garden, you will see our Japanese garden. I promised them the money would go to something with a Japanese flavour." So she is not as financially vague as she might like to appear.

She handed over her own collection of some two thousand fans to the museum and they make up the core collection, but she also got donations or long-term gifts from other collectors, especially the Fan Association of North America.

The fan museum opened its doors in 1991 and proved an immediate success, attracting a lot of enthusiastic visitors, and since then it has won many awards. And so it should. The setting is splendid, the displays beautifully arranged and explained, and of course the contents are world-class.

In 2009, Prince Charles's wife, Camilla, Duchess of Cornwall, became a patron, which was quite a coup. The Duchess's staff wanted to give her a gift and applied to the Worshipful Company of Fan Makers, still an important and wealthy livery body in the City, of which Helene is an Honorary Liveryman. "The Duchess's secretary came here to look at our fans and we suggested the design for one that could be made for her, which we did. After that, the Duchess herself made a visit and agreed to be our patron."

In 2009, Helene became an MBE. Yet despite royal patronage, all the awards, and its fame in fan circles worldwide, the museum averages only between eight and ten thousand visitors a year. I had expected more, given its excellent situation. Even more disappointing, after almost twenty years the museum is not yet self-supporting.

"I pay for the insurance of my own fans and we try hard to raise money through the shop and through fan classes and lectures and hiring out the Orangery for private parties. Despite all this, we still have to rely on grants from people like the tourist board and from the Victor Adda Foundation, just to keep us going. It would be nice to be self-financing, but we are still not there yet."

Her husband died in 1999 and now, in her late seventies, she feels she does not have the energy she once had. "When my husband was alive, we used to organise big gala parties and they used to encourage generous donations. My husband was at Cambridge with Mrs Runcie, whose husband was Archbishop of Canterbury. She organised a fund-raising concert at Lambeth Palace.

"I want the museum to go on for ever, in perpetuity, and be a seat of learning and excellence, so it has taken some heart-searching not to go down the path of vulgar tourism. I don't want to make it just another slick attraction for the kiddies. In these twenty years, all who come here have been enchanted. Only twice have we had a negative comment in the visitors' book."

And what was that, pray? "Oh some person complained that they had expected to see four thousand fans actually on display all the time, which of course was a ridiculous moan, how could we be expected to do that?"

She is determined the museum will continue and has made plans for its financial future, but the problem of finding someone with similar knowledge is a real one. "When I go, they will need three people."

The world of fan collecting, apparently, is rather in the doldrums. There are some very keen collectors out there, and big prices get paid for choice items — up to £300,000 for a fan hand-painted by, say, a famous Impressionist, or £50,000 for a fan with inlaid jewels — but the prices of ordinary fans, however ancient, are fairly stationary. So much so that the specialist fan sales, which places like Christie's used to hold once or twice a year when Helene first started collecting, have now ceased.

"They can't get the experts, that's one of the problems. The knowledge has been lost. The departments where people learned about fans have been closed. There are hardly any full-time dedicated fan dealers now in Britain at all." France appears to be the main centre of fan research, and there are still a couple of fan dealers in Paris, and some learned French experts and fan makers.

24

However, the Fan Circle in Britain soon became the Fan Circle International, which has about three hundred members, so all is not lost. Most fan collectors are women, but there are some men, drawn into it by the theatrical and dress connections.

"The one good bit of news is the Russians. They are suddenly becoming interested in fans, especially ones from their own culture, and they have a lot of money."

I began my tour downstairs, as one should, as that is where she has arranged the permanent exhibitions. Having talked to Helene first and learned about her background, I felt slightly better equipped to understand and appreciate the treasures. It's not of course how normal punters approach a museum, but I made a note to myself always to try, where possible, to see the museum creator before seeing their creation.

The ground floor seemed to be a mass of glass cases and cabinets, the contents all immaculately displayed, with extensive labels and explanations, but somehow a bit daunting and sort of complicated, despite telling myself I now knew a bit about fans.

Wandering round though, several times, and then starting in the proper order, as directed, it all began to make sense. As with so many things that appear at first sight rather limited in appeal and importance, when choice, rare objects are properly presented, and properly explained, one does begin to realise that fans are a rich subject with many varied uses.

I hadn't till then been aware of just how many uses there have been for fans over the centuries. Firstly, they were important as a cooling device, especially in tropical or hot countries, before the world got round to air conditioning. They could keep the flies away from bodies or animals. They could be used to fan flames, to keep fires going, to create a wind to separate wheat from chaff. They had a role in religious and ceremonial and regal occasions. They were cultural and decorative objects, painted to depict historical scenes and events. They have also been used as advertising boards, to sell products or carry messages.

When you think about it, which of course I'd never done before, fans are multi-purpose objects whose history can be traced back several thousand years. They appear in ancient Egypt, for example in the tomb of Tutankhamun, and were used in antiquity by the Etruscans, Greeks and Romans.

The word "fan", so Helene told me, comes originally from *vannus*, the Latin for winnowing. The French word for fan, *eventail*, and the Italian, *ventaglio*, have a similar derivation, from the word for wind, though when later I looked up the English word "fan" in my Chambers dictionary, it says it comes from the Anglo-Saxon *fann*. No doubt the Anglo-Saxons borrowed it from the Romans. Fan, as in football fan, comes of course from fanatic, and it first appeared with that meaning in the seventeenth century.

Thinking about fans, for the first time in my life, and looking at the Roman examples in the museum, it suddenly struck me that for about forty years I've had an ancient fan staring at me every day. On my desk I have a small statue that I bought at the Tullie House

Museum in Carlisle. It's a copy of a tombstone, found locally and dating from around the second century AD, which shows a lady, a child at her side, who is clearly holding a large fan in her right hand. Why would she need that in Cumbria? It wasn't exactly tropical, even all those centuries ago. I now realise it must have been ceremonial, presumably to depict her status.

In the fan museum, no flashlights are allowed near the fans and all the windows have UV filters. The electric lights are monitored and the temperature carefully controlled. Fans are quite delicate objects, though all the ones in the cabinets seemed in splendid condition, even the oldest ones, dating back to the eleventh century. Mostly they seemed to be from the seventeenth to nineteenth centuries.

Most fans do appear to be fan-shaped, like a half-circle, made so they can be folded, with or without handles, but they can also be flat. The variations are enormous. They can be totally round, with a long handle, or made of straw, or very large for the fanning of some important personage. They can be made of highly coloured feathers, often large ostrich feathers. As for the handles, they were often highly decorated with gold leaf, hand-painted or enamelled.

The main part of a fan is called the "leaf", and is usually made of paper, silk or some cotton material that has been laid out flat. The stick and the vertebrae — the skeleton of the fan — is known as the "monture". There is a glossary on the wall explaining all the terms, most of which are French, traditionally the world leader in the making of fans.

It was the Italians in the fifteenth century who are credited with popularising the folding fan, but it was the French who took over as the experts. Queen Elizabeth I brought fans into vogue in England and used both fixed and folding ones. Their popularity led to the formation of the Worshipful Company of Fan Makers in 1709. Queen Victoria was very keen on them and sponsored an exhibition in 1871. Art schools all over the UK were encouraged to enter examples and win prizes, in the hope that British fans would catch up with the French, but they never acquired the same status. Today, there is no fan-making in the UK.

The ground floor of the museum serves as an introduction to fans and contains the most interesting examples, taking you through their manufacture and design, explaining their history and art. It is incredibly detailed and well displayed but often I found my head going dizzy, trying to take in all the terms, understand the different types, materials, significance. I was in a daze of incomprehension mostly. I might just as well have been trying to learn calculus or Chinese. My little brain didn't seem up to the intellectual effort required.

However, there are quite a few exhibits that are easy to appreciate, such as a fan leaf painted by Gauguin in 1887 showing a scene in Martinique, and also one by Sickert. The Impressionists were very keen on fans, painting them as presents for friends and admirers. There are also some novelty fans, including a telescopic fan that expands and contracts, one that holds an ear trumpet, another a pair of spectacles. One is described as a "Swiss army knife for corseted ladies" and contains, secreted away, a miniature sewing kit, so emergency repairs could be undertaken. There is a Welsh fan, made of Welsh slate, and some naughty ones, with traditional scenes on one side but erotic or saucy pictures on the other.

Upstairs, there is always a special exhibition, which changes every four months. The day I was there it was the Adam and Eve exhibition, with fans depicting biblical scenes and characters. There are at least three mentions of fans in the Bible, but of course thousands of fans on which biblical scenes have been illustrated. The exhibition had its own, very erudite catalogue, some thirty-four pages, giving detailed descriptions of each of the seventy-three "biblical" fans on show. Over the years, other special exhibitions have been devoted to Children in Fans, Theatrical Fans, Advertising Fans and many other topics.

I found it amazing that Helene has managed to mount three different exhibitions on different topics every year for the almost twenty years during which the museum has been open. I was later allowed into the library, or study, a large drawing room on the first floor, not open to the public but available for scholars and researchers. Helene was working away on her next exhibition, which was to be on military fans. She slid open various cunning drawers to show me some of the examples she was going to display.

The room is filled on all sides with specially built sets of walnut-veneered drawers made with a little silver fan at the top of each row, each with a different letter so the fans can be easily located. This is where the majority of the museum's four thousand fans are stored, kept carefully in the drawers, wrapped in tissue paper.

The garden and the Orangery, which several times a week serves teas, are also immaculate. The walls of the Orangery are covered with hand-painted murals. Outside, the front half of the garden is in the shape of a fan, while behind there is that Japanese-style garden. It is all in exquisite taste and reeks not just of refinement and scholarship but of affluence. No expense seems to have been spared. No wonder the museum does not make a profit.

It does have an academic, learned feeling to it, and has been most professionally created and organised. I wondered if I would see another such clearly high-class, upmarket museum on my travels. I suppose I half-expected something a bit more amateur and informal, which is what I would probably end up with if I ever opened my own museum. I do tend to be a messy collector, which is how I feel most collectors are, caught up in the excitement of their passion. Helene didn't strike me as a messy person. And her reason for beginning her collection in the first place, with the loss of her daughters, was one I had never imagined.

So that was one thing I had learned — that I don't know what I don't know, that I can't possibly guess at all the reasons that might make people begin their own museums. There was nothing I particularly envied in her museum, no object I coveted, nothing I longed to take away and hug, and despite being so impressed, I wasn't inspired to start collecting fans for myself. My little brain, and my little house, are full of enough clutter.

But goodness, I did so admire what she had done and how she had done it, creating such a wonderful space out of two derelict houses. The thing I'd most like to spirit away would be Helene herself, to assist me if and when I ever get round to starting my own museum, to help knock it — and me — into shape.

I went back to say farewell to Helene and told her how much I admired what she had done. I felt in awe of what she had created. It made all my little collections seem piddling. And it had also let me see that there can be many reasons and motivations for creating a museum.

It was such an achievement, a work of art and scholarship, knowledge and devotion. All on one subject, yet vast and rich in range and content. It represents over forty years of her life, devoted to the study and collection of fans. The result, I said, of a totally magnificent obsession.

Sorry, just slipped out. I must not, she told me once again, describe her as an obsessive. That's not how she sees herself.

She does veer between pride, almost a superiority, in her knowledge and in the richness of collection, and coolness and detachment, as if above it all, removed from all such material possessions.

"I am not an obsessive because I know too much about the world — and I know that things are not as important as people. The fans took over my work, but not my life or being.

"If my daughters had lived, I am quite sure I would have never created this museum." Her two daughters had died as babies, but she did not want to go into the details, even after all these years.

"But that is why I have always known that an object is just an object, while a person is always a person."

The Fan Museum
12 Crooms Hill
Greenwich
London SE10 8ER
Tel 020 8858 7879
www.fan-museum.org

CHAPTER TWO

The Vintage Wireless Museum, Dulwich

The British Vintage Wireless and Television Museum is one of those unique places, world-famous in wireless circles, but set in an ordinary suburban house — and hellish to find.

The Fan Museum is in a house, but one beautifully and professionally converted into a museum, well signposted and in a very well-known street. The Vintage Wireless Museum was in a house that was still lived in by its creator and sounded to be a rather eccentric, messy museum — just the sort of place I felt sure I would love and identify with, even though, yet again, I was coming to a subject about which I knew nothing.

Over the years, so I gathered, it had grown to thirteen rooms, totally devoted to the wonderful world of wireless, filled with fifteen hundred different wireless and TV items — so you'd think it would be easy to find, or at least that the neighbours would be able to point it out.

It is one of those by-appointment-only museums, which is often the case with the more esoteric places.

Its founder and curator, Gerald Wells, is getting on a bit — he's now eighty years old — and doesn't want folks just turning up. You have to ring and book.

I did find him on Google, in deepest Dulwich, with an address and telephone number. I eventually got through to him on the phone, which was lucky, as he doesn't always answer, being far too busy. But he agreed to see me, next Friday morning, not too early, say about 10.30, he'd have the kettle on ready. I then asked how to get to his house.

"No idea," he said.

What about the nearest Tube station?

"There isn't one."

Railway station?

"Not the foggiest. I don't use trains."

Buses?

"I wouldn't know. I don't go out."

Thanks, I said, see you then. I hope.

From the map, his address appeared to be in West Dulwich, but I worked out that Tulse Hill, a place I'd never been to and thought might be fictional, was the nearest railway station. When I got there, I spotted a minicab office in the street outside. A driver took me straight to the address in Rosendale Road — and was absolutely amazed that there was a world-famous museum inside. First he'd heard of it.

The front garden of the house, a two-storey, brick-built detached villa, appeared a bit neglected. Mr Wells himself eventually opened the front door, wearing a rather dirty-looking white coat, the sort young doctors wear, which had clearly seen better days, and holding on to his walking stick. Rather tall and bulky, spectacles, quite well-spoken, if a little bit croaky and creaky. He had been ill, he said, in fact he'd been very ill many times in the last few decades, in fact he's surprised he's still here.

He is unmarried and has always lived alone, which is just as well, for from the moment you enter the whole house is covered with old radios, or bits of old radios. He led the way into his kitchen which didn't look as if it had been touched since the 1950s — linoleum on the floor, ancient sink and cooker, sensible-looking dark brown china teapot in which he made tea.

He was born in 1929 in this house, which his father, Frank Wells, an insurance assessor, had bought in 1916 for £750. It had formerly been owned by Dulwich College, along with another three houses in the same street, where masters used to live. There were two older sisters in the family before Gerry. His mother, so he says, was not best pleased when she found she was pregnant with him.

"She said to my father, if I am going to have another baby, I want some more luxuries this time, like hot and cold water and electricity. We didn't have any of those things until I was born. We just had gas. But that year a man called Percy Carlin went up and down the street canvassing, asking people if they would like electricity connected. When he got enough people saying yes, he went to the Electric Light Company and got them interested. They agreed to lay on cables, so he went back, took orders and starting wiring up the houses. My mother was terribly excited. We were at the top of

Percy's list, as she was pregnant. I've always thought that my love of all things electrical was therefore prenatally indoctrinated."

His passion became focused on radio, tinkering with crystal sets, which were then beginning to be popular. "Oh I was obsessed. I thought of nothing else, which meant I was a disaster when it came to school work, a total wash-out. I was sent to Dulwich Prep School, and hated it. I was a legend at the time, because I would never ever conform.

"There was a boy who lived near us called Trevor Bailey. He was also at Dulwich Prep but he was the model schoolboy, went on to play cricket for England, a shining example to little boys everywhere. My mother longed for me to be like Trevor Bailey. She was furious when I got into trouble and did awful things, such as during the war going round the bombed-out houses and stealing all their electrical equipment. My sisters were ashamed of me as well, but my father was a gentle man. Rather than being furious with me, he was bewildered. He just couldn't work out why I'd turned out as I had done.

"During the war, it was decided that all the boys at Dulwich Prep were to be evacuated to the country, but my parents didn't want to me to go, thinking I'd get into worse trouble away from home, so they sent me to St Joseph's College, a Catholic school. I was still raiding bombed-out houses, stealing any electrical equipment, fuse boxes, lamp holders, even light meters, and riding off with them in the saddlebag of my bike. I made a trapdoor in the floor of the shed in our back garden which I called my swag box and that's where in I hid my treasures.

"I then moved on to stealing from houses while people were still living there, like next door. I knew the people in the downstairs flat had a big Ferranti radio. While they were away, I went in and took it. I got it working and told my parents they had given it to me. I then took a Marconi from the upstairs flat, but was seen by my grandmother, who lived nearby, as I climbed over the garden wall. That evening the neighbour came to our house to report his Marconi radio was missing. He was very upset, so my parents gave him the Ferranti which I had stolen from his house earlier that year. Oh the disgrace.

"Alas, he had already reported the theft to the police, so I'd had it this time. Detective Sergeant Clutterbuck arrived at our house, searched the shed and found all the stuff I had stolen and I was hauled up before Lambeth juvenile court. I was sent to Stamford House remand centre in Shepherd's Bush. They told my mother I would be quite happy there. She replied that she didn't want me to be happy, she wanted me to suffer.

"Which I did. At the remand home, I was stripped and searched and made to wear this awful uniform made of canvas. For tea we had a mug of cocoa and a slice of bread with dripping, then got turned out in an exercise yard ringed with barbed wired. I was there several weeks. A psychiatrist examined me and decided I had an average IQ, so I was released under the care of a probation officer. St Joseph's College would not take me back, naturally enough. The only place that would take me after all that was a council school over in Brixton. The problem there was I didn't understand what the boys were saying, and they didn't understand me. I got expelled from there as well. More tea?"

Aged fourteen, Gerry was riding his bike one day along Norwood High Street, when he noticed Archie Root's radio shop. He went in, picked up a radio from the counter, ran out of the shop, jumped on his bike and rode off.

"I suppose it was worth about seven or eight pounds. I didn't have that sort of money, and anyway, it seemed good fun to steal it. I wanted it so much. Unfortunately I didn't know that Archie Root had an Austin 7 van. One of his boys who worked there jumped into it, drove after me and caught me in Chestnut Road. I was up in court and charged with stealing a radio. I remember one of the two women magistrates saying to me, 'You are behaving as though you are writing a book about yourself.' I didn't understand what she meant then — and I still don't.

"While I was on bail, I removed all the electrical fittings from a local vicarage that was empty. Every night, I'd been going in and taking stuff. On the last night, with my last load, they caught me."

The upshot was that he was sentenced to serve three years in an approved school. They decided to send him to one as far away as possible, out in the country, thinking this would keep him away from urban temptations, like wires and plugs and sockets. The school was called Redbank at Newton-le-Willows in Lancashire.

"I arrived on 1 January 1944 and was met by the headmaster, John Vardley. 'What's the trouble, lad?' he asked. 'I'm obsessed with wireless,' I replied. 'Oh we've got a master like that, Reg Yates, go and see him.'

"I did and he turned out to be a marvellous man, and an excellent electrician. I loved it there — the first time I'd met an adult who was as keen on my hobby as I was.

"At the end of that year, on 1 November, the head called me in and gave me a train ticket to Euston, saying my father would meet me there. They were sending me home. I didn't want to leave, as I was loving it. They said it was now safe to go back to London as the doodlebugs had finished, which was true, but they hadn't reckoned with the V-2 rockets, which made an even bigger bang and this time you didn't see them coming."

A job was quickly found for Gerry, now that he was over fourteen, and a week later he started as an apprentice joiner with a local building firm.

"My father didn't have to pay a premium, which you had to do in those days to get an apprenticeship. It was done as a favour to my father by the chairman of the magistrates who had sentenced me, Basil Aldus. He was quite nice really, unlike the two old ratbags who served on the bench with him. My father had done some insurance work for his building firm, so that was how I came to be fixed up with the apprenticeship.

"I stood it for about three years, by which time I was making more money by mending radios for the firm's customers than doing any joinery work. So I set myself up from home, repairing radios and doing electrical work. When I'd saved enough money, I built my own shed in the garden and used it as my workshop. My mother was still against all this but my father agreed, thinking it would keep me out of mischief.

"In 1951, I bought the Austin 7 van, the one that had chased me, from Archie Root. I'd become a friend of his. I didn't realise till I got it home that he'd been carrying accumulators in it and the acid had leaked and rotted the metal. You could push your fingers through the sides and floor. Anyway, I got it mended and set off to drive the 190 miles to Newton-le-Willows to visit my old alma mater, the approved school. I fancied a few days' holiday and couldn't think of anywhere nicer to go. My mother thought I was barmy. Took me six hours in that old van, with no heat and no radio. It was in late November, so it was very cold.

"I arrived to find that all the boys were rehearsing for a school pantomime, *Jack and the Beanstalk*. I was immediately given the job of doing all the lighting. If you ever want a good laugh, go and see boys from an approved school putting on a pantomime. It was hysterical. But I loved it, and stayed to the end and had a lovely holiday."

His radio and electrical business expanded and he was soon employing up to three other workers, with a girl in the house to answer the phone when they were out taking orders.

Then, around 1970, he started to have health troubles. He'd been smoking eighty cigarettes a day, and working round the clock, never trusting his own men to do a job, thinking it would be easier if he did it himself rather than explaining it.

"Eileen came in one morning and found me lying down there on the kitchen floor. I'd had a heart attack, though I didn't know it. The ambulance was there in minutes, so quick they must have been passing outside, and I was rushed to hospital. All the doctors had cricketers" names, but I must admit they were brilliant.

"I recovered from that, then had two strangulated double hernias, oh it was hellish. The pain was so loud you could hear it. I took months to get better and I was then told I should never work again, dammit, that I should give up my business and take it easy. They said I'd done my share.

"I realised I couldn't go forward any more so I thought, I know, I'll go backwards instead.

"I'd been to visit Lord Montagu's collection of vintage motor cars at Beaulieu, as I'd always been interested in cars. That got me thinking about starting a collection of old radios, the sort I'd worked on when I was young."

There was another moment of inspiration, or at least enlightenment, which happened around the same time.

"I was in the back garden one day and this big brash Yank was leaning over the wall, taking a photo of the back of our house. I asked him what he was doing and he said his mother used to live in this house. His mother then appeared and she was refined and ladylike.

41

She explained that her husband, Alfred Richard Taylor, had lived in this house. He'd been a master at Dulwich College, she said, and had been very interested in wirelesses.

"At once I realised who he was — THE Alfred Richard Taylor. I knew his name by now as I had been studying the early years of wireless. Everyone in wireless knows his name because he was one of the earliest wireless pioneers — a total amateur, but very skilful, who did his own broadcasts and in 1908 had his own call signal, 2AF, broadcasting from our house.

"I knew of him, that he'd been a master at Dulwich College, but until that day I never knew he'd lived here. All I ever knew was that my father had bought this house from Dulwich College, not the name of the man who had lived here."

Alfred Richard Taylor had started the first engineering group at Dulwich College. It was aimed at the dull types, who couldn't do Latin or Greek and were too lazy or slow to march.

"It was so strange to realise he had been living here all those years ago, in this very house, fiddling with his radios. That was the second big prenatal influence in my life, even though I had never been aware of it. But it must have been in the air. After all, there were no collecting genes in my family, and my father was never interested in radios, nor was my mother. My family, until me, had all been in banking or insurance or the church. I was the black sheep."

Gerry started collecting as many old radios as possible and got them operating, and also repairing them for other people. He also built repro models, complete with fancy woodwork.

"Eileen helped me with the fretwork. She turned out to be pretty nifty with a screwdriver.

"I started a vintage wireless society, the first in the UK, and members used to meet here. It then spread around the country. There were quite a few wireless clubs at that time, and some members had their own little museums."

His museum of vintage radios opened to the public in 1974, with proper opening hours, welcoming all-comers, and very soon was attracting a lot of people and a lot of attention. He appeared on a couple of TV magazine programmes in 1978, such as *Nationwide*. "It was only ten minutes, but afterwards I got sacks and sacks of mail. The National Theatre started borrowing my stuff for props and so did film and TV people. Did you ever see *The Russian Bride?* I provided all the props for that."

It was always a struggle though, with little money coming in. As the collection grew, he expanded into more rooms, adapting halls and corridors and any available bit of space, as well as creating a workshop for repairing radios. Eventually every bedroom got filled with his display, including his own.

But it was proving more expensive to run than he had expected, what with trying to equip the bedrooms with proper display units and shelves, even though he knocked up most of them himself. He was beginning to think he might have to get a proper job and run the museum part-time, when a saviour appeared.

In 1980, Christie's had a sale of EMI archives and collections which attracted quite a lot of publicity. One of the more interesting lots was a 1924 HMV Lumière, the world's first radiogram. It was bought by Paul Getty — the son of John Paul Getty — who later became Sir Paul Getty when he was knighted for his philanthropic work, helping various British cultural institutions.

He didn't bid for the old radiogram personally, but sent an assistant along. Alas, when he got it home, he found he couldn't get it to work. Someone then told him about Gerry and his work on old radios, and one day Gerry got a phone call asking if he could repair an old radiogram.

"There had been a feature on me and my museum in *Sounds Vintage* magazine — now no more — which someone must have read."

Gerry went along to Paul Getty's house in Cheyne Walk, the house in which Christina Rossetti had once lived. Getty was known as a bit of a recluse, staying indoors a lot, playing music on old gramophones, reading through his collection of rare books. When younger, he'd suffered from various problems. One of his neighbours was Mick Jagger, who became worried about him, especially when he seemed to stay in for weeks at a time.

Getty told Gerry that one evening Jagger had barged into his house and switched on the TV, insisting they watched the cricket together. And from then on, according to Gerry, Getty developed a passion for cricket, which resulted in him contributing to help rebuild Lord's cricket ground.

Back to the radiogram — which I managed to steer Gerry towards, as once he starts a story it is hard to interrupt or cross-examine him — what happened to that? Did he get it working?

"Oh yes, I got it working OK and sent him the bill, which I think was for £60. He paid up prompt. This was in the September. In December a food hamper arrived from Harrods and a cheque for £1000 towards my museum. It was just what I needed and came at a vital time.

"Then in the January I got a phone call from a Scottish woman who said she was a chief accountant at Deloitte's, Getty's accountants. She just wanted to come and check to see if the £1000 had gone to my museum, that I really did have a museum She said she'd only stop for a moment, leave the car running, pop inside, then out again.

"When she arrived she looked to me like a hospital matron, grey-haired bun, tweed suit, very smart and efficient. She asked me what my charity number was. I had no idea what she was talking about. I wasn't a charity.

"Anyway, on that first visit she ended up staying two hours. She went round everything and saw what I was trying to do. I did have a couple of sheds in the garden by then, but I needed more space. There was a bit of spare land adjoining the bottom of my garden which I was longing to have, but of course couldn't afford it.

"She must have told Sir Paul about this because the next thing I knew I was being given a cheque for £8000. The neighbours who owned the land were delighted to accept it."

Sir Paul then followed it up with further generosity, offering to pay all Gerry's council taxes — something else he'd been worried about — plus all his electricity bills. Sir Paul himself visited Gerry and his museum a couple of times.

This continued every year from then on, till Getty's death in 2003. "I went to his memorial service, as he was a wonderful man, and very knowledgeable about lots of things. But after his death the money stopped."

However, since Getty's death, Gerry has done the obvious and sensible thing, which many small-time specialist museums do, which was to turn the museum into a charity. With the help of a group of enthusiasts and supporters, a trust has been set up to look after the museum and secure its future.

During his lifetime, Getty did hand over to the museum the 1924 radiogram, the one he had bought at Christie's — and also another equally rare item, a 1937 television radiogram — the RGD 235DT, to give it its correct title. This is one of the world's first radio, gramophone and TV units, all in the same cabinet.

We were sitting during all this chat, or at least monologue, at a table in Gerry's front room — about the only space in the whole house to sit down, although even here we were surrounded by old radios and TVs. Along the whole of one wall was a massive 1930s TV radiogram, a huge piece of art deco-like furniture, made of walnut and highly polished. He opened the top and I could see the gramophone turntable and also a small screen, set flat into the cabinet.

Gerry went off into the kitchen where four elderly men were now sitting. They had been arriving in dribs and drabs, going into the kitchen and making themselves tea. Gerry explained that every Friday morning he had open house for a group of his supporters.

"I give them all rude names, but they don't know. I call them the Little Old Men Club."

I followed Gerry into the kitchen where he introduced me to the men. They were all supping tea and chatting while playing with valves. Each time the doorbell rang and another old man arrived, Gerry shouted, "See who seeks admission."

He went to a cupboard in the kitchen, switched on some plugs, and we returned to his front room where we stood in front of his monster TV radiogram. He explained that he had rigged up an ancient BBC transmitter, which had once been in use at the old Crystal Palace, and this was how he could get the 1930s TV screen to work. As we waited, it eventually did start flickering into life. I peered forward and the pictures on the screen were pretty good, in black and white of course, but also upside down. But ah ha, that is not the way you watched TV on this machine in the 1930s. Gerry opened up the lid of the cabinet to its full height and inside it was a large mirror on which the TV picture was reflected, the right way up, and much bigger. By moving the mirror around, you could watch the TV from anywhere in the room, without having to bend down and look inside at the actual screen. Damn clever, but why on earth did they do it that way?

"Ah well you should see the size of the transistor inside. It's about five feet long. To get it inside the cabinet, they had to put the TV screen in upside down, but they got round that with the use of a mirror. Ingenious, don't you think?"

He showed me how various other radios and TVs worked, not that I quite understood it all. Despite the room, like all the others, being crammed with stuff, he seemed to know where everything was, partly because he has made no changes and done no modernisation for many years. The furniture and wallpaper looked straight out of the 1950s. All the same, it seemed quite tidy.

"Oh, Eileen comes in every day, does a bit of cleaning, sees I'm OK, checks I'm still alive. It was Eileen who found me that time I had a fall, and it was she who called the ambulance."

There had been quite a few references to Eileen, who seemed to be a regular presence, so I wondered who she was.

He explained that she was a local girl who came to help in the days when he had his own electrical business and hired girls to answer the phone, look after things, keep the place tidy, when he was out on a job.

"When I was making repro radios and TVs, I discovered she could use a screwdriver, so she worked with me. She was very good. Excellent at woodwork.

We made a good little team. She's now married, has a family of her own, but she still comes in to keep an eye on me.

"I look upon her as my daughter, but she's not. When I was in my twenties and thirties, I did have a few ding-dongs, but we needn't go into them. So I have no children, as far as I know."

"The first time I fell madly in love was when I was about fourteen. She was called Barbara Alan and she was about twelve. I met her at a youth club and for a few months we used to go everywhere together. I felt I was walking on air. I knew she had other friends, and they all thought I was boring, playing with my radios. I was very jealous of them, but I was head over heels in love. We used to sit in my shed, kissing and cuddling for hours, which got my mother very worried.

"One day she came to my shed with her bicycle lamp. It had got broken, and she asked me to mend it. As we talked, it came out she was going to a party that night and I hadn't been invited. I was so insanely jealous that I picked up a hammer and smashed her bike lamp. She picked up the pieces, left the shed and walked out of my life for ever. That was on 5 January 1946.

"For about fifty years, I always held a little party on 5 January each year to cheer myself up. I suppose that was the biggest romance in my life. What it did teach me was not to be jealous of anyone and not to lose my temper — and I've tried to stick to both of those principles ever since."

We then did a tour of the museum, working our way round the old men in the kitchen, still deep in heated conversation about valves and transistors. In his bedroom at the back of the house, right beside his bed, Gerry had rigged up his own tape deck. He switched it on and instantly I could hear the sounds of palm court music from the 1950s, the Max Jaffa sort my parents listened to when I was a boy. As we progressed, the music followed us round the whole house and even outside into his sheds, as he has rigged up nineteen speakers to cover every room.

The tape deck was made of plywood, painted black, rather crude and amateurish, and clearly home-made, but it certainly worked efficiently — just as well, with perfect sound, as any modern whizzo sound system. He said he had a stock of five thousand records, all vinyl, each of which he could play at the touch of a switch.

"I used to make quite a few of these tape decks in the 1950s. It was when disc jockeys were first coming in, but they still had to make their own table and tape deck and rig up their own speakers. I sold them to various holiday camps, the cheap tatty sort. They would have hired a DJ for dances but had nowhere for them to play their records. So I made them a tape deck and worked out a way for them to mix their records.

"This one is the last one I ever made. Once mass production came in, no one wanted my home-made ones any more. This one has a pure valve sound, so it sounds like the sort of music you heard on the radio in

50

the 1950s, real music with melodies, not like this modern rubbish which I call council house music."

He also used to make working repro models of Britain's rarest radio, a green 1934 Ekco AD68. Original Ekco radios were sold in the 1930s for nine guineas each, which was expensive.

Only two were ever made in green, and they were exhibited in a plastics exhibition to show that Bakelite could be made in different colours. After the exhibition the two green radios were being chucked out, as they had been for display purposes only. However, a man who worked at the Ekco factory decided to save them, putting in the right parts from the factory to make them work. Then they disappeared.

"About twenty years later, one of them turned up in a junk shop in Honor Oak, priced at £150. A man contacted me to ask if it could be genuine, so I went to see it and said it was authentic, though by now it didn't play.

"It was then advertised for £15,000, and in fact it was sold for £17,500. That's a world record for an old radio. But the last time I heard, it had changed hands for £8000."

The market has apparently fallen out of old radios because all the systems have changed, the modern signals can't be picked up on old valves any more. Or something like that. Until about twenty years ago, you could repair an old radio, or build a repro one, if you were clever like Gerry, and tune in to present-day BBC stations.

51

"I used to do a good trade in repro Ekcos, making them in my workshop. People couldn't really tell the difference. I made about eighty in all and sold them for £150 each. Eileen helped me with the fretwork. Then it turned out the material we were using to fix the wood got banned. It was found to contain cyanide, so we had to pack that up. Anyway, once you can't play old radios, they become ornaments only and lose part of their attraction."

Upstairs, the house's original five bedrooms, and every nook and cranny and landing, have been converted into museum rooms. He was able to do this after 1957 when his mother died. She left him the house while his sisters got some money.

Each room has a different name, after a well-known collector, a sponsor of the museum, or a place name which means something to radio fans, such as Droitwich or Daventry. Sometimes he gives a room a rude name, which is self-explanatory, such as the Gas Smell room.

"I've never bought an old radio. Everything has been given to me — or, er, I nicked them, many years ago. When my museum appeared now and again on those old TV programmes, I always got masses of offers, people saying I could have their old radios if I took them away. That still happens now and again, but I keep a lower profile today, now I'm appointment only."

In the Sir Paul Getty room, he showed me the 1924 Lumière radiogram. This has a strange sort of cover above the turntable, shaped like a circular fan, which holds the needle. He explained this was to make the needle stable. He turned it on and the record started playing — Walter Glynne singing "Passing By". Ah, what memories. That used to be one of my mother's favourite songs.

In another room was a large collection of Roberts radios. "Dick Roberts began his firm in 1928. He was a good friend of mine." One room was named John Vardey, after the head of the approved school he liked so much. When he died, he left some money to the museum.

"I was born in this room," said Gerry, opening another door. Inside, it was arranged exactly like a 1936 radio shop, with an original counter and all the shelves and boxes and displays and illuminated period advertisements, which lit up when he pressed a switch.

The oldest item in the museum is an 1899 sparks transmitter, whatever that is. He also has an early Baird television set, dated 1933.

Gerry insisted we climbed up the final set of stairs to his loft, though his legs and voice appeared to be weakening, which was not surprising as he had not stopped talking for the two hours since I'd arrived. He had converted the loft himself, turning it into one huge room. At one time he used to have meetings here with members of the radio club, and also played table tennis.

One of the walls is covered with the ornate wooden honours board that once belonged to the Dulwich High School for Girls. "It was being chucked out when someone heard I was converting my loft and offered it to me to use as a wall." On the top, in ornate scroll, I could read the lettering "The Utmost for the Highest". Below are the names of girls from 1882 to 1937, mostly long-dead by now, but stars in their time, honoured by fellow pupils and staff for their academic achievements. Historic stuff.

"Oh it is, yet probably only once in about thirty years has someone asked to look at it, researching the history of their family. So many of those surnames were well known in Dulwich. I am glad I saved it, because no one else would have done. Councils and government bodies, they have no interest in the past."

I looked down the honours board, noting the Victorian Christian names like Florence, Amy, Fanny. "Yes, there were a lot of Fannys. Let's hope none of them became a gynaecologist."

Gerry's jokes, like his old radios, tend to be a bit of their time, and probably wouldn't go down well in mixed company today, but his Little Old Men, when we met them on the stairs or in one of the rooms, laughed heartily every time.

Finally, we went out into the garden to inspect the sheds. I hadn't realised there were so many. Once he got that extra bit of land, he went on to build a veritable village of sheds, some very elaborate, with gable roofs and internal courtyards. This accounts for the fact that, in all, counting both house and sheds, he has a total of thirteen different rooms devoted to his old radios and associated bits.

One large shed is a schoolroom, arranged with six little workstations, where he still has Sunday afternoon workshops for people who want to learn how to mend old radios and TVs. The workstations seemed very well equipped, with glass-blowing and welding facilities, though several did look a bit worn and dusty, as if they were not used as often as in the past.

As we wandered round, we found one or two of the Little Old Men crouched over a machine, or studying old diagrams, searching through drawers and cupboards. His store cupboards looked chaotic to me, with drawers and little cubby holes piled high and jam-packed, but Gerry maintained he knew where everything was. "Because we are not computerised, I guarantee I can find anything in three minutes flat."

One old man came over and wanted a certain valve. Sure enough, Gerry had located it in ninety seconds.

"Look at this HMV resistor," said another old man, handing something to Gerry. "They shouldn't go like that."

"They do, if they've had a bomb under them," replied Gerry. "Or a Radio Rentals engineer has tried to mend it."

The old man guffawed, then padded away, back to playing happily with his old radio. As we walked back up the garden to the house, across the large lawn, Gerry reminisced about all the good times he'd had in the garden.

"We have had lots of garden parties here, feeding over a hundred people — barbecues, tables laid out, cocktails, proper meals. We had a huge one in 1984 when twenty-eight members of the Antique Wireless Association of America flew over, with their partners, and they had three days of events and celebrations with our BVWS members. Oh it was a wonderful time, with music and dancing."

BVWS stands for the British Vintage Wireless Society, an organisation that has been going since 1976 and still has over 1700 members.

An impressive number, considering that many of them must be pretty old by now. "That's true, but people do have an emotional connection with their old radios. You'd be surprised how important they are, reminding them of times past, what they used to listen to, when and with whom.

Talking to the Little Old Men, I discovered that several had worked as BBC engineers in the old days, so had grown up with what are now vintage radios. The next generation will not have that experience and knowledge. Did Gerry worry about the future of the museum?

"Not at all. We have at present a very strong core of enthusiasts. They spend a lot of time here and help with the museum. They are determined to keep it going, whatever happens to me.

"In the past, we have had a few who didn't quite see eye to eye with each other. The trouble with enthusiasts is that some don't turn out to be the most reliable or, shall I say, stable, especially when you have a lot of old men. They can be very cantankerous. We have people who have fallen out, then they go away and try to cause trouble.

"We have an excellent committee and trustees and they will make sure everything is preserved and looked after when I am gone."

So who will take over running the actual museum?

"Eileen of course. She's a trustee and general manager. She knows where everything is and all about the museum, as she's worked with me for many years. Her own daughter, Nicola, is also getting very knowledgeable. I have no worries about the future. She and the committee have looked after me well in the past, and I know they'll look after all this in the future."

The Little Old Men had all come in from their various sheds where they had been pottering around and were waiting for Gerry to stop talking to me. "It's my big treat of the week. Every Friday, when they come round, I go out with them at the end of the day for my only outing of the week. They take me to a greasy spoon caff. I then get my cholesterol top-up for the week.

"Not that I'm totally helpless. I can do a roast dinner if I want to, but I do tend to stick to the same old things, like tea and biscuits. And when I go anywhere, it's usually just for a week's holiday at the same place — a geriatric holiday village on Hayling Island. They know me well there. I wrote my book while I was there, spread over about five years. While the other geriatrics were playing bowls, I got peace and quiet to get on with my book while the staff supplied me with constant tea and biscuits."

His book, *Obsession*, about his life in wireless, was published by the BVWS in 2002 — free to members or £6 to the public.

Unlike Helene at the fan museum, Gerry is proud to call himself an obsessive, which he clearly is, always has been, a prime example of someone whose obsession took over his life and who, in the end, made his obsession work, turning it into a career. Until then, many people had thought him a bit strange — perhaps mad, if not exactly wicked. Sending him away to a remand home did seem a bit excessive, but obsessives can sometimes appear a threat.

In the end, his obession gave him a life and purpose and amusement, for Gerry is full of fun and obviously enjoys looking like a mad boffin. I had arrived with no knowledge or interest in old wirelesses, but I have to admit I came away inspired to look out for them from now on. And there were quite a few objects I would like to have taken with me, if I could have carried them. Some were a bit big, such as the monster 1930s TV radiogram.

The thing about old wirelesses is that even when they don't work, they do look decorative with all the polished wood and fancy fretwork and nice bits of inlay. I would love to have his 1924 Lumière radiogram, the one he got from Getty, the fan-shaped one, along with the record of "Passing By".

What fun to wind it up and turn it on, how our smart dinner-party guests would love it. Except we don't have smart dinners or smart guests any more. But my four grandchildren — God, they would be in ecstasy. Far cleverer and more entertaining than any boring old computer game or Peapod or Blackcurrant.

Gerry's enthusiasm for his subject — I'd like to have that, and be able to rattle and prattle away to strange visitors, as if they were the first people he had ever told about his obsession. And his sense of humour, still intact after all these years. You need both these qualities if you are going to open your own museum, and keep it open.

Before I left, I asked if he wore his white coat all the time.

"Yes, every day when I get up I put it on. I started wearing them in 1946 when I had my business and was going round all the time mending radios and TVs and electrical things. I found that after six months I had to put it in the dustbin as it was covered in burn holes from the soldering irons, or from battery acid and other things. Since then, I've bought a new one every six months. I reckon I must have gone through a hundred of them by now. They're technically lab coats and when I first started buying them, they cost thirty shillings. Not sure what they cost now.

"I'm famous in the vintage wireless world for wearing them. It's my trademark. There is one collector who along with his vintage radios, has one of my old white coats displayed as part of his wireless collection. I won't tell you his name. Don't want to embarrass him."

How nice to think that not only will the museum Gerry Wells has created go on for ever, or so he fondly expects, but that somewhere one of his white coats is being carefully preserved.

The British Vintage Wireless and Television Museum
23 Rosendale Road
West Dulwich
London SE21 8DS
Tel 020 8670 3667
bvwm.org.uk

CHAPTER
THREE

Bath Postal Museum

Fans and radios were both new to me, subjects I'd had no knowledge of or interest in, but now of course I find them totally fascinating, oh yes, and always will, go on, ask me anything — but now I was on the train to Bath on the trail of a subject I like to think I do know something about. The world's biggest collecting hobby, or so they always say.

It was stamps I first came back to when I became a born-again collector in my forties, so I can't say I had always been obsessed by them, as Gerry had been about old radios, nor had there been some tragedy in my life to make me pick them up, as with Helene, hoping to find some sort of solace. Unless you count giving up football. That did throw me back, when I realised I was still fit enough to play football but not fit enough to recover from playing football. When I realised my knees had gone, I knew that was it, but what was I going to do at weekends from now on, to give myself another interest? Perhaps deep down I was looking for some displacement activity, to save myself from mischief, from getting into less wholesome pastimes. Collecting, after all, is a form of escape. But we needn't go into that.

So I decided to go back to collecting stamps, as I had as a boy, and found it had all changed. No more sticky gums, but little plastic folders. The language seemed to have changed as well — much more academic and scientific. I thrashed around all over the place, up different routes and alleyways, trying to get one of every GB stamp, trying to collect penny blacks with different letters on. I collected thematic stamps — meaning on one theme, such as railways. I collected Wembley stamps, from the 1924–5 Wembley Exhibition, and also postal history, envelopes — or covers, as they are called amongst collectors — showing Cumbrian postmarks.

I then did a really dopey thing, which I had never done before and have never done since, which I know is stupid and about which I warn every new collector I meet — never, ever buy as an investment, not if you really are a collector. I paid Stanley Gibbons £5000 to arrange a portfolio of stamps for me — and ten years later I sold them for £1500. I had bought at the height, which was bad luck, but I also allowed Gibbons to pick them for me, from places and periods I had no interest in, then I put them in the bank, so I didn't even get pleasure out of them while I had them. What a mistake. Always buy for fun. Then if stuff you have goes up in value, that's an extra bonus.

Would I experience a little flutter of excitement to see some really choice stamps once again? Would I get derailed when I realised just how many different and tantalising museums there are in Bath?

The whole of Bath is of course a museum. The Georgian streets and terraces go on for ever, even when you think this must be it, some council houses will be round the next corner, a sixties concrete tower block will soon rise up, Poundstretcher and Iceland can't be far away — but no, beauty and good taste and architectural wonders, as far as the eye can see. I wonder if Bathonians get so used to living in a masterpiece that going to an ordinary, run-of-the-mill British town, like, say, Motherwell or Margate, makes them think, hmm, how exotic, how unusual, I must have a long weekend here and really explore.

The only problem with living in a masterpiece is that everyone and his wife wants to visit the town, then stand and around and gape, getting in your way when you want to be on with the everyday business of living and working. Bath streets seem to hide their names, or do without them. I was constantly being asked the way by total strangers. I must have given the impression I knew where I was going. As if.

Outside the Jane Austen Centre in Gay Street there was a woman in a bonnet and period blue coat, standing beside a man dressed as an eighteenth-century gentleman. The man moved to greet some Americans going in, which was when I realised that he was real while the woman was a model.

"Is it Jane Austen?" I asked the gentleman, who had very fine side whiskers and an excellent West Country accent, straight out of a Radio 4 afternoon play.

"No sir, Miss Austen, I think you'll find, was taller and had hazel eyes, not blue eyes. This is Elizabeth Bennet."

Of course, silly me. And what about you — apart from a Gentleman of the Period, are you supposed to be someone in particular?

"Probably Dr Mapleton."

"Oh, which novel was he in?"

"He was real, sir, lived locally in Bath and looked after Miss Austen. As for fictional characters I could be Darcy, Mr Collins or Captain Wentworth."

Excellent, excellent, I said, do carry on.

I found the Bath Postal Museum at last, hidden away down some stairs in the basement of Bath's main post office, at the corner of Broad Street and Green Street. I did notice a Stannah stairlift, not working the day I was there, which must be a help to those with even worse knees than mine.

You enter a 1930s post office, complete with wooden counter and pigeonholes, plus adverts and packets of household goods from the time. Some jaunty period tunes were being played in the background to aid the atmosphere. It is a real post office, which used to be in the Wiltshire village of Neston, untouched till it ceased trading in 1961 and eventually moved to the museum as a job lot.

Before I could start poking around and exploring inside, Audrey Swindells herself, co-founder of the museum, appeared — a bustling, energetic lady in her early eighties. If I wanted to talk to her, she said, it was best to go across the road to the church. Her museum didn't do refreshments but the church had a good tea room where we could talk in peace.

Audrey Stephens, as she was, was born in Birmingham in 1928. When she left school she worked mainly as a secretary in various offices, then got married and had three children. The marriage collapsed and she moved back in with her parents, who by then were living in Bath. It was in Bath that she met Harold Swindells, some eight years older than herself. They married in 1957 and in two years had three children, including twins.

"Oh he did get teased. He'd been a bachelor all those years, then in the space of two years he was married with six children."

As a boy, Harold had been a chorister at Manchester cathedral, but his real passion in life, from the age of six, had been stamps. On leaving school he worked in the rag trade and in timber, till he set himself up as a stamp dealer, opening a stamp shop in Stockport. In those days, not long after the war, before TV, every half-decent-sized town in Britain had a stamp shop, if not two, and Harold's Stockport shop did quite well. Someone told him that a stamp shop in Bath was up for sale, which had a much better location and clientele, so in the mid-1950s he bought it and moved to Bath.

"I knew nothing about stamps till I met Harold," said Audrey. "As a girl, I was much more interested in the theatre. When we got married, I did the secretarial side, the bills and tax and all that, but gradually I became interested in the postal history side, rather than the actual stamps. I began collecting things like balances, which post offices used to weigh envelopes, and also prints of mail coaches. I became interested in coins as well, which we also began to sell in the shop."

She never found having the name Swindells much of an embarrassment, though Harold did tell her the correct pronunciation was Swin-dells, in two clear syllables.

"I've heard most of the jokes over the years. Luckily we never put Swindells" Stamp Shop over the door, it's always been the Bath Stamp Shop. It's not such a bad name, people do remember it.

"The funniest name I ever saw was when I was driving through Bridgnorth once and I saw a solicitors' called Dolittle and Dally. They must have had to put up with the same old jokes every day."

Talk of opening a postal history museum in Bath had gone on for some years, as Bath has played a vital part in the history of the postal service and there have always been many enthusiastic and knowledgeable local collectors, some of them quite wealthy.

"I remember discussing it with four people we knew, all millionaires. One was Charles Robertson of the jam firm and Karl Jaeger of the clothing firm. They were all keen collectors and keen on a museum, but when it came to getting any of them to put up the money, I got nowhere. I soon discovered that if you are setting up a museum, you don't really get much help till people can actually see it. When it's up and running, if it's any good, that's when you'll get lots of help."

In 1977, despite having a large family to bring up and support, Audrey and Harold put up their own money and bought premises at 51 Great Pulteney Street. They lived in the house and started to convert the lower ground floor into a postal museum, borrowing most of the items on long-term loans from collectors, establishing a charitable trust which would own and run the museum. It opened in 1979 with a grand ceremony, filling the streets of Bath with a liberation of 250 pigeons, a period mail coach with Martin Horler blowing the post horn, the landing of a helicopter from HMS *Birmingham* and people in nineteenth-century costumes.

They quickly acquired more material and soon outgrew their space. In 1985 they moved to bigger, council-owned premises in Broad Street, in a building that had been Bath's main post office from 1822 to 1853. They had an even grander grand opening this time, as Audrey does like a good party, and is also clearly a whizz at PR and contacts and organising people. She rang Clarence House, hoping to contact the Queen Mother.

"I got through and spoke to someone, explaining we were opening the Bath Postal Museum and I wondered if the Queen Mother would send a pigeon-gram to celebrate our opening. I explained that's a message sent inside a little metal container, the sort which pigeons used to carry during the war. I later heard from an equerry, Sir Martin something or other, who said Her Majesty would be delighted."

So, on the museum's opening day, a carrier pigeon left Clarence House and was in Bath three and a half hours later, carrying the welcome message from the Queen Mother.

Again, they had a real mail coach, gentlemen in period costume, plus this time two very popular celebs of the day — Leslie Crowther, star of a TV show called *Crackerjack*, and Richard Briers, greatly loved for his part in *The Good Life*. They agreed to perform the opening ceremony for nothing, thanks to Audrey, who knew that both happened to be stamp collectors.

"They were doing the opening ceremony just as the pigeon arrived, so all the crowds and TV cameras — we had two crews, from BBC Bristol and HTV in Wales — turned instead to watch the pigeon being carried in by his handler. I heard Leslie turn to Richard and say, 'Is this the first time you've been upstaged by a pigeon?' "

In 2005 came problems, the sort all little museums can face, even if they think they are making local waves and creating attention that will help them for ever. They were told they were having a massive rental increase — up from £5500 to £43,000. "I couldn't believe it. I knew we'd had a subsidised rent till then, but I hadn't realised what they thought the true rent should be. The council at the time was intent on getting what the government was calling 'best value' from all their resources. We just couldn't manage it. Despite our success, we had never run at a profit, so it did look as if we would have to close for ever.

"However, a local councillor told me about a property developer who might help us, Stephen Green, who was setting up something called Future Heritage. In an hour I was on the phone to him. The upshot was he found us premises very near, in the same street, in the basement of the present post office. He gave us a fifteen-year lease, which we'd never had before, at only £7500 a year."

Then came the problem of equipping the new museum, with up-to-date audio and visual displays, which all museums these days seem to be convinced they need, otherwise how will they ever attract anyone under the age of thirteen? The trustees worked out they would need £270,000 and three of them began applying to the National Lottery for funding. It took a year, but they got it, or at least 90 per cent of it, and the rest of it they raised themselves. The museum reopened once again — for the third time — in 2007. Such perseverance.

They don't have as much space in their present basement as they had previously, and a vast amount of their material is not on show but kept in their archives. Not surprisingly, visitor numbers have fallen slightly, from a high of about twelve thousand a year to around ten thousand. They are not making a profit, and struggle to raise money, but have always had excellent voluntary support, managing to run the museum with only two part-time paid staff and the rest volunteers. Audrey herself does around two days a week, unpaid, and she is clearly still the driving force. Harold, aged eighty-nine, rarely comes in these days as his short-term memory is not what it was, but he is eager to be kept informed about their activities and progress.

I asked if being in Bath was a help or handicap, with so many rival museums and attractions. "Bath itself is a huge draw, and there are loads of tourists, so the cake is bigger than in most places, but we all have to fight hard for our share. The trouble many places like ours have is getting volunteer help — there are not really enough volunteers to go round, as there are so many interesting places in Bath to do voluntary work. We have done quite well since moving here. Volunteers quite like telling people they work in the museum under the post office. It seems to be a sort of status symbol.

"Our biggest problem is actually the problem of stamps. When you tell people about this museum, they say oh, we don't collect stamps, no one in our family is interested. We then say it's not about stamps, it's about communication, the history of it over the centuries. Once kids are dragged along, they rarely want to leave, there's so many buttons for them to press, things to do. But getting them in, when they hear the word stamps, that's the big struggle."

Alas, I have to agree. Despite that boast about being the biggest collecting hobby, I suspect the great days of stamp collecting are over. All kids at one time collected stamps, every school had a stamp club. When I became a born-again collector in 1979, there were still thirty or so stamp shops and dealers in the Covent Garden and Strand area alone. Now at least two thirds have gone. I should think the demise of Woolies has added to the decline. That was where many children got their starter pack and cheapo album.

At the top end, philatelists do tend to appear a bit snobbish and elitist, with their arcane rules and awards, institutions and language. And at the bottom, collecting stamps projects a geeky, boring, speccy image. When almost all kids collected stamps in their childhood, they had had an involvement, a knowledge, which helped bring them back into the fold in their middle years, as happened with me. Now these possible returnees, who might be thinking again about some sort of collecting, have a mass of rival attractions — and also other new and unusual things they could be collecting. Adult collectors are more independent and original these days, willing to strike out on their own into new areas rather than boring old stamps. The fact that we no longer have a National Postal Museum in London is another sign of the times. I used to haunt it when I became born-again, as its collections were so rare. It closed in 1998, after a scandal involving some of the stamp treasures allegedly disappearing.

Audrey did not quite agree with all my observations, but she is well aware that the stamp world is in danger. "Which is very sad for future generations. You can learn so much from stamps, such as history and geography and politics. It teaches you about the whole world. I see my grandchildren collecting these stupid Japanese stickers, little trinkets, forgotten the name, but they are so expensive and so pointless compared with stamps. You can start collecting stamps for free, just by steaming them off envelopes."

I also told her about my bad experience as a stamp investor, which rather soured my love affair.

"Oh, I've heard that story all the time. It did such damage to the whole stamp world. Harold and I never sold investment portfolios in our own shop, so our customers did not get caught when the slump came. On the other hand, in good times, we of course gained by prices going up. At the moment, during this period of recession, stamps, strangely enough, have kept and even increased their value. That's what our son Mike tells us. He now runs the Bath Stamp Shop. It's nothing to do with us any more. We just do the museum."

After a couple of hours' chat, we went back to the museum and Audrey gave me a conducted tour. There appeared to be no other visitors, though by this time it was early afternoon.

I had been prepared to mock the audio-visual stuff Audrey had been going on about, but it turned out to be more useful, relevant and tasteful than I had feared. There are several short films about the history of writing, one of which is narrated by Richard Briers. "He did it for nothing, as a favour. It could have cost us £30,000 otherwise." There are also two portraits of eighteenth-century Bathonian gentlemen, in gold frames, which spring into life when you touch them, speaking from the frame itself, telling you who they were and their importance. Very cleverly done.

The first one was Ralph Allen who, in 1720, was the first person to set up a system of cross-country posts which did not go via London, as all previous postal services had done. He paid the Post Office £6000 a year for the contract, a enormous sum — about half a million today — and ran the inland postal system right to the borders of Scotland from his office in Bath. It didn't make him a profit for seven years, but then it came good, giving him enough money to invest in local quarries, the ones used to build Georgian Bath. He ended up very wealthy with a massive country estate.

John Palmer had an equally good idea, creating a system of very fast coaches which eventually carried the Royal Mail all over the country. In his case, he didn't become a millionaire on the proceeds, even though his Royal Mail coaches revolutionised communication. It was fifteen years before the Post Office repaid him for financing the entire project. Postal history does have its heroes and entrepreneurs and innovators, just as computers do today.

Another eminent Bathonian connected to postal reform was Thomas Musgrave, Bath postmaster from 1833 to 1854. He was responsible for posting the first-ever penny black, which he sent from Bath on 2 May 1840. He was of course jumping the gun as the first day of issue was officially 6 May, as every schoolboy collector used to know. The cover, with the stamp and date and postal marking clearly to be seen, came up for auction at Harmers in London in 1990.

Audrey went along to bid, knowing this was just the sort of prime treasure, with Bath connections, that would do wonders for the postal museum, but she failed to get it.

"It went for £55,000. It was an agent who bought it, whom I didn't recognise. I grabbed him afterwards to ask who he was bidding for, but he wouldn't tell me. We still don't know who owns it, apart from that it is someone in the Far East. If it ever came on the market again, it would probably fetch £1 million."

Other well-known Bathonians and events featured in the museum include Henry Cole, who devised the first Christmas card in 1843, and the first 100-mile airmail flight, which went from Bath to London in 1912.

The museum also has a collection of different letterboxes, including one that used to be attached to tramcars so that passengers could post their letters while travelling, plus franking and perforating machines.

One large display is given over to four thousand years of communication, from clay tablets carrying messages from Mesopotamia around 2000 BC, through papyrus letters from Egypt right up to the present day with mobile phones. Which enables the display to have the racy title Clay Mail to E-Mail.

I found the history of the mail coach very interesting, how they were allowed to race through toll gates, paying no tolls. A team of horses at a coaching inn had to be changed in six minutes max in order to adhere to the timetable. The post horn could be heard miles away, heralding its arrival. Coach travel was of course hellishly uncomfortable, with lots of terrible accidents as they clattered along at speeds of up to 15 mph on pot-holed roads.

One of the pleasant surprises to me was that the museum doesn't really have a lot of stamps, or even postal covers. Stamps can be a bit boring for the uncommitted. In fact it is mainly filled with objects, original artefacts to do with communication over the centuries. Audrey had boasted that, once inside, children do love it — which I had doubted, but now I could believe it.

She is not too worried about the future of the museum. She feels there is a strong and knowledgeable board of trustees and supporters who will be able to run it long after she and Harold have gone. None of their own six children, or eleven grand-children, wants to be involved in the museum and only one is interested in stamps, and he, Mike, has his own shop to run. The others went into a variety of careers — refrigerated vehicles, landscape gardening, music, art and journalism.

She must feel proud, having helped create such a museum, on a subject she knew nothing about till she got married, and seen it through all its various problems and struggles.

"I think the best thing about it has been the fun, not the pride. We have had so many wonderful events and I've met so many interesting people, and made so many friends, through the museum. It's given me a wonderful life."

So that's another reason for creating a museum. With a bit of luck, the world comes to you. Naturally, you have to be the right sort of person in the first place to want to meet the world, which not all collectors are.

Having been prejudiced against audio-visual nonsenses and interactive how's-your-fathers, I was quite impressed by some of her bits of modern techno-magic, particularly the portraits that come to life and start talking. I can see all ages finding that interesting.

Most of all, though, I was impressed by Audrey's promotional and PR skills — considering there was nothing in her background or training along those lines. She just did it. Now, should I hire a helicopter or an old stagecoach for the opening of my museum? Do I know any DJs or TV stars?

My wife and I did get invited, for some reason I never worked out, to a Buckingham Palace garden party several years ago. We never had her back. Very rude. I know, when I get my museum organised, I'll invite the Queen to tea and to have a look at my treasures. That should make a few lines in the local paper.

On the way back to Bath Spa station, I met an old woman in her eighties who looked like Mrs Tiggy-Winkle. I thought at first she might be a bag-lady till I realised she was struggling with her shopping. I asked her if I was on the right way to the railway station and she insisted on walking there with me, explaining that the roadworks were to do with a new bus station, which she hated, having campaigned against its design as it was not in keeping with Bath, absolute disgrace.

I told her I'd been to visit the Bath Postal Museum and she asked if I'd gone to the Museum of East Asian Art, as that was really excellent. She had worked there as a volunteer and loved it. She sounded from her accent and appearance as if she had always lived and worked around Bath, so I wondered how she had become interested in Eastern Art?

"Oh, I started collecting it when I was working in New York for the World Bank. I was in external affairs, PA to a director. The friend I shared an apartment with had lots of ancient Chinese plates, which we ate off!

"I've been round the whole world, you know, on my own — took a year, travelling with just one suitcase, to Afghanistan, Thailand, everywhere. My family are always telling me I should write my life story, it's been so interesting."

You should, I said, or at least get it down on tape for your grandchildren.

"Oh, I've got no children or grandchilden. I'm not married. But I'm still hoping."

She offered to sit with me till my London train came, but hers was just leaving, a local train to Westbury, so I bade her farewell — and good luck.

Working in a museum, even if it's just voluntary work, is also a way of meeting the world and having a social life.

During those ten years madly collecting stamps, I did make friends with many dealers, went to fairs big and small, and exhibitions, and joined various clubs and societies. It was an amusing distraction, kept me off the streets, till one day I woke up and said what am I doing? What's the point of all this?

I was still buying stamps, but not looking at them. Just shoving them in drawers. There's not a lot to look at anyway. I prefer items with more content, such as books, comics, postcards, letters, leaflets, magazines, which is why I have found myself with twenty or so other collections on different topics, including the suffragettes, first editions, the Lake District, the home front.

Most of all, I realised there were two areas where I really did feel actively passionate and genuinely interested, and also, I like to think, vaguely knowledgeable. That's when I decided to chuck in the stamps, sell up, even at a loss, and move on. I would concentrate on my other collections from now on, and on those two main ones in particular. Would I find museums devoted to them as I wandered around? Or perhaps museums on topics I would never have imagined could possibly exist?

Bath Postal Museum
27 Northgate Street
Bath BA1 1AJ
Tel 01225 460333
www.bathpostalmuseum.co.uk

CHAPTER
FOUR

The Baked Bean Museum of Excellence, Port Talbot

For about an hour, Captain Beany would not let me see his museum, keeping me talking in what he calls his interview room. I was beginning to think it was all a nonsense, I'd been conned by a joker or a fantasist, and the museum, if and when I was eventually allowed to see it, would be empty, or perhaps contain just one can of beans, ha ha.

Perhaps after all I should have gone to the National Coracle Centre up in Cenarth Falls in Carmarthenshire. That was on my list as another unusual Welsh museum devoted to just one subject, but it sounded a bit worthy and institutional, and also there didn't seem to be one person, one collector, behind it, which is what I had decided I was looking for, apart from unusual contents. And Captain Beany's collection did sound pretty unusual. After stamps — the most obvious, popular and longest-established of our modern-day collectibles — baked beans would certainly be a bit different.

I had spoken to Captain Beany on the phone and he sounded real enough, and looking at his website I saw he had had an official opening of his Baked Bean Museum of Excellence in January 2009 with a well-known TV and radio personality — so it said, though I didn't recognise the name, but that doesn't mean anything, I wouldn't recognise most TV stars if I met them in my porridge. I also noted he was a member of the Association of Independent Museums, which was a good sign.

On the phone he had asked if I wanted him to dress up. For what? For my visit, he said. Don't bother. I'll just be wearing my usual old rags. OK, good, he replied. I won't have to put on my Captain Beany costume then.

Which he had not. He was wearing jeans, an old shirt and a woolly hat which he kept on all the time. Aged fifty-ish, thin, slender, pale but fit-looking. Having said I am not up on TV stars, he did remind me of that bloke in *The Fast Show* who runs down the street shouting "Brilliant!".

He laughed all the time, which was a bit disconcerting, partly because I found his Welsh accent rather hard to follow and also because I couldn't always quite work out what he was laughing at. I decided it was nervous laughter, to put me or himself at ease. And yet, looking round at all the photos and certificates and newspaper cuttings on the walls of his very neat and tidy interview room, he has clearly received many visitors over the years.

TV crews from as far afield as Korea have traipsed to his little council flat in South Wales to capture what they believe to be a true British eccentric who has developed a passion for baked beans. In Korean homes, he's probably better known than our prime minister. But then we do much the same: all countries love Fancy That human interest stories about funny people abroad doing funny things.

Captain Beany lives in Port Talbot, on the top floor of a three-storey 1960s council block on an estate called Sandfields. Not scary or vandalised, just a bit sad and worn out. Port Talbot itself is pretty sad these days, having been for generations one of the industrial powerhouses of South Wales. On one side of the estate there used to be a massive BP chemical works, now gone, while the other way you came to the steelworks, which employed twelve thousand people only twenty years ago. Still going, but now Indian-owned and with barely three thousand workers.

Captain Beany lives alone in his two-bedroom flat. He originally lived here with his mother, nursing her till she died. He has turned his living room into the interview room and the main bedroom is now his museum — but before opening up he was insisting I had a good look at his personal memorabilia and heard the stories behind them.

He wasn't born Captain Beany, surprisingly enough. He was born Barry Kirk in 1954 and at school he was always known as "Captain", after the Starship *Enterprise*'s Captain Kirk.

"Aged five, at primary school I used to sit at my desk with plastic specs on and a false moustache. I remember one day another teacher coming into the class and remarking on the fact that the other kids were not looking at me. She was told by our class teacher that I was always like that, so everyone was used to me.

"I suppose I was trying to draw attention to myself. I did funny voices all the time, and impressions. At secondary school I did join the drama class, thinking it would be great having an audience, which it was. But I couldn't learn my lines. I hated having to work from a script. I have the attention span of a goldfish. So that was that. I felt I was a thespian inside — ha ha, hee hee — but it would never come out. I wouldn't be able to find a channel. I presumed I'd therefore end up putting away the false moustache, get a mundane job, get married and have 2.5 kids."

The mundane job part came true and he had a sequence of them when he left school, armed with five O levels. He reeled them off, almost having hysterics at the memory of each one. "British Constitution! Can you believe it! I have an O level in British Constitution! Brilliant. I also got art and design, drama, RE and pottery. Can you believe, pottery!"

For four years he worked not far away at the DVLA office in Swansea, as a machine operator, then he moved to Surrey as a signwriter, returning home to Port Talbot and his mum to work on a computer at the BP chemical works, where he stayed from 1978 to 1992, when he was offered redundancy.

While working there, he started doing a lot of charity work, going on sponsored walks, helping good causes. His moment of epiphany, his life-changing moment — or at least what became his name-changing moment — occurred on 11 September 1986. He got up to examine the framed photographs and cuttings of the event which happened that day, just to check the precise date, which of course he knew all along. "I had read somewhere that someone had got into the *Guinness Book of Records* for lying in a bath of custard for twenty-four hours. Then I heard someone had sat in a bath of spaghetti for fifty hours. I was wondering what I could do when I thought, I know, baked beans! I'll lie in a bath full of them for a hundred hours!"

It wasn't quite the totally original piece of inspiration you might imagine. He says he pinched the idea from the Who. He scurried off to find one of their old LPs, called *The Who Sell Out*, on the cover of which is a photo of Roger Daltrey in a bath of baked beans. It looks to me suspiciously like a photomontage, but the seed was sown.

Barry got sponsorship from people all over Port Talbot. Heinz, alas, ignored his appeals for help, or at least free beans, but a local businessman paid for 360 tins. Another provided a bath, which was set up in the foyer of the Aberavon Hotel. He got in, naked but for his swimming trunks, and children had to pay £1 to pour one can of beans over his head. In four hours, all the tins had been emptied and the bath was full.

"It's strange what the human body can endure. I got a shock with the cold at first but then I got used to it. Someone gave me a board which I put across the bath and laid my head on it and got about four hours" sleep that night. But a hundred hours is four nights! I was exhausted, unshaven and very tired by the end — but I got massive publicity, from TV and radio and the papers. I did create a record and got a certificate — look, on the shelf — from the *Guinness Book of Records*. Best of all, I raised £1500, which I gave to a local mental handicap charity.

"I had thought that would be the end, my last charity stunt, but for days afterwards, kids were following me in the street saying look, there's the bean man. I began to think I could turn him into a character. I thought of my childhood nickname 'Captain', added it to Bean and then made it Beany as two syllables flowed better, and out came 'Captain Beany'. I saw him as a super-hero from a *Marvel* comic. He had come from the Planet Beanus to help human beans. So after that, when I did other charity stunts, I dressed up as Captain Beany, in an orange jumpsuit and cape.

"In 1992, I legally changed my name. I went to a solicitor and asked him to do it. He laughed so much he let me off the £80 he should have charged. Then I went to Lloyds Bank with the documents and said my name is now Captain Beany, can I have a credit card in that name? They laughed as well — but I got one. I even changed my passport — look, here it is. It's in the name of Captain Beany. My driving licence is as well. Oh, if I only I had a car . . ."

Since 1992 he has run about twenty marathons, all over the world, including Boston, Los Angeles, New York, Dublin, Brussels and seven London Marathons, each time as Captain Beany, carrying a plate of beans on toast all the way round. "I love marathons and I'm now getting ready for the next London one. The spectators are my audience, that's why I love them." Over the last twenty years, he reckons, he has raised over £100,000 for charity.

He has stood for seven elections, local and national, as Captain Beany. "I stood in one general election against the late Screaming Lord Sutch, God bless his soul, but he did better than me. In one local election, I got 139 votes, beating the Lib Dem candidate who got only 124. She was so disappointed she gave up politics and never stood again."

On his walls he has certificates awarded to Captain Beany, medals won by Captain Beany, the Planet Beanus officially registered in his name by an American star-naming company, and an insurance policy that guarantees to pay Captain Beany one million pounds in the event that he is a) Abducted by Aliens, b) Impregnated by Aliens, or c) Consumed by Aliens. He says it's from a genuine insurance company, who agreed to it as a stunt, though they have since gone bust. On 1 April 2009 he was honoured by the Eccentric Club in London and received the 2009 Great Britain Eccentric Award.

Oh what larks — but I was getting desperate, becoming convinced it all was just a silly, if harmless, stunt to attract attention, that the so-called museum room would be empty, just full of space, ha ha. But eventually he got on to the origins of the museum.

"About ten years ago, as part of my Captain Beany character, I started collecting items to do with baked beans. I have always liked them, lived on them for years really, so I went on eBay and began buying any unusual beany items.

"When I'd got a few dozen, I decided to put them all in one room and call it the Baked Bean Museum and I painted all the walls orange. Then I thought I have to do this properly. I don't want anything tacky, so I contacted a professional designer and he got me some proper display shelves, made of Perspex and glass, shatterproof glass in case any tins of beans explode, ha ha. They weren't cheap. In fact he charged me £1500 just for the shelves. I think he saw me coming.

"I've been letting visitors see my museum for the last seven years, such as TV crews and parties of students. There's a Captain Beany Appreciation Society at the University of Aberystwyth, bless them, which has 560 members on Facebook. But the museum has never been officially opened.

"I was waiting for a celeb to arrive and cut the ribbon, but no one appeared. I was hoping for an A-list celeb, such as Anthony Hopkins, the actor. He comes from round here, you know, as did Richard Burton. We also have Katherine Jenkins and Michael Sheen, the actor who played Tony Blair. No, I didn't approach any of them. I just waited, thinking someone will arrive, present themselves, perhaps from another planet.

86

"In the end, Danny Wallace materialised. You haven't heard of him? Oh, he's very famous. He rang up one day to say he was doing a TV series about eccentric people and wanted to do a programme about me. So I asked him when he was here to cut the ribbon, and he also unveiled a plaque. I've put him in my Haricot Hall of Fame. Come on, I'll show you . . ."

At long last we went into the hall and I admired his Hall of Fame. It consists of Polaroid photos of all the TV crews and media people and groups who have been to see him and his museum over the years.

Finally, with a lot of pretend blowing of trumpets, he opened the bedroom door marked Baked Bean Museum of Excellence. He added the "of Excellence" for the opening ceremony, thinking that, as he had waited so long, it was bound to be really excellent by now.

The door was thrown open wide, but I couldn't see much at first as the window blind was down. It was quite dark till he switched on the light.

I expected to be underwhelmed, though ready to make polite noises and affect delight, but I have to say I was really impressed. It is indeed what he had said it was, a baked bean museum. It is a whole room, full of display units, neatly ordered and arranged, totally devoted to baked beans.

The blind is kept down as he doesn't want sunlight to enter and perhaps affect his treasures, and the radiator is always off. "Some of the cans are still full, so I wouldn't like them to overheat and start ponging. That could upset the neighbours."

The display units do look very professional, self-standing, about six feet high, in white with glass shelves, arranged in a logical order as you proceed round the room. On the top shelf of the first unit is a collection of Mr Bean merchandising, a slight cheat I suppose, as his character is not directly connected to beans, but permissible. It includes film stills of Mr Bean, Mr Bean toy cars, videos, clocks, dolls and a signed photo of Rowan Atkinson as Mr Bean. He paid £25 for this on eBay.

I was surprised to see how many merchandising products and spin-offs there had been from Mr Bean. Captain Beany obviously thinks so as well — he's a bit jealous that his own character has not yet spawned as many. However, on a shelf below he has a collection of Captain Beany merchandising which he himself has created for his own character — not quite as numerous and some of the stuff looked a bit home-made, but the Captain Beany keyrings and fridge magnets appeared professional enough.

Next, you come to a most interesting and extensive collection of American items all to do with the origins of what we now call baked beans, which, as Captain Beany tried to explain, began in Boston, hence the fact that they are often still called Boston baked beans. When the Puritans arrived in Boston, or was it the Pilgrims, he couldn't quite remember, but a lot of them were very religious and wouldn't do any cooking on Sunday. So every Saturday they would make a big pot of beans, perhaps throw in some pork, and that would be the dish eaten on Sundays.

Lots of different manufacturers of baked beans set up in New England, and then throughout the USA, most of which I had never heard of — such as Bush Baked Beans, Grandma Brown's Baked Beans, M and B Baked Beans and the Old Fart Baked Bean Co. Along with examples of their produce, like any good museum curator he has also collected their associated advertising and merchandising — dolls, jigsaws, plates, bean pots, tea towels, bed warmers, space hoppers, postcards, Frisbees and clocks, all to do with the various baked bean producers, complete with their logos.

"Look at this clock — it keeps Greenwich Bean Time, ha ha."

Moving round, I came to collections of European baked beans, with tins and other items from countries like Germany and Holland, and also Britain. In his British display area, there is a tin of Biba baked beans. I remember going round Biba in the seventies, wondering at all the amazing clothes, and my wife still has a pair of purple canvas boots from there. All I kept was a Biba plastic bag and Biba bill. But I don't remember them doing their own baked beans, or any sort of processed food. Wow, I said, you've got an unusual piece of modern British consumer history. "I had to pay £40 for it — the most I have ever paid for a tin of beans. Lots of people were after it because it's an iconic label."

There was another British baked bean I had somehow also missed, one sold at Asda. This was baked beans in chocolate sauce. Ugh. "Yes, that was what

89

most people thought. It was taken off the shelves after about one day, so it's very hard to find. Again I bought it on eBay."

His British section includes quite a few items related to HP baked beans, which he says is the only truly British manufacturer. One of his most touching HP items is a set of cufflinks, still in their presentation box, with the engraved message "Cufflinks Presented for 20 Years" Service to HP Baked Beans, Wisbech, Cambridgeshire'.

"Just think of the poor soul who got them. Knocking himself out all those years on a baked bean production line and all he gets is a pair of measly cufflinks. Poor bugger, bless him, whoever he was."

The biggest single display in his whole museum is, naturally enough, devoted to Heinz beans, which is of course a US company, though they have been manufacturing in England since 1886 according to the centenary booklets in his collection. He has a vast range of all their different sizes and types of tins, plus aprons, tea towels, soft toys. When they decided to start spelling the name "Heinz Beanz", he had to start again, getting all the same sorts of items only with a Z. Ah, once you become a collector, it never stops.

He has a copy — not the original — of an historic photo that shows Herbert Ponting, a member of Captain Scott's Antarctic expedition, in 1911, sitting in a snowy wasteland on top of a box on which you can clearly read the words Heinz Beans. How's that for product placement?

Most of his baked beans-related stuff has been bought quite cheaply, because, so he says, there is no one else collecting it. I told him this was his fantasy. There will be dozens of others out there, there always are, only he hasn't met them yet. But it does appear old tins of baked beans are very inexpensive, if you can find them. He has also been given a lot of stuff by people clearing their shelves. Tins of old beans are, I suppose, a bit awkward, not to say worrying, to keep.

But as with that Biba tin, he often finds himself up against more mainstream collectors who are after the same objects, but for different reasons, which puts up the prices. This happens particularly with things like Dinky and Corgi toys, which include delivery lorries for various baked bean firms. He has, for instance, thirty different examples of Heinz beans die-cast vehicles, still in their original packaging, which is how all true collectors want them. They were not cheap. The single most expensive item in his whole museum is a Dinky Supertoy of a Heinz lorry from the 1960s, which cost him £200.

I reckoned, looking round his museum, that he has about five hundred different items, though he himself wasn't sure. He clearly dusts them, as they were all sparkling, but he doesn't count them. Nor has he labelled them, tut tut, which all good curators should do, though as he only does one-to-one tours he does his own commentary.

Overall, he thinks, he has not spent more than £1000 so far on the actual contents of his collection, making the glass display shelves still the single biggest outlay.

So where does he get his money from? He doesn't appear to have had any sort of job since 1992 when he was made redundant from BP, though he does live simply and frugally and has no family to support.

"When I took the redundancy money and ran, I did have enough to live on for a while and was able buy things for my baked beans collection. I did apply for jobs, but didn't get them, so I was entitled to benefits. I began to realise that one of the problems about my getting any sort of work was being called Captain Beany. When people saw that was my name, they didn't want to know, thinking I'd be a weirdo.

"So, yes, I was on benefits for a long time, which allowed me to do all the work for charity, raising money. But four years ago I went self-employed. I am now technically a small trading company. And what I am trading in is Captain Beany merchandising. Every so often, I order about two thousand or so Captain Beany keyrings, fridge magnets and dolls, made to my design, and try to sell them. I don't charge people to look at my museum, but I hope they might buy some of the goods as souvenirs. It means that for the last four years I have not taken any benefits."

So how many people visit his museum in a year? "I'd like to say tens of thousands, but the truth is probably around a hundred or so a year — always by appointment."

He would of course have a bit of problem with his local council if the museum became a professional concern, and probably also with his neighbours if queues and cars suddenly started appearing outside and people were traipsing up the communal stairs to his flat, though he does seem to be well loved and popular in the area.

He would ideally like more space for his museum and more money to buy more items, but even if he were to win the lottery and own his own big house he doesn't think he would open up his museum to the general public. He doesn't have that sort of yearning. Captain Beany, he fondly hopes, will one day become a public figure, a character taken up by comics and films, but his actual museum is more of a private thing, an act of love and devotion to a persona he has created to save himself from, well, whatever has been troubling him in his life. He did hint at various problems and dramas he has had, mainly to do with the death of his mother and a younger brother. His relentless public cheerfulness would appear to be a cover for something or other, though he rarely let it slip. If nothing else, Captain Beany has probably saved him from boredom and depression, given him an audience and a purpose when life otherwise had not given him very much.

"Captain Beany did take over my life. No one knew who I was till then. But it has begun to feel as if I have a dual personality. I am now going back more to being Barry Kirk as well. Two years ago Barry Kirk became a born-again Christian. Barry now goes to church, an evangelical one in Port Talbot — but Captain Beany, he has not yet seen the light. Coming from Planet Beanus, he has his own bean of light . . ."

His mobile phone rang, which rather alarmed me because all I could hear was a disembodied voice echoing round the room.

"Planet Beanus to Planet Earth, please communicate. Captain Beany, are you there? Require your immediate assistance!"

He then had hysterics at his own wit and cleverness, letting it ring and ring, doubled up with laughter, before answering the call from a friend. He created the ringtone himself, as of course in his working life he was quite handy with computers and technical stuff — which you will see if you study his website.

It is the only ringtone he has, so when it rings in public places like the post office, strangers are very surprised, much to his delight. "I love their surprised expressions — but I carry on as Captain Beany, saying Captain Beany here, then I say I must go off into a private corner to take an urgent message."

He insisted on coming back to town with me in my taxi, wanting to show me where he normally sets up his museum souvenir shop. Every museum, of any size or sort, national or private, has to have a souvenir shop. Some are often as big as the museum itself, for this is how they attempt to make an income, apart from entry fees. By the unusual nature of his museum, and having it located in a council flat, he is a bit limited when it comes to cash flow. As we wandered round Port Talbot's shopping centre, he pointed out all the shops and stores where the owners or managers allow him set up a little stall for a few hours at the weekend. He sits there selling Captain Beany keyrings and magnets and dolls to local families and kids.

Everywhere we went, people did smile when they saw him, shouted over and said, Hi Captain, Hello Beany. He does seem to give pleasure to people, and he has raised all that money for charity.

There was a friendliness about the town, despite a rather deprived, run-down feeling, the sort of ordinary, rather impoverished, pound-shop kind of place that only ever makes the national headlines when something awful happens there — or something wonderful. Which in fact did happen, the month after I had been to see Captain Beany.

In November 2009 a couple from Port Talbot — the man unemployed with £68 overdrawn at the bank — won the astounding sum of £45.5 million on the Euromillions lottery. I felt a bit jealous — not of the money, certainly not, I won the lottery when I met my wife — but of the copy. I did a book about the National Lottery when it started, following the winners of ten jackpots over the first year after their win. The biggest win amongst my lot, in fact for many years to come, was £22 million. Piddling really. I don't think Captain Beany would be jealous either. He seemed content with how he had his museum, what he had done in his own modest way, and probably wouldn't want a few million to buy better baked bean treasures or build a bigger museum.

He came into the railway station with me, right on to the platform, saying he would wait with me till my train left, as if he didn't quite believe that I was going back to

London and that really I secretly lived in Port Talbot all the time.

I thanked him for all his time and help and told him I thought his little museum was a gem.

I had perhaps come slightly to scoff and mock, thinking it might all be nonsense, but I really thought it was a worthwhile if rather unusual topic. He'd made a good fist of it, creating something out of nothing. It made me think that opening my own little museum, showing my collections, might not be so silly or unrealistic after all. But I don't think I would ever open a museum in my own home, let alone my own bedroom. My wife would not be at all amused. She gets cheesed off as it is, with my clutter all over the place. Having strangers walking round the house, making inane and fatuous comments — I had a tin of those, only bigger, oh, so you haven't got the full set — that would really cheese her off. Cheese — I bet there are loads of cheese museums. But I think one comestible museum is enough.

So what about the future of Captain Beany's museum? As he is a single man, what will happen to it all? "I would hate it all to be chucked in a skip when I die, which is possible. My fantasy is that a local museum in South Wales might accept it, put some of the items on display. That's my hope. But whatever happens, collecting the stuff has given me such a lot of interest and pleasure.

"When I go, I have left instructions that I want to be buried in a coffin shaped like a baked bean can and my inscription will read 'Bean there, done it, got the museum . . .'"

Baked Bean Museum of Excellence
6 Flint House
Moorland Road
Sandfields Estate
Port Talbot
West Glamorgan SA12 6JX
Tel 01639 680896
www.bakedbeanmuseumofexcellence.org.uk

CHAPTER
FIVE

The Casbah and the Beatles, Liverpool

The large imposing house, No. 8 Hayman's Green, was much as I remember it, even though I was last here over forty years ago. Detached Victorian villa with fifteen bedrooms and one acre of garden in a very quiet residential road in the suburb of West Derby, about four miles from the centre of Liverpool. At one time it had housed the local Conservative Association.

It had looked rather neglected in 1967, with the garden overgrown, a bit mysterious and forbidding, perhaps a haunted house, kept a bit scary to frighten away kids or intruders. It still looks rather ill-kempt, though I couldn't see much. The trees in the front garden have grown huge and obscure the front of the house so you can see little of it from the road.

I went through the gate and down the driveway to the left of the house, stepping carefully as someone appeared to have been at the drive with a pneumatic drill and left jagged slabs of concrete sticking up. At the end of the drive I noticed an expensive-looking Jaguar that had managed to get through. As I approached the front porch, which was peeling and chipped, two fierce-looking dogs rushed out to greet me.

In 1967 I was working on a biography of the Beatles and was desperate to get into this house. It was the family home of Pete Best, the drummer who had been ditched in August 1962 after two years of playing with them in Liverpool and Hamburg, his place to be taken by Ringo just at the moment when they were about to conquer the known world.

His mother, Mona Best, had at first refused to see me, saying that, as my book was going to be the authorised biography, I would be taking their side and she was still furious with them for what they had done to her Pete. I said I would not be taking sides, just trying to tell the truth. I desperately needed to hear what happened from Pete himself. No chance, Pete was giving no interviews. He didn't want to have anything to do with anyone connected with the Beatles after what they did to him. In the end, though, she agreed to see me herself.

I was very pleased because I knew that Mona had figured highly in the Beatles saga — as all true believers now know, which means millions all over the world today, though in 1967 there were not many who knew anything at all about her.

It was in this large, rambling house that Mona had opened a little coffee club, which she called the Casbah, in August 1959. The Quarrymen, as the Beatles were then, played there as the opening live group, and later, when they had become the Beatles, performed many times over a period of two years. By this time her son Pete had joined them as their drummer — till the axe fell.

I remember we sat in a large upstairs room and she glared at me for a long time before agreeing to answer any questions. She was a very attractive but formidable woman, small, rather olive skinned. She had been born in 1924 in Delhi, where her father was in the army, and brought up with servants. She married an army officer, John Best, had two sons, Peter and Rory, both born in India, in 1941 and 1944, and then after the war they all returned to Liverpool. The Best family had for many years owned the Liverpool Stadium, famous as a venue for boxing and wrestling, and John Best became a boxing promoter. He did quite well, but not well enough to move from a smallish house to this vast villa.

The legend in the family was that Mona had spotted the house for sale, set her heart on it, and, without telling her husband, pawned her jewellery and put the money on a horse called Never Say Die in the 1954 Derby — which came in first. It was thanks to this money that they were able to buy the house.

In 1959, Mona's two teenage boys were into pop music, which she encouraged as she liked it herself. She happened to see a TV programme about the 2i's coffee bar in Soho, where the early skiffle groups and embryo rock bands were playing, and thought Liverpool should have one. She bought an espresso coffee machine, the first in Liverpool, so she claimed, and decided to clean up the cellars under her house, which had been unused and were full of junk, and open a coffee club for the local teenagers. She called it the Casbah after hearing

Charles Boyer utter the line "Come with me to the Casbah" in a film called *Algiers*. It also sounded suitably exotic, in keeping with her own Indian background.

She told me all this as we chatted. After about an hour, I asked again if I could possibly see Pete sometime. She said he's here, he's been listening in the next-door room.

Pete sheepishly emerged, wearing a white, dusty coat. He had just finished shift work in a bread factory, slicing bread for £18 a week. He sat down, sighed, clearly not really wanting to talk about the Beatles and what had happened. But he did, slowly and patiently.

On 15 August 1962, Pete and Neil Aspinall, the Beatles' roadie, who lived at Pete's house, had said to John that they would pick him up the next day in the van, as usual, for their next engagement. John said don't bother, he had made other arrangements. It seemed odd to Pete, but not remarkable.

The next day Brian Epstein called Pete in and told him the news — the Beatles wanted him out and Ringo in. Pete asked why. Brian muttered something about George Martin, with whom they had had their first audition, thinking Pete wasn't a good enough drummer. He had been good enough for two years, in Hamburg and Liverpool, so why were they doing this now? But that was it. They went on to fame and millions and Pete went on to, well, nothing very much.

Hundreds of Beatles fans had protested in 1962 when the news came out, holding placards, some blaming John, others blaming George, who got a punch in the eye during one demonstration. Pete had been very popular, as all the contemporary accounts reported, described as the handsome one, if very quiet and retiring.

A few weeks later, back in London, I was with the Beatles. I told them about the people from their past whom I had seen in Hamburg and Liverpool. When I mentioned I had seen Pete and said he was now slicing bread, they all fell silent, then changed the subject. Some time afterwards I was with John, on his own, at his house and he brought up the subject again. "We were cowards when we sacked him. We made Brian do it. But if we had told Pete to his face, it would probably have ended in a fight."

What I didn't know that day I saw Pete in 1967 was that some time after the sacking he had been so depressed that he tried to commit suicide, turning on the gas fire in a locked room at Hayman's Green. Fortunately he was discovered in time by his brother Rory.

I also didn't know that day — though John Lennon later told me, sniggering but swearing me to secrecy — that at the time of the sacking, Mona, aged thirty-eight, who had been separated from her husband for some time, had just given birth to another son, Roag. And the father was Neil Aspinall, then aged twenty. It gave an extra emotional element to the whole drama, though no one outside the family circle knew at the time, nor in fact for many, many years. (Mona died in 1988. Neil went on to be the head of Apple and died in 2008.)

I never knew what happened to Pete afterwards, though he did write his memoirs in 1985. So I had a lot of catching up to do when Pete eventually appeared. He doesn't live in the house any more, but nearby. He looked very fit for his age, lean and healthy, good head of grey hair, neat moustache, and seemed confident and happy, more so than he had done forty-odd years ago.

After the dead-end bakery job he joined the civil service. Like John, Paul and George (but not Ringo), Pete had passed the eleven-plus exam for grammar school and had gone to Liverpool Collegiate, where he had passed five O levels. He started at the bottom as a clerk and worked his way up to training manager, taking early retirement in 1993.

And then he went back to drumming, after playing at an anniversary event to celebrate thirty years since the Casbah had first opened, which had attracted huge crowds, encouraging him to start his own group, the Pete Best Band. It is still going strong, making records and performing around the world. These days, he says, they try to limit their tours to five weeks and to be away for no more than five months a year. They play heavy rock and roll, not skiffle, anywhere from clubs with audiences of two hundred up to open-air stadiums in front of twenty-five thousand.

Also in the Pete Best Band, and also on drums, is Roag Best, his half-brother, son of Neil, now aged forty-seven, smaller, stockier, and bearded, more outgoing and extrovert than Pete. Roag acts as manager of the band, and of Pete.

The house still belongs to the Best family, to the three brothers, left to them when their mother Mona died. Roag, like Pete, lives elsewhere, but one of Roag's sons lives in the house, as do various other people. Upstairs they have a recording studio and editing suite and people who work there usually doss down in the house. It did have a bit of a feeling of a sixties squat. One room is the office for the Pete Best Band, and also the office for the Casbah Coffee Club. Yes, it is now open again — this time as a museum.

It was Roag who thought of it, incensed when he was walking down Mathew Street in Liverpool one day and saw notices saying "Welcome to the Cavern Club — Home of the Beatles". The original Cavern Club, which is where the Beatles went on to appear, was demolished in the 1970s, at a time when the city authorities didn't seem to be interested in, or even aware of, the tourist goldmine on their doorstep. The Cavern was later rebuilt, but not on the same site.

"So it's not genuine for a start, nor was it the Home of the Beatles," says Roag. "The Casbah club, if anywhere, was their home. They played here as the Quarrymen and then came back later for their first performance in Liverpool as the Beatles. In all, they played here about forty times. This is where it all happened, this is the place that really matters. I couldn't let the Cavern get away with that statement. You know what happens. If something gets repeated enough times, and nobody counters it, it becomes a fact."

Roag and his brothers and family started clearing out the cellars, which had not been used as a club since 24 June 1962, the Beatles having been the last group to perform there before Mona closed it. Since then, they had been used for storage. They opened three years ago and now have a rather swish website and each year attract between five and ten thousand visitors. Bookings are by appointment only, with everyone getting a guided tour, usually with either Roag or his brother Rory. They want to keep it an intimate, family affair.

Roag and Pete took me down the stairs to give me a conducted tour together. The public today, as in the past, enter from the back garden, which leads into the cellars at ground level. They run the whole length of the house and are far more extensive than would appear from the outside.

The first room is a cloakroom, where membership cards were shown, for Mona was very strict, and coat tickets were taken. So popular was the club that they quickly had to have two cloakrooms, one for the girls upstairs. On the wall on the right as you enter are the large, white-painted letters CCC, for Casbah Coffee Club, and a large insect, covering the whole wall. It's rather clumsily painted and hard to make out if it's a spider or a beetle. Naturally Roag likes to believe it is a beetle, though when the club opened the Quarrymen were some way away from changing their name. Mona had hired them a few weeks before the opening night, when the club was still not quite ready, so all of them were given paintbrushes and told to start painting the walls and ceilings.

In the second, much bigger room, which they call the Aztec Room, John was made to paint the ceiling three times. First of all he covered it in hideous figures, pot-bellied men, crippled women, children with three arms, the sort of crude cartoon figures he was doing for his own amusement at the local art school. Mona was furious and made him paint over them and start again. This time he did the whole ceiling in green. Mona didn't like that either. She said she wanted something African or Aztec. John covered the ceiling with lots of little patterns, thinking perhaps of the decoration on an African warrior's shield, which he'd probably seen in a boy's comic. This time Mona approved.

Low down on the right-hand wall, which is wood-panelled, you can clearly see that someone has carved the name John. Mona was furious when she saw it and gave John a slap, but it was too late to remove it. The wood had just been newly installed and painted, in black, and she didn't have time to start again as they were working against the clock to get everything ready in time.

She also discovered, at the last moment, that John had done some of his painting work in gloss, not emulsion, as he had been told. Being unable to see much without his glasses, he had picked the wrong pot. Mona was in a panic that it would still be wet on opening night — but it dried in time.

The third room is the where the Quarrymen played on that opening night. It's hard to believe they could have stood up in here, never mind play. It's little more than a corridor, just over five feet in width, but of course they didn't have a drummer or a drum kit that evening. This room is now called the Rainbow Room, as the ceiling was painted by Paul in a rainbow pattern.

Next door is a much bigger room, which became the Band Room when the club grew more popular and the Beatles, when they returned, had a proper drummer, namely Pete. Lots of well-known local groups played here apart from the Beatles, including Rory Storm and the Hurricanes, with whom Ringo used to play in Liverpool and Hamburg, in the same clubs as the Beatles, which is where he got to know them. Rory Storm was very tall, around six foot three, and you can still see the hole in the ceiling that he made while jumping up and down too enthusiastically. In this room, there is another carving by John, on the ceiling this time, which says John I'm Back.

The Beatles' first spell at the Casbah, while still calling themselves the Quarrymen, ended in a row. Mona was paying them £3 a session, which meant fifteen shillings each for John, Paul, George and their fourth member at the time, Ken Brown. One evening Ken arrived feeling ill, so Mona offered him a bedroom upstairs to rest in. When the time came to pay the band, she paid the three who had played fifteen shillings each, and also gave Ken his fifteen shillings. They maintained the three of them should have shared the £3. It ended in a row and they stormed out, threatening never to return.

Sometime later, when they got their first Hamburg booking and were still without a regular drummer, Paul rang Pete and asked if he was still playing and, more importantly, had he got his own drums? Since the Casbah had first opened, Pete had learned to play the drums and was playing in various groups. He said yes and went off with them to Hamburg.

On their return, they performed at the Casbah, this time as the Beatles, with Pete as their drummer. Hence John writing on the ceiling that he was back.

It was at the Casbah that John persuaded his art-school friend Stu Sutcliffe, who had just won an important art prize, the John Moore's prize, worth £45, to spend it all on a guitar — even though he couldn't play the guitar — and come with them to Hamburg. (Where he fell in love with a German girl, Astrid Kirchherr, and then in 1962 suddenly died of a brain tumour.)

All these stories and incidents are well known to Beatles fans everywhere, and now, with the Casbah opened up again, they can visit one of the Beatles shrines in the flesh, stand on the holy spots, imagine where the magic first emerged, relive the dramas, inspect the relics.

Well, relics is perhaps a slight exaggeration. There are not a great many artefacts to see, apart from the hand-painted walls, ceilings and carvings done by John, Paul and George and also a silhouette of John painted by Cynthia, then John's girlfriend, later his wife. But they do have on show some chairs that were there at the time, a coffee machine, some crockery and the original Dansette record player that was used at the club.

Their more valuable relics have been locked in their archives, such as a guitar played by Paul, a Vox amplifier, microphones and other sound equipment used by the Beatles while performing in the Casbah. Most were on display when the Casbah first reopened, but they feared wear and tear from people handling them — or worse, disappearing with them. The conducted tour lasts roughly sixty minutes, then visitors are allowed to wander back and forth around the cellar rooms and look at things again for themselves, ending up in the coffee bar — the same one that was there in the sixties, which now doubles as souvenir shop. It contains a huge Philco fridge, which came from America, with a massive handle, which can be opened on either side. Beatles fans will enjoy the excellent display of photos and documents, posters, cards and tickets from the 1959–62 period that covers the walls in every room. None is original — they are photocopies — but even so, I found them fascinating. There are many I had not seen before, such as the handwritten biographical notes each Beatle wrote while in Hamburg, a letter written to the Hamburg police by Pete after they had been expelled, and letters from Pete to his mum describing what the Beatles were doing in Hamburg. Well, some of it.

Sticking to that period and gathering enough material is quite a challenge, as of course it was post-1962 that Beatlemania started and there were suddenly billions of images. They have also tried to arrange the rooms and the displays chronologically, so that you begin with the history of the Best family, descriptions of coffee bars of the period, the creation of the Casbah, the history of the Quarrymen, before moving on to Hamburg and the Beatles.

There are five main interconnecting cellar rooms in all, plus corridors and alcoves, and everything has been painted as it was in 1959, which means mainly in black. There are quite a few steps up and down between the cellars, with yellow and black warning lines and notices saying Mind Your Head. These notices used to read Beware the Casbah Kiss — Mind Your Head, but every single one of them got stolen as souvenirs. Now they now stick to the simpler wording.

Although the cellar rooms are more numerous and spacious than I had imagined, it's still hard to believe that three hundred members crammed in on that opening night to hear the Quarrymen. The record, later on, for one night's attendance, when there were two sessions, was 1331. The noise, the sweat — my dears, it must have been unbearable, for there was no air conditioning.

Upstairs again after the tour, I sat with Roag and Pete in their office as they described the endless meetings and form-filling that lasted a year before they got all the necessary planning, health and safety permissions. They were now in discussions once again with the planning people about putting up a sign at the front of the house. At the moment there is nothing to tell people this is the Casbah, though when you get into the grounds, down the drive, round at the back, there is an arrow pointing to the Casbah Coffee Club.

"We are hard to find," says Roag, "which is a problem. The Beatles tours, which take people round

110

the Beatles sites, don't include us because they say we are too far away, on the wrong side of the town. People have to make their own way here. So a board at the front is vital — but to put one up, we'll have to cut down some of the trees. They've just grown wild, but apparently you now can't cut down any trees in your garden without permission.

"My fantasy, when we do get a proper sign up, is to have a courtesy bus running here straight from Liverpool Lime Street."

One thing that did happen, without them applying or even knowing, was that in 2006 the house was officially Grade-Two listed, giving it official status as a building of historic interest. "It was a local historian who looked into it, investigated the whole history of the house, and applied to have it listed." It means of course that they will have even more paperwork, should they ever want to make any changes, but the house and the cellars should be preserved for ever.

As we were talking, I noticed people outside in the garden, stumbling around. They got nearer and started staring through the window. Because of the overgrown nature of the front garden, it is possible to assume the house might not be occupied. Roag sighed and said it happens all the time. People don't realise entry is by appointment only. When the doorbell eventually rang, he said he would have to go and send them away, tell them to book a time for tomorrow, he was too busy now — talking to me. When he came back, he said they were ten Canadians, taxis waiting, this was their last afternoon in Liverpool, so they couldn't come back tomorrow. I said he must let them in. Don't lose customers because of me.

I followed Roag out and talked to two of them, men in their forties, one said he was an academic with a PhD and the other an accountant with Deloitte & Touche, both from Edmonton, Alberta. Their accents did not sound totally Canadian — and they said that was because they were originally from Yugoslavia. They knew all about the Casbah history and that it had now opened to the public, but hadn't been aware you had to book. They were clearly thrilled to be allowed in and to meet an actual Best, not Pete alas, but they did know who Roag was.

I went back upstairs and talked to Pete. I wondered if in his civil service life he had ever had to sack people. "You can't, not in the civil service," he said, laughing. "It's almost impossible. But I did have to discipline some people, which wasn't pleasant."

What about the Pete Best Band, any discipline problems, rows, fallings-out there? "Luckily people have only left voluntarily, natural progression. And we don't have people going on the piss, getting drugged up and can't perform. We are all too experienced to behave like that — or perhaps too old."

Pete has two daughters, Beba, aged forty-five and Benita, aged forty-one, and has been married to his wife, Kathy, since 1963. "And very happily," he added emphatically.

In one way, he has done better than any of the Beatles. Paul not long ago went through a nasty divorce, which means that all four Beatles got divorced at some time. Then of course there have been all the other tragedies and dramas.

"Brian Epstein and Stu, they died young. When John got shot, and George got attacked in his own home, I did each time think to myself, there but for the grace of God go I. Yes, I have been very lucky."

It had been a terrible blow to his pride and self-esteem when he was sacked — and he still doesn't know the real reason, who did the dirty deed. It took a long time to get over it, but now he can't believe he was so depressed as to contemplate taking his own life.

Now, approaching seventy, he can only look back with fondness to his time with them, especially the wild Hamburg years. He enjoyed the girls and the drink, as they all did, but says he took no drugs, no pills of any sort, unlike the others. Perhaps that was something that set him apart, made the others think he was perhaps a bit boring, not as amusing as Ringo. No one at the time thought his drumming was inferior.

"I had two brilliant years during which we achieved so much. We became kings of Liverpool and kings of Hamburg. We did our first radio appearances, our first recording. I knew we were going to be huge because the signs were there. Unfortunately, I was the one forced to change direction — but the benefits have accrued later on. I am very happy. I have had a good life, with some great experiences few people have had. I have no regrets."

He has never met any of the Beatles since he got the sack in 1962. "I've made no approaches. It's up to them. The doors are always open."

His mother, Mona, was contacted by John in 1967. He remembered from his Casbah days her father's military medals and wondered if he could borrow them to wear on the *Sgt. Pepper* cover — which he did. When the *Beatles Anthology* was broadcast in 1995, Pete got some royalties as it was realised he had played on one of the "Love Me Do" recordings.

When the Casbah reopened in 2006, Roag approached Paul McCartney for any memories, which he gave willingly and was filmed by Roag. "It's a good idea to let people know about the Casbah," said Paul. "They know about the Cavern, they know about some of those things, but the Casbah was the place it all started. We helped paint it and stuff. We looked upon it as our personal club."

When Roag returned from guiding round the Canadians, I asked if Pete himself ever led any of the tours.

"Of course he doesn't," exclaimed Roag, indignantly. "Just me and Rory or another member of the family does it. Never Pete. He's Pete Best, one of the Beatles. It would be demeaning. It would be like Paul McCartney giving guided tours round the Abbey Road studios."

I can see why Roag enjoys doing personal tours, booked in advance. It saves on staff and you can control times and numbers. And charge a lot more. Something to bear in mind when I open my museum. I suppose it might be amusing and distracting when I am really old and out of work with nothing else to do, a chance to meet new people and chunter on to strangers — but dear God, I'm banking on that time never arriving. I asked about the future, when he and Pete have hung up their drumsticks, what will happen to the Casbah?

"I am passionate about it," said Roag. "I see it as our mum's heritage, so I want to do it for her. It's also a matter of credit where credit is due. I want the world to recognise what once happened here.

"However, I can't force the next generation to keep it going. I won't say to them you have to do it. If they find the house becomes a pain in the arse, and they want to get rid of it, it's up to them. But I would hope they will try to keep it going, open to the public for ever, or as long as the Beatles are remembered . . ."

Which of course they will be, as long we are on the planet and have the breath to hum the tunes. So I think. But I'm biased.

All the same, I am surprised that everything connected with the Beatles, however humble and humdrum, should now be valued and revered like holy relics — worshippers charged to look, and touch if they are lucky — even when they are just scratches on a wall or roof done in an idle moment by callow youths, hanging about.

But that is the nature of so much of collecting, and of museums of collections, ever since ancient times. Scratches in neolithic caves or daubs on suburban ceilings can end up being considered priceless, yet they have no real intrinsic value. It's the context, the story, the associations, the history, and of course us — the fact that we impose importance upon them and invest them with value and power.

I would hate to tell you the notional market value today of some of the unconsidered Beatles trifles that I was fortunate enough to gather. They would look good though, if I ever get round to my own museum. Still thinking.

Meanwhile, let's roll on to another museum — which, in its own way, is definitely a cut above the rest.

Casbah Coffee Club
8 Hayman's Green
West Derby
Liverpool L12 7JG
Tel 0151 280 3519

CHAPTER
SIX

The British Lawnmower Museum, Southport

Never been to Southport — been missing from my town collection. Collectors can collect experiences as well as things, such as visiting all ninety-two of England's league football grounds, or groupies notching up how many pop stars they have shagged. There's a lot to recommend collecting experiences. You don't have storage or display problems. Though there were groupies, allegedly, who took plaster casts of their conquests' private parts as souvenirs. I wonder where they kept them? Perhaps donated them to that museum in Iceland that displays penises. They have over two hundred and fifty, but mainly of animals. Not been to the museum, or Iceland.

I often look at maps and think, been there, been there, not been there, must go there sometime. I've done Blackpool, which is the bigger, brasher seaside town further up the Lancashire coast, and of course just done Liverpool again, which is to the south, but never managed to enter that bulky, bull-nosed peninsula between the two, even though it does contain such famous sporting places as Aintree and Haydock Park, and loads of golf courses, such as Birkdale.

I was early for the museum, which is on the outskirts of Southport — deliberately early as I wanted to have a look at the town, add it to my portfolio. I parked in a street near the museum, as there did not seem to be any parking restrictions, and decided to walk into town.

I had been smiling to myself all the way here, thinking about the museum I was going to visit. Lawnmowers! I don't know why I found it so funny. Do you want to see my lawnmowers? Got any lawnmowers to swap? In here I keep my lawnmowers. I had been saving it up for ages, like pudding.

Very foolishly I had arrived without a map, assuming I would pick one up when I walked into town, wherever that was. I asked a woman where the town was and she said keep walking, right down Duke Street, you'll come to it. Took ages and all the time I was thinking I'll see the sea soon, then I'll get my bearings. Silly name, Southport. It's neither in the south nor is it a port. Not even got a harbour, but I had heard boastings about a pier, the second longest in the UK. If it's so long, why can't I find it?

I asked a man where the pier was and he pointed along an empty, rather ugly road. I kept walking and came eventually to a sort of esplanade and there, lurking in the background, miles and miles away across empty sands, I could definitely see sea. Then to my right I spotted what must be the pier, long and low and very plain, not nearly as handsome and ornate as the piers in Brighton — OK, there's only one left in

Brighton, but even in its death throes it retains an architectural charm.

Close up, Southport's pier was more attractive and I was delighted to see a tram chugging along it, heading towards what looked like a glasshouse at one end, out to sea, whereas at the other end the pier just seemed to disappear into the town. I climbed up and walked along it. It is long — 3,600 feet, I discovered later — but it's a bit of a cheat as half the pier goes over land. In my book, a pier should go over water. I don't actually have a book, but I do have a collection of postcards of seaside piers, about fifty in all. I bought a job lot of thirty once and started adding to them, along with a job lot of angry seas, till I decided it was a sheer con. Whoever manufactured them, back in the 1900s, had just taken one photo of an angry sea and then inserted the name of whichever seaside town he was trying to sell them in. Very smart.

At the end of the pier — or the beginning, for I should have started here — I found myself in Lord Street, and goodness, that was a surprise, a sheer delight to come across something so grand and impressive after the dullness of the blank sands and the tattiness of some of the seaside amusements at the end of the pier. Lord Street is about a mile long, wide and handsome, with lots of green spaces and gardens and classic public buildings on one side, while the other side consists of shops, hotels, restaurants, most of them with Victorian glass-topped canopies and arcades. At one time it must have been clarty posh, as we say in Carlisle, and attracted the quality and wealth of industrial Lancashire. Even today, despite day trippers strolling the broad pavements in shorts and skimpy tops, it still has a certain dignity and style.

I eventually found the tourist centre, in a glass conservatory on the other side, and discovered that Southport is a pure nineteenth-century invention. It didn't exist at all till 1792, when the first hotel was built near what is now Lord Street. It was purpose-planned as a seaside resort, of the classier British kind, hence all the arcades and covered walkways.

I also discovered that Prince Louis Napoleon, nephew of the great Napoleon, had lived on Lord Street in 1846. He had been imprisoned in France, then escaped, dressed as a workman. He lived in Southport the best part of two years, then returned to France in 1848, becoming president of the republic and then, a few years later, the Emperor Napoleon III.

It was under Napoleon III that Baron Haussmann rebuilt Paris, creating those magnificent boulevards with covered glass canopies and arcades. Very like Lord Street. A professor of architecture, according to a leaflet I got in the tourist centre, has argued that Napoleon must indeed have been influenced by Southport. Could Paris's grand design really have been modelled on Lord Street? And what on earth was Louis Napoleon doing in Southport in the first place?

However, it was time for my real appointment, and to try to understand an even bigger and more intriguing mystery — how come this rather remote seaside town has got the world's one and only lawnmower museum?

The outside of the museum gives an immediate clue. It turns out to be a shopfront, housing Stanley's Discount Garden Machinery Warehouse. I went in and was confronted by rows and rows of gleaming new lawnmowers of all shapes and sizes. An elderly gent was at the counter, arguing that he had bought his lawnmower here two years ago, so surely it was still under guarantee.

The lawnmower museum is upstairs. I didn't want to go straight in, as by now my rule was always to talk to the creator first, if at all possible, or if it not him or her then to the present curator. Having done that, I aim to talk them into going round with me, so I can ask them endless dopey questions.

Brian Radam was on the premises, dealing with a customer, but I was told to go right up to the museum and he would see me soon. Might as well, I thought, have a quick look on my own, see it as others see it. Even if I have to pay. Naturally, if I have rung ahead and arranged a meeting, I don't usually have to pay. They take me in. I'm not daft. Just careful.

Entrance was only £2 and even I was prepared to splash out — a bargain in this day and age for any sort of museum. I pushed past a little turnstile at the bottom of the stairs and went up.

The moment I entered the landing, I was confronted by five rooms crammed with all sorts of vintage lawnmowers and related relics, and immediately from somewhere unseen music started playing. Then a TV screen sprang into life and a commentator with a broad

Lancashire accent started giving me an explanation of all the delights before me.

I was alone in the museum, having passed through the unattended turnstile and up the stairs, so I reckoned I must have activated some infrared starting mechanism on the stairs which sparked off this delightful audio-visual explanation. Just for me. The music was sort of mock country and western, with a jaunty singer telling me about the man who invented the first lawnmower — rather informative, if not exactly musically distinguished. The commentary itself was packed with fascinating facts, which I tried to take down in my notebook, but it was all a bit quick and overwhelming. The video display turned out to be mainly slides of old and modern lawnmowers, but jolly interesting all the same.

I watched it to the end, then Brian Radam himself appeared, small, slender, big specs, small pointy beard, while I was still getting my bearings. I asked him to turn off the audio-visual stuff, if he wouldn't mind, as I'd like to talk to him first, before touring the museum properly.

I sat on the stairs, while he stood beside me and asked him questions for about half an hour, till suddenly the music and audio-visual stuff burst into life again, making me jump. An elderly foursome, all smiles and giggles, were coming up the stairs, having paid their £2. We then went downstairs to his little overcrowded office where his wife, Sue, was sorting through what looked like bills, invoices and contracts.

Brian is the son of Stanley Radam who opened the shop in 1945 as Southport's first DIY outlet, specialising in selling and repairing garden implements. It started in one shop, then, when business expanded, he bought the adjoining shops till he had the whole corner. Brian was born in 1951, left school at sixteen and went to be an apprentice with Atco. He also did an apprenticeship as a locksmith, becoming a Fellow of the Master Locksmiths Association.

Atco, one of the best-known names in lawnmowers, stands for Atlas Chain Company and began in 1865 in Birmingham, making chains for ships before moving into lawnmowers. In the late sixties, when Brian joined them at their repair centre near Preston, it was just one of eight Atco depots across the country. All they did, all year round, was service and repair lawnmowers.

"At our depot, there was a staff of over fifty and we repaired 425 Atco lawnmowers every week. Originally they had mechanics who drove a motorbike and sidecar and when they went out on a job, if they couldn't repair it there and then, they would bring back the lawnmower in the sidecar. Oh, those were the days. I felt proud to work there.

"British people have always taken great pride in their lawns. We have always had the best in the world, oh yes. You don't get our sort of lawns in California and in France and Italy they don't care the way we do. I'm talking about ordinary people. If you are a rich Californian, then you can throw a tanker of water over your lawn. If you are really rich, you can paint it green. But ordinary folks abroad are not obsessed by lawns like the British. We always have been. It's part of our culture. We have the right kind of grass and the right kind of climate and the right kind of mentality. The old adverts for the early lawnmowers used to say 'Gentlemen will find it an amusing and healthy experience'. That's still true.

"I would say that out of every hundred people in Britain today who have a lawn, about half of them find it a drag, a real chore, to mow it. But the other half, well, they love it, they take pride in making it look as good as possible, with perfect lines and stripes. It is still a pleasurable thing to mow a lawn, and very healthy.

"Oh, it were great days at Atco, wonderful to work there. I felt proud it was a British company and that all our competitors were British companies, with generations of service to British lawns behind us. The quality of our lawnmowers was the best in the world and we had the best mechanics."

Alas, poor old Brian didn't at that time realise he was about to witness the end of the traditional British lawnmower industry. By the 1980s it had practically crumbled away

"I remember the day I discovered that the new supermarkets were selling lawnmowers for £6, while we were charging £10 to repair an old one. That signalled the end. These mass-produced, cheaply made plastic lawnmowers were soon everywhere. Even though most fell to pieces after one year, people didn't care. They just bought another, they were so cheap. In the old days, if you bought a good lawnmower, you would never buy another one. If serviced once a year and cared for properly, they would last you a lifetime. Many people really did only ever have one lawnmower. Once the disposable age had come in, that was it. It's like cameras and mobile phones and computers. It's normal now to get a new one every year, as new models come in or the old ones pack up and can't be repaired. People don't do repairing any more. They just want to sell you a new model.

"And all the new models are mass-produced cheaply abroad — at least they are with lawnmowers. Atco is still going but is German-owned. So is Qualcast. Ransomes is American-owned and so is Shanks. All these great British names, all gone from our shores. I find it very sad."

Just before Atco closed he returned to Southport to work with his dad in the shop. He got married to Sue and together they eventually took over the running of the shop when Stanley retired. (He was still alive, by the way, aged eighty-six, coming into the shop a few times each week, but I never saw him.)

"I found a lot of old lawnmowers in the back, perhaps kept originally in case their parts might come in handy, but mostly they had been scrapped, waiting to be chucked out. Looking through them, I found some famous names, like Royal Enfield, Vincent, Hawker Siddeley and Rolls-Royce, firms most people don't realise ever produced lawnmowers. I got some of them cleaned up and in working order and put a few of them in the shop window, just for interest.

"I found other even older ones lying around and I thought, we can't scrap this or that, we must keep them, do them up and preserve them. Then people started bringing in their old ones and giving them to us, perhaps one they had inherited or had had for up to sixty years, after they noticed what we had in our window. And that's really how it all began. No one else was keeping old lawnmowers. No one else was bothered about old machines. We felt we had to, it was our duty. So, that's when we thought of the idea of having a proper museum."

They opened in 1986 and over the years the British Lawnmower Museum, as it proudly calls itself, has had quite a lot of national publicity, considering where it is and what it contains — but I suppose its novelty value does attract interest, makes people smile and perhaps, though I would not dare say it in front of Brian, who is a true believer, allied with amusement there is often a tone of mockery. It does seem very British, very eccentric, very daft.

Brian himself has appeared on *Blue Peter* with some of his lawnmowers, though this was about fifteen years ago. (*Blue Peter* itself has now gone flash and modern and superficial.) He took along the very latest robot lawnmower, as well as some vintage ones, and did a demonstration. "It worked all right but *Blue Peter's* sheepdog was on the programme and it got very confused, thinking the robot lawnmower was a sheep and trying to chase it."

He has also appeared on a TV programme with Robbie Coltrane, on his tour of Britain, and on other shows, though most of them seem to have been some years ago. The sort of TV magazine programmes that all regions used to have, featuring odd quirks of British life, seem to have dried up in recent years. For all its fame, the museum still has an amateur, enthusiast, home-made, do-it-yourself, provincial feel to it — which is how it should be, as that is how lawnmowers first began.

The first one was patented in 1830 by Edwin Beard Budding of Stroud in Gloucestershire. He had noticed in a local cloth mill how some cylinder blades, fixed on a bench, were being used to trim the nap on finished cloth, to smooth out all the rough and bobbly bits on material such as guardsmen's uniforms. He thought a similar principle could be applied to cutting lawns and invented a machine, carrying cylinder blades, mounted on wheels and which were rotated by the motion of the wheels. He is reputed to have made his first trial runs at night, fearful that the locals would think he was mad. It worked, and he went into partnership with a friend and they patented the first lawnmower. Budding is also credited with inventing the first adjustable spanner.

Lawns had existed before, but only around stately homes for until that moment only aristocrats and the wealthy could afford to have them mown. This was done by hand, using scythes, usually by a team of eight men with eight women and boys following behind, picking up the grass. They worked non-stop in the grass-growing season. Each grown man had his scythe hand-made to match his height and strength. It's all in the angle and the sharpness of the blade, not just brute muscle power, as anyone who has tried to scythe thistles will have found out. You often see eighteenth-century illustrations of teams of scythers, in fields as well as on lawns, looking knackered.

Early cricket pitches were also mown by hand, though on the edges, in the rough, sheep were allowed to graze to keep the grass down. Naturally they also deposited sheep shit, so when a fielder ran into the rough ground he would often slip on it. Hence the term "in the slips". I'm not sure if this is true, but it should be.

Budding built only six hundred lawnmowers — for one man, and also a bigger model for two men, one to push and one to pull — but the lawnmower he invented basically stayed the same from the late 1830s to the present day. Other forms of mowing lawns have come along in the meantime, but the old hand-pushed rotating cylinder system always remained. In this environmentally friendly age I am sure they will soon come back into popularity again as they are so morally and ethically correct. No nasty petrol or electricity or carbon footprint. What can be more desirable than that?

One of the early lawnmower manufacturers, using Budding's patents, was Ransomes of Ipswich, who were making lawnmowers from 1832. Budding's patents ran out in the 1850s and lots more makers piled in, bringing their own variations, but until the end of the nineteenth century most lawnmowers had to be pushed or pulled by hand or using horses. The big houses had big lawn-mowers, pulled by teams of men and horses. One of the early Scottish lawnmower manufacturers was Shanks of Arbroath, who called one of their best-known models Shanks's Pony. This was because it was pulled by a pony, but it also needed a man to walk behind to guide the machine and the pony. And yes, the walker also became known as Shanks's Pony, hence the well-known phrase.

"Not long after I started the museum," says Brian, "I got a call from an old lady in the Lake District. She was ninety-six and had been brought up in a stately home but had now gone into a care home and was clearing out her possessions. She had vivid memories of their family's coachmen using the same horses to pull the lawnmower. In some old stables she still had an 1880 lawnmower made by Green's of Leeds, the sort that was pulled by a pony. She asked if I would like it. She also gave me something I had never seen before, special leather boots that were put on the horses before they started mowing the best lawns. This was to protect the lawns, stop them leaving marks.

"She also told me that her coachman had devised a system for stopping the horses shitting while on the best lawns. He would drive them to the side, on to the rougher stuff, and blow his whistle, and they would perform. They would then return to the main lawn. Obviously he must have known their habits — or perhaps he really had trained them."

Hand- or horse-drawn mowers had no rivals until towards the end of the century, when at long last someone invented a steam-driven lawnmower. I was surprised it had taken so long, when you think that George Stephenson had perfected a steam-driven railway engine as early as 1825. However, when they did eventually hit the market they were almost immediately replaced by another invention, the internal combustion engine. A similar thing happened with canals as a mode of transport, they were really getting into their stride when railways were invented.

"Very, very few steam-driven lawnmowers were ever made. Leyland made their first in 1892 but only about a hundred, that was all. I would dearly love one. The Leyland transport museum haven't got one — all they have is a replica."

Karl Benz, one of the two Germans who invented the petrol-driven engine around the year 1886, originally worked on lawnmowers, among various other machines. (The other inventor was Gottlieb Daimler, who lived just sixty miles away from Benz in the Neckar valley, yet, amazingly, they never met.)

By the 1900s petrol-driven lawnmowers, as well as motor cars, had arrived, but their mass use came in the 1920s when prices came down and cheaper lawnmowers, made by firms like Atco, flooded the market. The suburban gardener became as proud of his manicured lawn, complete with stripes and perfect edges, as the old aristocrats had ever been. Social equality, you see, had been made possible by the use of lawnmowers.

Flymo introduced the hovering lawnmower in the 1960s, with a single blade that rotates — but of course it does not create stripes, nor does it have a roller, so boo to that, say all true lawnmower purists. They were, however, produced in massive numbers and very cheaply and were light to use, being made mainly of plastic. They were bought by people who just wanted the job done as quickly and easily as possible — i.e. women. The early ones came in blue, but Flymo then did a survey of two thousand of their female customers asking them which colour they would prefer. The answer was orange, still Flymo's signature colour today.

Ride-on mowers, big enough to be climbed on and driven like a car, date from 1904 and were first developed by Ransomes. They are very popular with wealthier or more macho gardeners, with big or rough gardens, who like a bit of showing off.

After all these decades there are still only three basic lawnmower cutting systems. Cylinder blades turning against a fixed blade and the rotating spinning blade are the two most common. The third one is the reciprocating knife — like those scissors barbers often use, with the two blades interlocking. You don't come across this much in domestic use but they can often be seen on rough, overgrown areas.

All these systems, and all possible forms of power, are faithfully and lovingly preserved by Brian in his museum. On show in his five rooms he has at any one time around two hundred models on display, all in spanking, gleaming condition, plus another six hundred behind the scenes.

I got him to take me round, which anyone can do, as he loves doing guided tours so long as the shop is not too busy, and for this he charges £6 as opposed to £2 for the automated audio tour.

The biggest lawnmower on show is a 1926 Dennis, which at the time cost about £75, the same as a small house. The smallest that works is a six-inch mower from the 1930s used for graveyards. Strimmers, by the way, go back many decades, but they were not called strimmers until recent times. The longest-serving mower ever was a machine made by Green's in the 1860s and called the Silens Messor, meaning silent cutter. They were very fond of having Latin names at one time, just to make them sound classy. Another smaller one was called Multum in Parvo — much in a small size. The Silens model was sold for over seventy years, until the 1930s, and is in the *Guinness Book of Records* as the domestic machine that remained unchanged for the longest period of time.

One of the biggest lawnmowers on show is one presented by Atco to Prince Charles and Lady Diana on their wedding in 1981. It's a large, ride-on machine and was used at Highgrove until fairly recently, then became redundant and ended up with Brian.

He is clearly fond of celeb mowers, machines once owned by the famous, presumably believing that in this day and age a celebrity name will bring in punters who would otherwise not be interested in a lawnmower museum. I couldn't quite see the point, as an old lawnmower owned by, say, Hilda Ogden (or at least the actress Jean Alexander) is exactly the same model owned by millions of others, but Brian enjoys collecting them. Amongst his celeb items, all neatly and reverently marked, are mowers once used by Lily Savage, Alan Titchmarsh, Vanessa Feltz and Ainsley Harriott. Brian is particularly pleased to have a mower donated by Brian May of Queen, complete with a handwritten letter. As a teenager Brian played in a rock band as a semi-professional, before realising that mowers were the way to national fame, if not fortune.

Nicholas Parsons promised to donate his lawnmower but it got stolen and he had to send a pair of secateurs instead. I was amused to see in one cabinet a fairly boring, Woolworths-style trowel with a wooden handle, which had formerly belonged to the poet Roger McGough. I wonder if he handed it over as a joke. I also learned that Charles Darwin used a Samuelson Donkey mower on his lawns in 1857, though they don't have the exact one.

In various cabinets and display cases are toy lawnmowers, lawnmower models, books, advertisements, posters and lawnmower memorabilia — but all a bit thin, when you think how long lawnmowers have been going. Perhaps they had never been considered exciting objects, compared with, say, steam trains, till Brian came along. There is not even a proper history of lawnmowers, which seems a great shame, and only a few children's stories featuring lawnmowers.

Electric mowers are not as modern as I had imagined. On show is a Ransomes electric model from 1926 that you plugged into the mains in your house, at a time when most ordinary houses did not yet have electricity.

The robot lawnmower, solar-powered, the one Brian demonstrated on *Blue Peter*, looks very weird and space-agey amongst all the solid, wrought-iron Victorian contraptions. It was made in Sweden and cost the company £1 million to develop. Each costs £2000 and it can cut any lawn of any shape without supervision, avoids obstacles and plugs itself in when it needs recharging. Truly a wonder, but they didn't do very well in Britain, not just because we are too mean to spend that amount of money but, according to Brian, because we still like our mowers with old-fashioned cylinders so we can make pretty patterns — and also we like the exercise.

One of the oddities is what looks like a miniature sports car, which Atco made in 1939, converting a lawnmower into a motor car to be used for training motorists. Not many of these were ever made, as the war came along, and so today they are greatly prized by lawnmowerists — if there is such a word — who will pay up to £7000 to have one.

There are of course many lawnmower collectors — as I had expected, though without ever having come across one. Out there somewhere Brian estimates there are about two hundred keen collectors, most of them members of the Old Lawnmower Club. There's also the Atco Car Owners Club, of which he is a member. Brian has rarely ever had to buy an old machine as almost all of them have been given to him or assembled from old parts. He estimates that the total cost of his museum has been about £10, which covers both the cost of converting the old upstairs rooms and all the lawnmowers on show.

He was once about to splash out when he saw a particular lawnmower on sale at Sotheby's. He reckoned it was worth only £40 but decided at the last minute to leave a telephone bid of £200 as he very much wanted the parts for mending similar machines. "When I told Sue what I had done she was furious, said I was being really silly. But I didn't get it. It was sold for £1200."

That's about the most Brian has ever heard of being paid for a traditional old lawnmower, though specialist or one-off rarities can command much larger prices, such as a silver Qualcast mower that was produced in a limited edition of only ten.

The only time he has spent real money was on documents not machines, buying a collection of five hundred original lawnmower patents from the early nineteenth century, some from as early as 1799, on parchment and including many that had belong to Mr Budding. They came complete with drawings and full details and are of course a vital part of engineering history. It took me a while to get out of him how much he had actually paid — he eventually admitted, in a hushed voice, that they had cost him £5000. I said that was nothing compared with what people will pay for old motor cars, or even an old wireless.

Going round, I was very surprised to learn about the existence of racing mowers. I sat in one, wearing a crash helmet, just in case it burst into life. Brian used to be a champion but has recently retired, having reached his fifties. There is a British Lawn Mower Racing Association, which holds races once or twice a month, all over the country. "It's the cheapest form of motor sport you can find. Most of the races are run for charity, but it is taken seriously, people do want to win.

135

One of the regular races is over 350 miles and is run like the Le Mans race and can take twelve hours."

The rules insist that each lawnmower must have been able to cut grass, though in actual races the blades are taken off for safety reasons. You can't make the engine bigger than it actually was and it must still look like a lawnmower, however much you modify it.

"Many of the bigger, more expensive lawnmowers have 320 cc engines, which is quite enough power really. They are designed to do only 6 mph while cutting grass, but they can easily be made to do 30 mph. Over 30 mph, well, it can be pretty hairy. They develop a mind of their own and do what they like. I've done 65 mph myself but the world record is about 90 mph. We're still working here in the workshop on a lawnmower that will beat that and reach 100 mph, but I haven't had the time to work on it recently."

When the sport was first established in 1983 it received quite a bit of attention and several well-known people took part, such as Stirling Moss and Oliver Reed, the actor. "Oliver Reed ran over someone who was in the toilet tent at the time, so he wasn't exactly in complete control. It was said he was half-cut."

Probably true, as he was a notorious drinker, but also a well-known joke amongst lawnmowerists — along with the mower the merrier, a cut above the rest, don't let the grass grow under your feet, many of which appear in the audio commentary about the museum, which is spoken by Brian's brother-in-law.

The song, a country and western ditty about Mr Budding, which can also be heard on a DVD sold in the museum, is sung and written by Doug Miles, a direct descendant of Edwin Budding. "I got this call one day from someone I didn't know offering me some music he had written about lawnmowers. He sent it to me and I thought it was pretty good. He said I could use it if I wanted to in the museum. That was when he told me he was related to Budding." Another example of Brian getting things free for his museum, because people like his enthusiasm and expertise so much they want to help him.

So does his museum make any money? Each year he attracts about six thousand visitors which, at £2 a time, in theory might pay one man's wages. He doesn't directly employ anyone in the museum, but he himself is always on hand.

"We still run on a shoestring, but no, we are not struggling. Overall we make a profit. Naturally I would like to win the lottery and do the museum out properly, make it professional, but that's not going to happen. I did get all the forms for a Heritage Lottery Fund grant. I spoke to some woman and she said we ticked all the boxes — part of engineering history, teaching young people, as we get a lot of school parties and engineering students in, and other things, but then when I saw all the forms I couldn't cope. None of us had the time to work on them. So we've got no grants of any kind, from the government or the local council or charities. We are totally on our own."

The reason he makes money is that, thanks to the museum and its fame around the world with lawnmower enthusiasts, he gets a lot of vintage mowers sent in for repair or requiring parts. Over the decades he has collected hundreds of old lawnmower manuals from long-gone manufacturers, which are now unavailable anywhere else. He sells copies of these for a flat fee of £10, and that's a very good earner. On the retail side, downstairs where they sell and repair new lawnmowers there is a staff of three, all trained experts.

Repairing lawnmowers is of course a dying art and Brian gets very depressed when he has school leavers approach him for work experience or to learn about lawnmowers. "Do you realise, they don't do metalwork or even woodwork in our schools any more? Shocking. I get kids coming here, not thick kids, who can't use a screwdriver — except for stabbing each other. One of them the other day was handed a nut and bolt and told to put it on a lawnmower, and he had never seen a nut and bolt before and had no idea what it was.

"This country invented the lawnmower, produced the best ones ever, and we had the best engineers, of all kinds. Now we don't know anything and we don't care any more, I don't know what's going to happen in the future."

Many museum people have said similar things to me on my travels, such as the wireless man and the fan lady. They fear their knowledge and enthusiasm will die with them, and so probably will die items they have collected — or else they will get shoved in store in some dusty municipal museum.

I believe, however, that the attitude of mind that breeds obsessive collectors and preservationists will always be there, as it is in the human spirit. It's just that the Brians of the future will fall in love with different things, such as old mobile phones, computers, digital cameras, stuff that is being dumped but that they realise has a fascinating history. It's probably already happening, only their museums have not yet opened.

There were lots of lawnmowers I would gladly have taken away, as he has restored and painted and polished them so nicely. Nothing too big of course, just something to put on a shelf along with, say, an old blow football game or vintage Subbuteo. It would be a neat cross-reference.

Most of all, I will definitely take away his clever entrance scheme whereby you let yourself in on your own and instantly it's all singing, all dancing. Dead smart.

So what about his own future? He and his wife Sue have no children, so no obvious person to inherit his little empire, but he hopes that whoever takes over the shop side will always keep the museum going. "I want it always to be kept together as a museum, even if that does mean it being shipped to the USA after some rich American has bought it. Not that I want that to happen, but it would keep it all together and give it purpose-built premises.

"I have a friend who runs his own microbrewery, which is doing very well, but he now wants to expand. We have this daft fantasy that we discuss all the time, half as a joke, about buying an old barn together, out in the country, and converting it. One half would be the brewery and the other half the lawnmower museum. Imagine looking at all the old lawnmowers then sitting down and having a pint. Wouldn't that be a really wonderful and unusual attraction?"

Well, it would certainly put Southport on the map, and perhaps help the museum keep going for ever. As it should. Lawnmowers are not funny, not really. If asked, in future I will still smile, but add quickly and seriously that their history is fascinating.

Lawnmowers are not sexy or exciting, nor do they come with their own natural fans — like, say, the Beatles or football — so it's unlikely that anyone will ever again collect enough to open a museum. Unlike old motor cars. There are museums of vintage motor vehicles all over Britain, and the world. New ones are always opening and rare vehicles fetch millions of pounds. Old cars can be very attractive and even beautiful while poor old lawnmowers can be a bit plain and lumpen. But lawnmowers are part of our social, engineering and economic history, part of what we think has made Britain British, our Sunday afternoons, our rolling lawns, our green and pleasant land.

Now, when I watch Premiership football on TV I often find myself clapping in delight when I spot a well-mown, well-cared-for pitch with exact lines or, even harder, perfect concentric circles radiating from the centre spot. Pretty — but pointless of course, as players and refs don't need such magical, almost mystical markings on a football pitch. I find myself wondering what sort of mower — scissor blades perhaps — has been used and what sort of roller and I think, ah, some of our traditions have not been completely lost.

British Lawnmower Museum
106–114 Shakespeare Street
Southport
Lancashire PR8 5AJ
www.lawnmowerworld.co.uk

CHAPTER
SEVEN

The National Football Museum, Preston

Football is my joint first collecting passion, along with the Beatles. Visiting the Casbah was amusing, a trip down memory lane, but what is mainly being museum-ed there is the building itself, the preservation of a stage in Beatles history, of memories and atmosphere rather than an actual collection, as they don't have many Beatles-related items.

But visiting the National Football Museum at Preston, oh my God, to me it was overwhelming, stupendous, unbelievable. Every football fan, of any age and sex, from any country in the world, should visit the National Football Museum for there is nothing like it, anywhere.

At the same time, I came away depressed, fed up, thinking what is the point? My stuff is so piddling and petty, why do I bother? They have got so much, and in such wonderful condition, thousands and thousands of items, most of which I never even knew existed. Bugger it, I might as well go back to stamps.

As with stamps, I became a born-again football collector. I'd cut out my football heroes as a boy, stuck them in home-made albums, then forgot about them. My return was sparked off by the World Cup final of 1966, keeping my ticket as well as the programme, but I didn't actively go out looking for footer stuff until I gave up stamps. When I sold all the stamps, I deliberately put the proceeds, such as they were, into the Beatles and football.

With programmes I concentrate on Spurs and have got them back to 1910, and with England — Scotland games I go back to 1927 — but now the prices are so great I probably won't go any earlier, though I might be tempted if something reasonable comes along. I have very low standards when it comes to condition, and am always willing to buy tatty examples as long as I can read them.

I also collect football books, and now have most of the classic examples from 1890 to 1910, and football magazines and football postcards. I tend in the main to go for memorabilia that I can read and study, that has content. I have always avoided shirts, suspecting they might be frauds, especially the autographed ones, and anyway they are hell to keep or display, whereas books can be on shelves and postcards in albums.

I had half-imagined I was one of the few football memorabilia collectors till I heard about the football collection assembled by Harry Langton. He was born in Yorkshire in 1929 and became a sports journalist and football collector and dealer. He started collecting football items in the early 1950s, when his wife gave

143

him an old football print as a present. He went on to acquire thousands of football items. I never met him, but was in contact once about going to see his stuff. I never did. Can't remember why.

In the early 1990s he had done a deal with FIFA, the world governing body of football, based in Switzerland, and sold the main part of his collection. In 1996 they produced a beautiful, lavishly illustrated book, in several languages, called the *FIFA Museum Collection*, based on Harry's material. It totally amazed me when I first read it. He had tracked down and acquired so many beautiful, artistic objects connected with football that I had never once thought of looking out for — such as paintings, drawings, prints, ceramics, games, toys, along with the more obvious football memorabilia like boots and balls. He had gone right back to the beginning of football, back to the foundation in London of the FA in 1863, when the rules were codified for the first time — the rules that the rest of the world went on to adopt — and even further back to the evidence for some sort of football games having been played in ancient China and Japan and in sixteenth-century Italy.

He was collecting these sorts of historic and artistic football treasures and documents at a time when no one else seemed to be aware of their value and importance, or even of their existence — although gradually they did become aware once the big auction houses like Christie's and Sotheby's started regular football sales in the 1990s.

Harry Langton's ambition was that his collection should be kept together and made the basis of a national football museum in Britain. It was discussed from the mid-1990s onwards but looked unlikely to happen, for lack of money and also because of disagreements about where such a museum should be located. Several museums in other countries were interested in acquiring the collection. Despite the collection being largely English, football of course now belongs to the world and its origins and history and treasures are of interest everywhere. The possibility of it leaving these shores for good did help galvanise the campaign for a national football museum in England.

In the end, it came to pass, at a total cost of £15 million, of which £9.3 million came from the Heritage Lottery Fund. The collection was bought and brand-new premises built and the museum opened in February 2001. Too late, alas, for Harry Langton to see it. He had died the previous year.

How it came to be located in Preston is a saga in itself, but it was a huge coup for the town and all the action groups and deputations behind the campaign. The government liked the idea of a national museum, of which there are twenty or so in all, not being in London for a change but up in the North-West. Real football fans will know the importance of the North-West in the history of football, as the early professional clubs that formed the world's first football league in 1888 were mostly based up there or in the Midlands, not in London and the South.

And really true fans will know that Preston played a pretty big role in the early years of football. Preston North End was a founder of that first league and ran away with the title in the first year, thus becoming known as the Invincibles. And Deepdale, the home of Preston North End, is now the oldest football league ground in the world. Preston have played there continuously since 1881, the year they were formed. (Notts County is our oldest existing professional club, founded in 1862, but they have had several different grounds in their history.)

The museum was built as an integral part of Deepdale, located under the new stand when the ground was being redeveloped in 2000. I went to visit it in the summer of 2009, getting a taxi from Preston station, which was a pretty depressing experience. I don't know the town, perhaps there was a scenic route I missed, but there seemed to be so many buildings closed or derelict, such as the Passion Palace — what passions could once have gone on there? — and the Ethical Spiritual Church, also boarded up, though perhaps its spirits were hovering elsewhere.

There was lots of action and excitement around the museum itself, which was reassuring. It was getting towards the end of the summer holidays and many families were clearly taking the chance to have a fun day out — and all for free.

The first thing to see, down a long corridor, was a Football Hall of Fame where they put up large portraits of famous players and managers who have achieved this accolade, awarded by the museum itself. I couldn't

146

quite work out the rationale, but a new batch gets announced every year and a big fuss is made — or so they hope. Being in Preston they have to work hard to make any sort of fuss, as the English media is so London-orientated.

One area was devoted to kids' activities, where lots of families were sitting painting or decorating dishes with football stars and scenes. There were quizzes and questions on the wall for them to answer, and a Subbuteo game they could play. All very popular, attracting lots of children. I caught sight of a large photograph of the Beatles on one wall. How had they dragged them in? Then I read a quiz question underneath — Who was known as the fifth Beatle? Answer: George Best. I suppose it is as good a way as any of introducing a player whom modern kids might not have heard of. Elsewhere in the museum children were allowed to dress up in ancient strips and have their photographs taken, and upstairs there were lots of interactive attractions for slightly older kids, such as taking penalties.

At the heart of the museum, which is what I had come to see and ogle at, are the real objects, the genuine historic artefacts, so many of them, and so well displayed and explained. I could have stayed for days, weeks even, without properly exhausting them all. They have some two thousand items on show at any one time, with another thirty thousand behind the scenes for researchers and academics to study.

Forty years ago, doing a degree in football would have been laughable, as silly and unlikely as, say, doing a degree in vintage radios, fans, lawnmowers or the Beatles. Now both football and the Beatles, which just happen to be my fave collecting areas, are studied at universities all over the world. Lawnmowers, alas, have yet to make it.

In the case of football, there are now fifty universities in the UK where you can a get a first degree or a postgraduate degree in football. Who would have thought it? The National football Museum is the prime research venue to which students come, not just from England but from all over the world.

Scotland has its own very good museum of football, located at Hampden Park, and one recently opened in Brazil. There's also one in Norway. That's about it, so far, on the national level, but in the UK there are seven leading clubs with their own museums, including Manchester United, Liverpool, Arsenal, Chelsea, West Ham, Newcastle and Celtic, with another four being planned. We football collectors are really spoiled.

Since the National Football Museum opened, many other valuable collections have been acquired, gifted or loaned, along with hundreds of humbler items provided by members of the public. One of the biggest acquisitions in recent years is called the Priory collection. I kept on seeing that name in the credit line on many labels as I wandered round, but the donor, when he handed it over, wished to remain anonymous. (I now gather it was Nigel Wray, the owner of Saracens rugby club, who is a keen collector of all sporting memorabilia.)

148

Naturally enough, the museum has lots of nineteenth-century balls from the early years of football, some in very odd shapes, used by public schools like Harrow, before the balls were standardised and the rules codified. And also balls from famous Cup Finals, and from the very first World Cup final in 1930. Uruguay and Argentina played each other in the final and each side insisted on playing with their own ball. A compromise was reached whereby the Argentinian ball was used in the first half and the Uruguayan in the second. Argentina were ahead with their ball at half time, 2-1, but Uruguay went on to win 4-2 with their ball. Which proves something. Or could just be balls.

For several years, the museum had on show the Argentinian ball. When the Priory collection was offered, it turned out to contain the other ball, so now, after all these decades, they have both 1930 World Cup final balls on show together. They do in fact look marginally different, with the leather panels in slightly different patterns.

Amongst their football shirts is the oldest surviving shirt, part of the Langton collection. It was worn by Arnold Kirke Smith, playing for England in the world's first-ever international, against Scotland in 1872, which ended in a 0-0 draw. They also have Bobby Moore's 1970 World Cup shirt, with the number 6 on the back. He swapped it after that game with Pele and for many years it was on display in a Brazilian bar before coming on the market and ending up at the museum. If you look carefully, you can still see the tobacco stains — from the bar of course, not from Bobby, as he was our blue-eyed clean-living hero. Other famous shirts include the one Maradona was wearing in the 1986 World Cup when he scored the so-called Hand of God goal against England, and also Stanley Matthews's shirt from the 1953 Cup Final, still known as the Matthews Final.

The day I was there they had a special display of Matthews memorabilia, which included a pair of his boots dated 1953. I was surprised to see how small and light they were, without the usual ankle protection pads of the period — the sort I thought everyone in Britain used at that time, including the professionals. I'd always believed that so-called continental boots, which real men dismissed as being more like slippers, did not come in till the 1970s, but apparently after playing in the World Cup in 1950 in Brazil, Matthews had acquired for himself a pair of the latest lightweights.

There was also a special display of items belonging to Sir Tom Finney, one of Preston North End's greatest-ever stars. Apart from boots, shirts and programmes, his knighthood medal was on display. In a display of Tommy Lawton memorabilia — another of the all-time English greats — they also had his ashes in a special cask.

One personal item that intrigues and rather shocks the younger generation is the large and rather cruel-looking neck brace once worn by Bert Trautmann. He was Manchester City's heroic goalkeeper in the 1956 Cup Final who played on, helping them to gain victory, not realising he had broken his neck. Trautmann was a German, held in a prisoner-of-war camp during the war, which in the end proved to be to his advantage. The FA at the time insisted on stringent residential qualifications for foreigners before they could play for a league team, but it was judged that Trautmann's years as a POW gave him residency.

One of the more recently arrived oddball items is a coracle. They have it near the entrance — a small, black-painted boat, tipped up on its side. What on earth could that have to do with football? Shows how much I know. It's world-famous, at least among Shrewsbury Town supporters. For decades it was the job of a man called Fred Davies to jump into this little boat whenever a ball went into the nearby river and retrieve it. When their ground moved from Gay Meadow, where they had been since 1910, into a new stadium in 2007, the coracle was no longer required.

I was particularly interested in all their items to do with Dick, Kerr's women's team, as I have my own little collection of women's football. People think women playing football, which is now incredibly popular all over the world, is a modern phenomenon, but its origins go back to 1895 when the British Ladies Football Club was formed and they held their first matches. As with the men's game, the early players were from the upper classes, public school and county types, but then the working classes arrived and took over. For the women the spur was the First World War, when one million women went into munitions factories, and started their own works football teams, just as the men had done.

One of the most successful of which was Dick, Kerr's Ladies, who came from Preston. I'd always assumed there must have been a man called Dick Kerr, but it refers to two men who had founded a Preston factory, a Mr Dick and a Mr Kerr. Grammatically, the team should always be called Dick, Kerr's Ladies, but the comma usually gets missed out. In 1920 they attracted a crowd of fifty-three thousand to Goodison Park, home of Everton, to watch them play St Helen's Ladies.

But then in 1921 the rotten old FA banned women from playing. Ostensibly this was on medical grounds because it was feared women would ruin their health by playing football, that it wasn't natural, that it would make them incapable of giving birth. There were also suggestions of financial fiddles to do with gate receipts — as if the men's game was not even more corrupt. The women believed it was just jealousy, because their game was proving so popular. It was not until 1971 that the FA finally recognised the women's game.

But in the years before and just after the First World War the women's game was incredibly popular. It featured in magazines and stories and was in a way part of the suffragette movement, in that it was an attempt by women to gain more independence and freedom. In 2002, Lily Parr, who was the star striker for Dick, Kerr's from the age of fourteen till her mid-forties, was inducted into the museum's Hall of Fame, their first female player.

So Preston figures large in the history of the women's game as well as the men's — and also in

152

football games of the toy variety. The oldest-known board football game, amongst the many the museum has on show, turns out to have been made in Preston in 1884. So good old Preston — the national home of our national game. But will it always remain so?

You would imagine that what has become, in less than ten years, a world-famous museum, with the distinction and honour of being termed a national museum, would have no worries about its future — attracting a hundred thousand visitors a year, with a handsome modern building, highly professional staff, lots of events and educational facilities, and thirty thousand historic objects. However, being big and national and apparently successful does not guarantee its future any more than the future of our little lawnmower museum is guaranteed. As I discovered when, at the end of my tour, I met Kevin Moore, director of the National Football Museum from the day it first opened. In fact even earlier, as he was involved in the many dramas that took place before it all kicked off.

Kevin was born in Nantwich in 1960. He remembers collecting 1970 World Cup stickers as a boy — the sort where you bought a packet then tried to swap your doubles with other boys. One day he got a letter from Gordon Banks, England's goalie, and naturally was well thrilled — till he rushed to school to show off his signed letter and found that half the class had had the same letter. However, it didn't put him off football.

He read history at Liverpool, then did an MPhil and worked on a museum project on Merseyside. After a few years, he realised he should have a proper qualification and went off to Leicester to do an MA in museum studies. "It was about the first and also the leading place for museum studies, attracting people from all over the world. I remember a man who was deputy head of the national railway museum in Zambia, who had left his wife and family for a year to study at Leicester. He said he had to do it or he would never get anywhere in Zambian museums."

Kevin then worked in a museum in St Helens, returning to Leicester as a lecturer. He wrote an academic book on museums and popular culture, arguing that subjects like football and pop music were just as valid for museums to display as any other. "It shouldn't be a matter of 'this is as good as that', but that football or pop music is important in its own right. Museums for too long suffered from stuffiness and elitism, which was why ordinary people were not going there. I still think, by the way, there should be a national museum of popular music."

When the campaign for a national football museum got going in the early 1990s he was roped in and in 1997 was appointed director, even though they still had no funding and no contents. FIFA's Harry Langton collection had never in fact gone to FIFA's headquarters in Switzerland, as I had always imagined, but was in Harry's garage in North London when Kevin first saw it, before it was moved into proper storage, but still in London.

"One of the many problems we had was that FIFA had bought it in partnership with a US sports company, and they did not agree on what should

154

happen to it. We lost about a year with all the arguments. In the end, we bought the FIFA collection for £580,000, using funding from the Heritage Lottery Fund."

That came out of the total of £15 million they received to get them opened and running, but after that they were on their own, hoping to live by generating income from admissions, the shop and the cafe. They had projected eighty thousand paying visitors but managed only forty thousand.

"We got tremendous coverage and plaudits for what we had done. I had been determined not to make it into a theme park, some sort of football Disneyland, but to put football in its social context, though we did have lots of fun and interactive bits. While everyone loved us, no one would give us any more money and not enough people were willing to come to Preston."

They had to trim their expenses, which meant no money for things like marketing and publicity, which would have helped them reached their eighty thousand target.

In 2003 the whole system changed. All national museums were now free to the public. In return for free entry, the museum was to receive a total of £450,000 a year from various football and government funds, leaving them to find £300,000 themselves. They did this by staging corporate events and organising foreign tours, such as exhibiting some of their treasures in Japan during the World Cup. The effect of free entry was immediate. Gates shot up to a hundred thousand and have stayed there ever since, though of course they

155

have had to work hard to keep up the excitement and activities, as being in Preston was never going to make it easy for a national museum.

In 2008, Lord Mawhinney, chairman of the Football League, was quoted as saying that he thought the national football museum should in fact be at Wembley — the new Wembley. When it was being constructed there was a plan to include a museum as part of the new stadium, but nothing seems to have happened. I suspect some of the opposition to Preston over the years has been snobbish, based on the thinking that all such national institutions should be in London, not stuck out in the wastelands of the North-West. It is probably true that visitors would have been more numerous if they had been nearer to London, though in fact, since the museum opened, Preston has been getting nearer to London. In 2001 it took well over three and a half hours to get to Preston by train from Euston. By 2009 it was down to two hours and is expected to become even quicker in the next few years. Why, soon Preston will be just a suburb of London. What's the problem?

"Ah, we still have several," sighed Kevin. "Even though everyone agrees we have done brilliantly, when you think of all the obstacles. Until now . . ."

What do you mean? I asked. What's happening now? He'd seemed such a cheerful chap, rather civil-servantish in his dark suit, spectacles and slightly sticky-out ears — but clearly an enthusiast. Why the sudden gloom?

"It's being announced next week that we are going to have to close . . ."

Oh my God. Have I just been round your most wonderful museum, going rave rave rave, and now you tell me it's going to cease to be?

"In Preston, probably. I don't see how we can continue here in our present form."

Poor old Kevin. For twelve years, since he got the job, which to any football fan in the world would have seemed a dream come true, he had been in constant meetings, battling with endless bureaucrats about funding. Now the plug was being pulled, mainly by something called the Football Foundation. Apparently they had been funding them out of their stadiums budget and now they needed the money for that.

I asked why, to make money, they didn't start charging again? Kevin said it wouldn't work. Attendance would probably drop from a hundred thousand back to forty thousand, which would not give them nearly enough income, as they now need £500,000 a year at least — but also as a national museum they have to be free; that is the system with all national museums.

The upshot was that at the end of 2009 most of the treasures were put into storage. There was a slight possibility that some sort of presence would be kept in Preston, perhaps a small local exhibition, plus the bulk of the artefact collection and the archive, which of course is enormous and would still attract hardy academics and brave researchers more than willing to trail to Preston. But Kevin didn't seem to hold out much hope that that would happen.

As for the National Football Museum itself, that would have to find a new home. Or close for ever. Impossible, I said. I'll sign any petition, storm the barricades, throw stones through the FA windows. Why, I'll even clear space amongst my treasures and look after some of your stuff. That 1872 England — Scotland shirt, that would look good with my collection of England — Scotland programmes.

I found it all pretty depressing. Just shows you. A purpose-built museum, devoted to a topic the whole world understands and most of the world loves, with national status, costing millions to create, with unique and amazing contents, attracting crowds of a hundred thousand every year — and yet, whoosh, it suddenly has to close. What hope therefore for all the piddling little museums devoted to one small subject, created by amateurs and run on a shoestring like some of the ones I had seen? And I was about to see another one, not far away, unless I got too fed up and went into mourning.

But it taught me not to envy too much the big, purpose-built museums — they can end up with big problems. Best to think small, best to stay modest. If I am going to display some of my own football treasures, I had better not boast about them.

However, a few weeks later things seemed a bit more optimistic when I met Kevin in London. He was now confident that they had had a serious offer that they were going to accept, subject to various details still to be thrashed out.

"Manchester City Council have made an offer to relocate the museum to the iconic Urbis building in central Manchester and provide substantially more annual revenue funding than the museum currently operates with. The Urbis building was funded by the Millennium Commission to be a museum and currently houses temporary exhibitions. There would therefore be great benefits for both the National Football Museum and Manchester City Council from this proposal."

It could take a year before the new site will be ready, so we football fans will just have to be patient. But it now looks as if at long last the museum's future will be secure. Even better, being in Manchester, in a prime location, in the middle of a vast metropolitan area and at the centre of a football-mad heartland, with famous Premiership clubs all around, attendance figures should shoot up. Kevin thinks that in their new location, they will immediately attract three hundred and fifty thousand, rising perhaps to four hundred thousand visitors a year. I can't wait.

The National Football Museum
Sir Tom Finney Way
Preston PR1 6PA[1]
Tel 01772 908421
www.nationalfootballmuseum.com

---

[1] See conclusion, page 381

CHAPTER
EIGHT

The Laurel and Hardy Museum, Ulverston

In the long, hot, humid summer of 2009 there was a photo in most of the newspapers of a statue of Laurel and Hardy being unveiled by the comedian Ken Dodd on a pavement in Ulverston — a nice bit of comic relief from the credit crunch and hard economic times. Probably made many people smile, as the sight of Laurel and Hardy still makes people feel happy, remembering their enjoyment of films past. At their heels their little dog Laughing Gravy is nipping away at their trousers, all part of the life-size bronze sculpture. Such fun, such innocence, we were happy then — yes, it was naive and childlike, and you didn't get bad language or anything nasty at the cinema in those days, not like today, tch tch tch. Then people moved on. Ulverston? I wonder how many people took that in and thought, now where's Ulverston when it's at home and why is a statue of Laurel and Hardy being put up there?

Ulverston is a lovely little town of some twelve thousand, surprisingly pretty, surprisingly thriving — at least that's how it feels, wandering round, looking at the shops, the cafes, galleries, indoor market, the nicely painted and preserved buildings. It just happens to be rather remote, stuck in a deep, hidden corner of what was the northern extremes of Lancashire and is now, since 1974, the southern peninsula of Cumbria. It's not in the Lake District National Park, being too far away, but it is just a short walk from the coast, along a very clean and green little canal to Morecambe Bay. Nearby towns like Millom and Barrow can feel depressing, left-over industrial wastelands, but Ulverston smacks of middle-class care and contentment. Despite its size, it has a cinema and a large, handsome theatre, the Coronation Hall, built in 1915, which seats six hundred. It does music, arts and literary events, as well as touring shows. That day, so the posters announced, it was going to be Freddie Starr Live! And I'd half-thought he was long dead.

The Laurel and Hardy statue is in front of the Coronation Hall. There were quite a few couples, of a certain age, standing in front of it, talking each other's photographs. Naturally I had my photo taken as well, asking a rather bulky couple to take me with my camera. I then followed them round the corner to the Roxy Cinema, a typical 1930s picture house, still going as a cinema though most of its vast space has now been carved up, to house a nightclub and also — taran taran — Britain's first-ever and still only Laurel and Hardy museum.

The museum was the creation of Bill Cubin, who died in 1997. In the 1950s he had a shop in Ulverston that sold some of the earliest washing machines, and he

161

was known in the town as Billy Twin Tubs. He had previously been a door-to-door salesman, a regular in the RAF, and for a while had a little cafe. None of the ventures made him a lot of money, but when he had any he spent it on his real passion in life — Laurel and Hardy

"I remember when I was little girl," says his daughter Marion, who now runs the museum with her son Mark, "that he told me that Stan Laurel had been born in Ulverston — but I didn't really believe it. At the time most reference books said he had been brought up in the North-East, in North Shields. There was also a problem about his real name, no one was sure what it was. But my father was insistent and he managed to dig out Stan's birth certificate, which proved that he was born Arthur Stanley Jefferson on 16 June 1890 at 3 Argyle Street, Ulverston, in the County of Lancaster."

Bill Cubin started collecting photos and memorabilia and anything else to do with Laurel and Hardy. When the house of Stan Laurel's birth came up for sale, he didn't have enough money to buy it, which he would have liked to have done, but he managed to acquire most of the furniture, which had once belonged to Stan's grandparents and had been in the house when Stan lived there.

Bill shoved the furniture and his other L and H memorabilia into his shop's storeroom. When he acquired any interesting old photos or copies of press cuttings, he stuck them on the walls and ceilings of the storeroom.

162

He joined the Laurel and Hardy fan club, went to Hollywood, met and made friends with other enthusiasts. When they came to visit him, Bill would take them into his storeroom to see his treasures. Local people heard about his collection and they too asked to see them.

"From about the early 1970s," remembers Marion, "he started to open up the storeroom on Saturday afternoons and charge people a few pennies to look at his Laurel and Hardy things. Fans came from America to see what he had and several donated some of their Stan Laurel items. They loved what he was doing, and his enthusiasm.

"It's hard to say exactly when his museum first opened — it was just a hobby at first then opened in dribs and drabs. I can remember several official openings when I was young, usually when he had acquired something new. Dad was a shameless self-promoter."

He was also a strong Tory and served as a local councillor. In 1974 he became the first ever mayor of Ulverston. Ulverston is an ancient town, but the reason why it had never had an official mayor was that it was in the wilds of Lancashire. When it joined the newly created Cumbria, formed from the old counties of Cumberland and Westmorland and a chunk of Yorkshire, its status was upgraded. In 1974 it was allowed to appoint its own mayor, who happened that first year to be Bill Cubin. "Practically the first thing he did as mayor was to have a special plaque put on Stan

Laurel's birthplace. That first plaque got stolen, so another one had to be put up."

It was of course good publicity for his museum, and Bill was always keen to draw attention to it, cutting many corners to put it on the map. From around 1975 onwards he began running it as a museum full-time, still in his old storeroom. He managed to cram in a little cinema, with 1920s cinema seats, and showed old Laurel and Hardy films.

When kids and teenagers came in — rather sceptical, perhaps not having seen a Laurel and Hardy film before — he would sit them down and say that if any of them did NOT laugh once during the film, they would get their money back. He never had to pay up.

But he did run into some trouble from showing these films. He had assumed that as they were all over fifty years old they would be out of copyright. "But a new company had appeared on the scene," says Mark, his grandson, "some company who said they had acquired the rights. Grandad got into right legal trouble. He had to hire a solicitor and the upshot was, I think, he lost about £10,000 in all — more than he was taking from the museum in a year. It did look as if he might have to close, but somehow he managed to survive.

"He then started showing the films again, but this time said the film show was free. All that people were paying for was entry to his museum. He was a bit of a character, always up to something."

"But most of all," says Marion, "he was an enthusiast for Laurel and Hardy. He just loved them. Many a time when I was younger, helping out in the museum, I would have to go in front of him and make a wind-up sign — he was talking so much a queue had formed behind him and people couldn't get in."

He then had some unexpected help when one day a young Dutchman called Nico Monitz, a Laurel and Hardy enthusiast, arrived to look at the museum — still just one little room crammed with stuff, with no proper displays. Nico had just won a big prize on a Dutch TV quiz show and he offered Bill the money to expand his museum, to help him build another room and so double its size.

"He gave Dad about £1000 — in Dutch money, so we had to exchange," says Marion. "It was a generous gift."

I asked Mark how many people visited the museum every year, and he said he wasn't sure. "All I know is that my mum pays me £8,000 a year to work here." My guess is about thirty thousand a year — double what they had in their old premises, where they were for over thirty years.

In 2009 the museum moved to what was once the old stage of the Roxy Cinema. They don't have a lot more space, but it is a better shape to exhibit their treasures and in a better position in the town.

"The old museum was getting tatty and run-down," says Marion. "It was a struggle running it after my father died and I wasn't sure about its future. This has been a big step, moving here, and I hope it works, but I thought it was the only way to keep it going. I want Mark to carry on running it, so it needs to attract more people, enough for me to pay him. We are totally self-supporting and get no grants."

Marion had been ill and had heard the news that day that she would soon be confined to a wheelchair, and would therefore not be able to run the museum as she had done. So in future Mark will do it, helped by a volunteer called Alan.

Mark had been in the old museum that morning, still taking Laurel and Hardy memorabilia from the walls and ceiling. "Some of the things had been put up with wallpaper paste, others with Blu-tack or drawing pins. It's been hell to get them down, but I'm going to have one wall covered with them, in honour of grandad."

You enter the new museum up some narrow, angled steps, which were originally the steps up to the main stage of the Roxy. There still is a vague air of a home-made museum, the sort that amateurs create, putting up their own displays and handwritten notices, which of course was how Bill created it in the first place, but they have gone a bit more modern this time. Since moving into their new site they have got a professional designer in to create an informative series of storyboards, with photos and cuttings, which take you through Stan Laurel's life.

Stan's father, Arthur Jefferson, was a music-hall comedian turned theatre manager. At the time of Stan's birth in 1890 he had returned to Ulverston, staying with his parents-in-law, having taken on the lease of the local Hippodrome and put on variety shows. "There's no money in being a comic," he told young Stan. "You have to get into management."

166

When he moved over to the North-East, to take over other theatres, Stan was left for a while with his grandparents in Ulverston, living there until he was about six. Later on, till he was about twelve, he still came to Ulverston for his summer holidays.

His father, known as AJ, then moved to Glasgow, where young Stan first trod the boards as a boy actor. He then joined Fred Karno and his company in Manchester. I'd heard of them but always thought they were a circus, as I used to hear my own father say, "It's like Fred Karno's circus in here," whenever we were all making a noise and fighting. It was in fact a music-hall troupe, extremely popular, which toured all the main cities and theatres. Karno's real name was Fred Westcott. In 1910 Stan set sail for the USA with Karno's troupe, along with the young Charlie Chaplin. For a time Stan was an understudy to Chaplin, doing the same sort of put-upon little man roles. Chaplin, once he reached America, never came back, but Stan did on that first occasion. He did another US tour later, and this time he reached Hollywood and started appearing in silent movies.

He changed his name sometime around 1917 during a period of bad luck, when he didn't appear to be making much progress. He decided that it was his name, Stan Jefferson, being thirteen letters long, that was holding him back. According to a copy of a letter on the storyboard, a young actress with whom he was then appearing took credit for his new name. She was in a dressing room with him, reading a book about Roman emperors, when she noticed that they wore

167

laurel wreaths on their heads. She suggested to Stan that he should call himself Laurel, then he would earn his own laurels. On stage and screen, Stan called himself Laurel from then on, and in 1931 he legally changed his name to Laurel.

It was while working for the Hal Roach film studios that Stan first met Oliver Hardy, a jobbing actor doing character parts, though Stan had already become a director. Ollie, however, was always content to do what he was told on the film set and was more interested in playing golf. When asked later on where the ideas had come from, or how the stunts had been done, he would reply, "Ask Stan."

Oliver Hardy had been born Norvell Hardy in Harlem, Georgia, in 1892, the son of a lawyer with no show-business connections in his family. The family had originally come from England and Ollie maintained he could trace his ancestors back to Admiral Nelson's colleague Captain Hardy, to whom he is reputed to have said, "Kiss me, Hardy."

As a boy Ollie had a good voice and once thought of becoming a singer, but his weight led to him getting the heavy roles, despite the fact that his nickname was "Babe". This originated from a gay Italian barber who fancied him and, every time he had finished shaving him, would rub his checks and say, "Nice-a bab-ee, nice-a bab-ee." This so amused Ollie's friends that they began to call him Babe, and the name stuck with him throughout the whole of his life.

They started making Laurel and Hardy films together in 1926. They used their own names from the beginning, which was unusual in those days, when film characters were often called things like Lonesome Luke or Hickory Hiram. If the studio sacked you, they could then hire another character actor to play the same role. Laurel and Hardy realised they could always take their own names, and characters, with them. Stan invariably played the dumb character, but in real life he was the clever one, thinking up gags and stunts. The plot for *Duck Soup*, one of their classic films, made in 1927, is said to have been inspired by a routine Stan remembered his father doing onstage back in his Ulverston days.

They made 106 films together — both silent and talking, twenty-minute reelers and full-length films — between 1926 and 1954, and were incredibly popular all over the world. They got mobbed when they toured the UK in 1932. They came back in 1947 and Stan visited his birthplace in Ulverston — but, alas, Bill Cubin was in the RAF at the time and missed the visit.

Hardy died in 1957 but Stan lived on till 1965, supposedly suffering some sort of collapse after the death of his friend and partner. Later he had a stroke. Hardy was married three times, while Stan managed five marriages — though two of them were to the same woman. When he was very ill in hospital he told the nurse that he was thinking of going skiing. "I didn't know you were a skier," she said. "I'm not," replied Stan, "but anything is better than lying here having needles stuck in me." Half an hour later, when the nurse returned, Stan had died peacefully in his sleep.

Stan, unlike Ollie, was always available and affable, kept his name in the phone book long after he had become world-famous, and was always willing to meet fans and talk about his films. "If any of you cry at my funeral," he once said, "I'll never talk to you again."

On the walls of the museum are copies of some interesting letters he wrote to his fans. And in little alcoves there is some of the furniture from his grandparents' house, the stuff Bill bought over thirty years ago. One alcove is arranged as an outside wash house with a huge mangle, and a repro 1904 comic in the corner. This is supposed to represent, so Mark explained, the wash house where young Stan was sent if he was naughty, but he had hidden his comics there, so he didn't mind. I said surely they could get a real comic from the 1900s, they are not all that expensive. As a collector, always on the lookout for something new to collect, I offered to look out for a real one and send it on.

They don't have a lot of personal belongings from Stan himself — prices have risen and there are a lot of wealthy L and H collectors out there, in the USA and Germany. What they have is in a little glass showcase — his cigarette lighter, a special ashtray he used after he had had his stroke, his razor, a fiddle he used on stage, his bowler hat and also some letters and photographs, which were presented by Stan's daughter Lois when she visited the museum.

Amongst the Laurel and Hardy souvenirs are bars of soap, a salt and pepper set in the shape of Laurel and Hardy, and some Italian wine bottles, also shaped like

170

them. It's always interesting how cheap souvenirs, issued to cash in on a current craze, can in the end become museum exhibits in themselves if the subject continues to be of interest.

Laurel and Hardy certainly are — they are regularly rediscovered by new generations and have their films revived. They feature on the cover of the Beatles *Sgt. Pepper* album, as John Lennon, like millions of other boys and girls in the 1940s and 1950s, had watched them at Saturday morning children's cinema shows. In 1991 they appeared on some US stamps.

There is today a worldwide fan club, the Sons of the Desert, which has thousands of members and lots of branches, known as "tents". (Because you have tents in the desert.) This was established in 1964, one of the founders being Dr John McCabe who had written a biography of Laurel and Hardy first published in 1961 and reprinted many times since.

"My father used to go over to the USA to their annual conventions," says Marion, "and when people visited his museum, and seemed to like it, he would encourage them to start their own tent when they got back home. In the 1970s, when he began the museum, there were only two tents in the UK, one in London and one in Scotland. Thanks to Dad badgering anyone who seemed enthusiastic, there are over thirty tents in the UK today."

There's a world conference every two years and in 1984 it was held in Ulverston, the first time it had been held outside the USA. There's also a European conference and a regular British national conference.

They had just had the annual UK one in Ulverston, which attracted 125 members. There are also a couple of magazines in the UK and the USA. In Harlem, Georgia, Hardy's birthplace, there is a Laurel and Hardy museum similar to the one in Ulverston.

So what's the attraction? "Oh well, Laurel and Hardy are such fun," says Marion. "Gentle humour, with no vulgarity. Everyone knows a Hardy figure — the one who thinks he's clever but he's not. And we all know someone we think pretty slow and dumb. Most of us know a relation who bumps into things. Generations grew up remembering their films from their childhood, but now you can see the films on telly or buy them in boxed sets from the internet. They are just as popular as they have ever been."

I said I had noticed quite a few people outside on the pavement having their photos taken in front of the new statue, proof they were still loved.

"That statue was my father's idea, something like twenty years ago. He tried so hard to get approval for it and then to get the money, but he died in 1997 without ever managing it. I hadn't really got the heart to take it on, but at his funeral some members of the Sons of the Desert offered to take on the task of fund-raising.

"We applied to all the usual places for grants, including the National Lottery. It took years of form-filling, but no one would give us a penny. All we wanted was a straightforward statue of them, as everyone knows them, not any artistic interpretation of their art. If we had gone for something arty, I think we might have got funding from some arts body. In the end the Sons of the Desert raised £60,000, all by themselves. That paid for the sculptor, Graham Ibbeson, and to have it cast in bronze.

"Every time I go past it, I can't believe we eventually did it. I did used to dream about it. My dad would have been so pleased. I see it as a monument to him and what he did for the town by opening this museum, as well as a monument to Laurel and Hardy themselves."

It is also a monument to amateur enthusiasm, creating something for other enthusiasts, something that never existed before and that no one had ever thought of doing, overcoming all the problems, legal and financial, that beset such home-made enterprises and have to be solved without any outside help. I'd like to pinch the idea of showing old films when I get round to my own museum, such as Beatles films, they would go down well — what am I saying? I must be mad. The lawyers would have a field day. I'd spend the rest of my life in court.

So far, a lot of my museums have been like the Laurel and Hardy one — a do-it-yourself, go-it-alone museums, like the vintage wirelesses, fans, lawnmowers, baked beans. The postal museum, you could argue, was not quite in that mould, not totally unusual or seen as daft by other people, as stamps are an established, mainstream hobby. The Beatles — well, for a start their name has enormous pulling power. Football likewise has always had a massive following, so in theory it should not be all that bizarre or difficult to create and run a football museum. In theory. In practice, we now know otherwise.

Coming up, folks, something totally different. A museum spawned by an industry.

Laurel and Hardy Museum
On Stage at the Roxy
Brogden Street
Ulverston
Cumbria LA12 7AH
Tel 01229 582292
www.laurel-and-hardy.co.uk

CHAPTER NINE

The Cumberland Pencil Museum, Keswick

About twenty-five years ago I took my children to the Cumberland Pencil Museum in Keswick. A wet day probably. Something to do while we waited for it to clear so we could take the steamer across Derwentwater and climb Cat Bells. It hadn't long opened, so it was still something of a novelty, but I'd been dying to go for a long time as I thought it was so unusual, eccentric and funny — how could there be a whole museum devoted to something as small and simple as a pencil?

I was delighted with it, came away raving — which I tend to do quite often, as my wife frequently warns me. I will oversell things, she says, which can rebound when other people then expect too much. My children, alas, were less than impressed, couldn't see why I'd found it so interesting.

The entrance fee in 1984 was 60p, for I have it in my diary, and that year they attracted seventeen thousand visitors. I remember it as small, fairly dusty, with low cases, one containing a Second World War pencil that particularly fascinated me.

175

Just been back for the first time since — and it was raining again this time, but goodness, what a difference. There were queues outside, as if it was a football match and I half-expected touts to be selling tickets. Instead there was free entertainment — jugglers amusing the crowds, most of them families with young children, as they waited, while at the little covered entrance hall an artist was doing cartoons with what appeared to be watercolour paints. Yet I thought it was supposed to be a museum of pencils, not painting.

Inside it was heaving, so much activity, so much going on, so many attractions. And there was also now an excellent and attractive cafe, doing light meals as well as drinks and snacks. No wonder today the pencil museum attracts a hundred thousand visitors a year. It is still the only one of its type in the world, and it still makes people smile at the very idea of it, imagining, as I did, that it must be a bit of a joke, not to be taken seriously.

"The average visitor still has little idea what to expect," says Alex Spencer, the curator. "They pick up a leaflet at the tourist office in the Moot Hall, or get told about it when they ask what else there is to do on a bad day. They come along expecting to stay half an hour and end up staying two hours. We have done surveys and we know this is true. That's the average duration."

It's not just the fun and the interactive elements that keep the punters amused for those two hours, but the discovery that pencils are a fascinating subject, part of

Cumbria's, and in fact Britain's, social and economic history. Oh yes.

The first discovery in the world of graphite took place around the early 1500s in the Borrowdale valley, near Keswick. Graphite is a natural form of pure carbon — the other, much harder, version is diamonds but alas we have not found many of these so far in Cumbria. According to local mythology, after a violent storm during which trees had been uprooted, some shepherds found that lumps of blackish rock had been exposed. They thought at first it was coal. They failed to get it to burn but found it was ideal for marking their sheep.

Sometime later, another use was found for it — making canonballs using graphite moulds, as the graphite did not melt at high temperatures. These were vital armaments during the Elizabethan age. Stagecoaches took the graphite under armed guard to London, where at the Tower of London, then an arsenal, the canonballs were made. Graphite was also used for medicinal purposes.

During the sixteenth century, there was a sort of mini gold rush in the Borrowdale valley. Graphite mines were opened and miners used to digging such materials brought in from Germany — who then settled down and over the centuries became — Cumbrians, which is why today you get quite a few German-sounding surnames in the Keswick area. When I was at school in Carlisle there was a boy called Reinbeck, whose ancestors had probably been German miners. I have often wondered if Paul Scholes, the Manchester United footballer, had a similar background.

Locally the graphite was known as "wad", and when it was used for marking or writing it was known as a wad pencil. Originally, after the discovery by the shepherds, a piece of graphite, which is easy to cut and shape, was simply wrapped in a piece of sheepskin to be used for marking. The Italians are the ones first recorded as using Cumberland graphite encased in wood. During the Renaissance, graphite from Cumberland was greatly prized all over Europe, by artists in the Low Countries and then in Italy, and was used by Michelangelo and other old masters when doing their drawings.

Graphite was therefore very valuable, so much so that guards were kept on the mines and the miners were searched after they came off a shift. All the same, there was an illegal trade in lumps of black wad smuggled out of the mines, most of which centred around the bar of the George Hotel in Keswick. This illegal trade was known as the "black market", a phrase that has passed into the language.

So not only did Cumbrian graphite help the old masters — and many of our great lady novelists, who did much of their early scribbling in pencil at the kitchen table — but it has had an influence on the English language. Quite an achievement for such a humble substance, which over the centuries has hardly changed its shape, its size, its purpose. Early pencil-making, using a wood casing, was for many years purely a cottage industry in the Keswick area. It was

178

easy to do, using minimal tools and machines, and could be done in ordinary farmhouses — and in essence the manufacturing process is still much the same today.

Most visitors to the pencil museum, if they have ever thought about the subject, if asked how the lead gets into a pencil, would probably say, er, isn't it done by boring a little hole through a bit of wood, then shoving the lead through? In fact, a pencil consists of two halves stuck together. A piece of wood has a ridge made in it, the lead is inserted, then an identical piece of wood is stuck on top — but so well done, so skilfully, that you can't see the joins, especially if the pencil is then varnished or painted. The shaping of the lead, the cutting of the wood, and the sticking together could therefore be done by almost anyone at home, using a saw and a chisel. But of course pretty slowly.

Pencil factories arrived with the Industrial Revolution and the Cumberland Pencil Company, which owns and runs the pencil museum, dates back to 1832. For many years there were four main pencil factories in the town, but by around the 1900s, after various takeovers and closures, there was only one left, which formally became the Cumberland Pencil Company in 1916.

David Sharrock, today's managing director, joined the company as an accountant in March 1981, just a few months before the museum opened. "I can't really take credit for it as it had already been pencilled in . . . it was there on the drawing board," he says, getting in the jokes before anyone else can — as of course he has heard all the possible pencil jokes by now.

Over the decades there had always been a steady stream of visitors asking to see round the pencil works, included royal visitors, but health and safety regulations were coming in, making it harder to allow the general public into the actual workshops, so they opened a small museum on the same site and put on display some of their extensive archives.

"At the time we were the only visitor attraction in Keswick — apart from the town museum in Fitz Park, which wasn't exactly, er, a massive attraction."

Keswick Museum used to be very fuddy-duddy and old-fashioned, with the usual mixed collections of unrelated stuff given to them over the years and shoved in dusty display cabinets, typical of many small-town local museums across the country. In Keswick's case they did have some truly exotic items, such as a 500-year-old dead cat, the original manuscript of *The Three Bears* as written by Robert Southey, one-time Poet Laureate, and a set of musical stones — stones on which music could be played, and had been played before Queen Victoria. However, it was always on the verge of closing, running out of money, attracting very few visitors, until relatively recently when a band of volunteers brought it back to life again. Keswick is now blessed with six different thriving museums.

The pencil museum is the only one which is an industrial museum, connected to a specific industry — a type of museum you find all over the UK — and the pencil factory itself is still going strong, the only factory in the UK still manufacturing pencils — and only pencils, that's all they do.

The death of pencils, like the death of books when radio and TV came in, is often being predicted, but so far they have managed to survive the arrival of biros and felt pens and, more recently, computers.

"Fortunately we have always been strong in the arts and crafts field, rather than the technical. One of our rivals was more affected by computers and has now closed its UK factory. Architects in the old days used a lot of pencils, high-class expensive ones, but CAD came in, enabling them to do drawings on computers, so that market has dwindled. We never sold a lot to the commercial and scientific world, we have been strongest in coloured pencils used by children, schools and also artists.

"Parents still start off their children on coloured pencils, from about the age of three, as they are too young for computers and they are not to be trusted with biros or felt pens because of the mess and marks they leave. So pencils are still a natural thing which we all grow up using. Children and schools still love them and use a lot, which is lucky for us.

"But we have also been lucky in that in the last few years there has been a boom in arts and crafts, especially amongst older people. Many retired people are taking up drawing and painting, something they did as a child and then forgot. They decide to go back to it, and need modern materials, help and guidance."

To cater for their needs, the Cumberland Pencil Company now produces one million pencils a week, in a thousand different types, covering ten different ranges and uses, including water-colour. Watercolour pencils?

181

I'd never heard of them, which shows how little I know. They have been going for some years. They look like ordinary coloured pencils, but having done your drawing of a flower or an animal you then paint over it with a waterbrush, which contains just tap water, or with a conventional artist's paintbrush, and bingo, the pencil drawing jumps into new life as a watercolour painting.

They have a full-time research and development department that is permanently working on new uses and forms of pencils, such as charcoal pencils. The latest is called Inktense and is an advance on the watercolour pencils in that once the water is applied the painting becomes permanent, as fixed as an oil painting.

"We lead the pencil world in innovation. At the world level, we have two main rival firms, one in Germany, which is part of a bigger group, and one in Switzerland, but we like to believe that no other pencil company in the world has the range of different pencils we have. Over 60 per cent of our production is exported and we sell to eighty different countries."

Until very recently the pencil factory was on the same site it had occupied since 1832, right beside the pencil museum, but in 2008 it relocated to Workington, some twenty miles away. They had wanted to expand their old factory, and the museum, redeveloping the whole site, adding some new buildings and residential houses, but they couldn't get the appropriate planning permissions, so in the end they sold the site and built a brand-new factory, costing £5 million, at Lillyhall, an industrial estate outside Workington. It was formally opened by HM the Queen on 5 June 2008 and today employs eighty-five people — it was the biggest industrial employer in Keswick till it moved. Fortunately, 75 per cent of the workforce ended up with a shorter journey to work as most were already living in Cockermouth or on the west coast, except for David himself. He happens to live in Penrith, so his journey to work has doubled.

None of the graphite used in Cumberland pencils today comes from Cumberland — and it hasn't for the last hundred years or more. The Borrowdale graphite mine ran out in about 1890, though the factory had enough supplies in stock to last till 1905. Since then, all their graphite has been imported. Today they get stocks of the quality they need from Sri Lanka, though China and Korea also produce graphite.

Even sadder in a way, the Cumberland Pencil Company is not Cumbrian-owned, but then it hasn't been for several decades, having been part of Rexel. Today it is owned by an American company called ACCO Brands, which produces office supplies, located near Chicago. They are clearly very pleased with the success of the factory, and of the museum. They have plans to expand the museum if they can get the right permissions, increasing its size and contents by 50 per cent as they still have large archives in store. So what is there to see today?

I went round with Alex Spencer, the curator, the person responsible for having introduced many of the interactive features. She comes originally from Leicester and for ten years was manager of a women's fashion store called Etam in the Metro Centre in Gateshead. "I woke up one day when I got to thirty and thought, what am I doing? I don't want to spend the rest of my life in retail. She saw an advert for a job with English Heritage in the North-East, looking after nine of their properties, then three years ago she heard the pencil museum job was vacant. Her experience in the retail trade, as well as tourism, obviously helped her get the job, and she has introduced the cafe and greatly expanded the shop — two elements that any half decent museum, however small and idiosyncratic, needs to survive. A cafe had been thought of before but it was viewed as a distraction that would require endless regulations to be overcome in a building that is not exactly modern — in fact from the outside it looks a bit like a Nissen hut left over from the last war. Alex managed all this, as well as the new features, and the museum now has a staff of twelve, double the number it had when she arrived.

The main development has been in the interactive activities, laying on demonstrations and courses in drawing and painting. Going round, there seemed to be groups everywhere, children and the elderly, busily engaged in drawing and painting. Children get free materials and prizes for the best efforts each day. Adults were being offered a free hour with a trained botanical artist who was instructing them how to draw flowers and fruit, using of course Derwent watercolour pencils. For a whole day's workshop — on a wide variety of subjects, including landscapes, seascapes and animals, and using different materials, such as pastels — inclusive of the materials, the charge is £40. They are trying to offer as many of these as possible in the winter months, as the summer months are the best times for visitors — especially if it rains. Given a really hot, brilliant, sunny Lakeland summer, which of course we are all longing for, their annual attendance can drop from a hundred thousand down to nearer eighty thousand.

You approach the exhibits via a tunnel, which is a bit naff and corny and is meant to recreate an old graphite mine, complete with miners and picks lying around. It did include suitable noises and at one time water dripping, to show how tough the work was, till they had a flood.

But all the displays were splendid, so attractive and colourful, epecially the old boxes and tins of Derwent pencils — their main trade name — from the 1930s and earlier. There are old machines and explanations of how pencils are made, using the same wood today — Canadian cedar — as in the nineteenth century, when it all began. They have pencils from 1840 onwards. One of the ways of dating them is that in the very early ones, when pencils were still a cottage industry and were made by hand, the lead inside was rectangular in shape, the way it had been cut with a saw. From 1912, when factories took over, the lead was round, having been machine-extruded.

There are lots of special commemorative boxes, sold over the years to mark important national occasions, and which they still produce. In 2007 to celebrate 175 years of pencil manufacturing in Keswick, they made 175 sets of a box of 350 different pencils, which sold for £500 — all the boxes were made of mahogany and contained repro items from the museum as well as the pencils. Only one of them is left, in a display cabinet. There are some very keen pencil collectors — as I should have expected, since there is nothing in this world that can't be collected — who will buy old pencil memorabilia. Most of the collectors are in America, where there are pencil clubs and websites.

The museum now has its own little video theatre where a ten-minute film takes you through the manufacturing process, but I suppose the single most fascinating item is still the one I was most interested in twenty-five years ago, on my first visit. This is the Second World War secret pencil that contained a compass and a map and was given to RAF pilots in case they had to crash-land over Germany or were trying to escape from a POW camp. I can stare at it for ages, marvelling at the titchy but real compass that was hidden inside, along with the little map made of what looks like a silk material. Each map had a code, depending on which region of Germany you might happen to be wanting to escape from, with the best routes over the border into Holland or Belgium.

They were created by a wartime boffin called Charles Fraser-Smith who was the real-life version of Q from the James Bond films. Officially he was employed in the clothing department of the Ministry of Supply, but unknown to even his own secretary and boss, he was

186

secretly working for MI6, providing equipment for special ops agents who were going behind enemy lines.

He started with counterfeit uniforms for them to wear when dropped into enemy territory, then moved on to other and more ingenious devices, such as a miniature camera hidden in a cigarette lighter, plus a shaving brush with a hollow handle to contain the film. He invented steel shoelaces which could be used as a garrotte — very handy for strangling baddies. He secreted torches and knives inside the heels of boots and the rims of hats — all devilishly ingenious.

The order to make the special pencils reached the Cumberland Pencil Company in around 1942, but it was so secret that only a handful of the managers knew about it. They returned to the factory after all the workers had gone home and made the special pencils themselves.

David Sharrock says that all trace of the order has disappeared from their archives, which are normally very good. He suspects that all written reference to and details of their manufacture had to be returned to the government, so no one now knows how many were in fact made. Twenty are known to exist today, two of which are in the pencil museum. Did they really work? Did the Germans ever find out? Did they have their own fiendish forms of secret devices? It's not often on my museum trail that I've come away still asking myself questions.

When I first went to the museum they also had on display what was then described as the world's biggest pencil — some seven feet long. It got the museum quite

187

a bit of national publicity when it got into the *Guinness Book of Records*. It had originally been made in 1978, before the museum opened, to raise money for the Keswick mountain rescue team. It went out on tour, to schools and clubs — oh, life was simpler in those good old days, before B-list celebs took over from giant HB pencils. It has since been superseded by rival attractions elsewhere in the world, such as Kuala Lumpur, where they are keen to make their own mark, ha ha.

Today, the pencil museum has its original biggie, standing straight up on its end so visitors can pose beside it and have their photos taken, as naturally I did, but they also have, lying down on its side like a stranded whale, a monster 25-foot-long yellow pencil which they boast is the longest *coloured* pencil in the world, so sucks to Kuala Lumpur. It demonstrates that Cumberland Pencils, after all these years, is still a world force.

It does, though, take up such a lot of room in a museum overflowing with so many small-scale goodies, that it seems a waste of valuable space. But I suppose it does make a point. OK, that's the last pencil joke.

The thing I'd like most would be the little pencil with the map and compass inside. That would amuse my grandchildren and would be a talking point of any collection I decide to display in my own museum — not that I'm sure yet what I am going to allow the world to share. Perhaps I should just stick to one theme. The pencil museum shows how it can be done — one simple everyday object, yet they have expanded

188

backwards and frontwards and sideways, using lateral thinking, good research and audience participation.

The success of the pencil museum shows that so-called industrial museums can be fun and fascinating, and that they can become big places with lashings to see and do, despite being devoted to just a single small object.

I did worry, though, about including pencils in this book because of their association with a factory and an industry — though of course the museum fitted my main brief perfectly, being genuinely concerned with just one apparently humdrum object. My other worry was that it hadn't come from the collecting of one single, obsessive collector, which is what I had been looking out for, ever since I left London. But, ah ha, there is another museum in Keswick with a collector and collection that certainly did appear to fit all of my self-imposed criteria . . .

The Cumberland Pencil Museum
Southey Works
Keswick
Cumbria CA12 5NG
Tel 017687 73626
www.pencilmuseum.co.uk

CHAPTER TEN

Cars of the Stars, Keswick

In 1982 a thirty-year-old dentist called Peter Nelson was driving from his home in Applethwaite, just under Skiddaw, in the heart of the Lake District, to his surgery in Keswick. Suddenly, in the road ahead him, he found himself being flagged down by a total stranger. Was it a cop and had he been speeding? Someone who had broken down and needed help? Could it be a hold-up? Dentists, as we know, are pretty well paid these days, so someone could be after his wallet.

It turned out to be a researcher from Granada TV. They were filming scenes nearby on the shores of Derwentwater for a popular TV series of the eighties called *Spoils of War* and they needed a car just like his — a 1947 MG TC — to use for ten days. They offered him £100 a day for the loan of his car, and he said, done.

After it was all over and he'd had his car returned and watched it on TV, he found himself thinking — I wonder what happens to all the other cars that have been used on TV and in films over the last five decades or so? Where do they end up? Do they go back to their owners or what?

And then he forgot about it and went back to concentrating on dentistry. He was running a successful practice in Keswick, doing very well despite having started with no family money or professional background. He was born in Carlisle in 1951, where his father was a policeman, a fairly humble one, working as a dog handler, though in his family he did have an uncle who had risen to be Chief Constable of Cumbria. During his childhood, his father was constantly being posted around Cumbria, to Wigton, Kendal, Penrith, plus a spell in Liverpool. "I think I went to twenty different schools in all, which rather knocks your education." He ended up in Whitehaven, where he did his O and A levels, then wondered what to do next, perhaps be a policeman like his father.

"The only thing I'd really enjoyed at school was art, though I was quite good at science subjects. I'd also enjoyed things like collecting stamps, coins, cigarette cards and birds' eggs — a bit galling now to admit it, but that's what boys did in the fifties, not realising how harmful it was to the birds. My uncle, the Chief Constable, advised against the police and said the two best, safest professions to get into were to be a solicitor or a dentist. My dad liked the idea of dentistry and a teacher at school, who was Welsh, encouraged me to apply to the Cardiff dental hospital as it was new and supposed to be very good."

So off he went to Cardiff to do a five-year degree in dentistry. He did get grants, but not quite enough to live on, so he looked around for a spare-time job. He applied to a music shop and when they asked if he could repair guitars, he said yes, which was a lie. His father, however, had been a joiner before becoming a policeman and he sent him down some special glues and clamps.

"The first guitar I repaired turned out well and I found myself spending my time repairing them instead of selling them on the counter. I got well paid and was in great demand. So much so that I was able to buy myself a sports car while still a student. It was a Triumph Spitfire, which I bought from one of my lecturers."

He was a good student, so he says, and had finished the course in four and a half years. "The day after I graduated, I was head-hunted, in a sense, as my professor arranged for me to start work immediately in Brighton. He had a dentist friend who had been involved in a terrible car accident, running over a child, and had had a bit of a nervous breakdown and was being forced to take six months off. They needed someone to fill in. So I left Cardiff on the Sunday and started work in this busy practice on the Monday. At dental school I was doing four people a day — suddenly I had to do up to twenty. But it went well, and after six months I was offered another six months as a locum with another practice, then a spell in Birmingham and in North Lancs.

"After only two or three years of working I was earning very good money, around £20,000 a year, when I saw this advert in the *British Dental Journal* for a dental practice for sale in Keswick. I wanted to return to my home county and this seemed ideal. It was the best practice in Keswick, partly because the dentist had two brothers who were local doctors and they referred patients to him. I bought the practice and the large Victorian house in the middle of Keswick where it was situated, with a flat on top, though I had to get a massive mortgage."

Once again, he did well, earning good money, and was soon running the latest Porsche 911, as well as his old MG.

"One day a friend told me that the old Royal Oak Hotel was selling off its garage, just behind Main Street, and they had got planning permission to build twenty flats on the site. I suppose I had always been a bit of an entrepreneur, without quite realising it, so I got a bank loan and bought it. I had a good cash flow from the dental practice, so that helped. But in the end, I discovered that building twenty flats would cost a lot more than I had anticipated. It would mean massive borrowing and uncertainty, so I just kept the garage empty, as it was, except I put my MG and Porsche in it."

Thanks to that incident with the TV people, which had got him thinking about what happened to old cars in films, he decided not to use the empty garage for flats but instead to track down as many ex-film and TV vehicles as he could, store them in the garage, and then, if he got enough, perhaps turn it into a museum. He saw it as a hobby, an unusual if rather mad form of collecting, which would provide relaxation from his real work as a dentist.

Having made this decision, he bought all the car magazines he could find, ostensibly for his waiting room, for patients to read, but mainly to study the small ads for cars for sale. He made lists of films and TV series where cars had been a major feature. "There were a lot in the seventies, such as *The Prisoner* and *The Saint*, and of course the Bond films, all of which I had watched and enjoyed.

"There was an article in one car mag about a Jaguar dealer in Weybridge who had acquired the original Robin Reliant as used by Del Boy Trotter in *Only Fools and Horses*. This dealer had specialised in providing Jaguars for a company called Action Vehicles, which was used by the BBC and ITV when they needed specific cars for their shows. I didn't know at this stage that such companies existed. Anyway, it had been offered to this Jag dealer, after the series had finished. He had bought it and now wanted to sell it.

"I rang him from my surgery, heard how he had got it, which seemed to be genuine. I asked what his price was and he said £995. I agreed, without trying to get him down, and put the cheque in the post. He arranged transport up to Keswick, which was extra. I put it in my garage — so I now had two cars which had appeared on TV, my own old MG and Trotter's Robin Reliant. They looked a bit lonely in that huge space.

194

"Two weeks later I got a call from the BBC — they were going to make another *Fools and Horses* series after all and wanted the car. Could they hire it from me? I said fine, and they asked how much. I said £995 for the series. That figure came into my head because it was what I had paid, and they agreed.

"When it was all over and I got my car back, they said I could also have another one which didn't run as the engine was bust. They had only used it for static shots — oh, and they also gave me half a vehicle, which they had again used for background shots. So not only did I get my own vehicle back, having got back what I paid for it, but another one and a half vehicles too."

Meanwhile, by this time Peter had got married to Debby. She had first come into his life as a schoolgirl aged eighteen when she had been a patient at his Keswick surgery. She had told him she had just sat her A levels and if she got three As she would be going to Cambridge. Later, when he heard she had got the right grades, he rang to congratulate her and invited her out for dinner. "I know as a dentist you shouldn't have personal relationships with patients, but I just wanted to help her celebrate."

That's how it started anyway. Over the next three years, she did go off to Cambridge, got a degree in modern and medieval languages, came home to Cumbria and they got married, moving into a house in Applethwaite, and soon had a baby on the way. He continued to flourish as a dentist, while throwing himself into his hobby of buying old cars. His next

195

purchase was the Triumph Roadster used by the hero in the TV series *Bergerac*.

"I heard about it one Friday while I was in the surgery and immediately decided I had to have it. I explained to Debby that with this sort of hobby, you only get one chance. The cars tend to be unique and they only come up once in a lifetime, so you have to act at once.

"I rang the owner, who turned out to be a policeman living in Ipswich. He said he already had one person interested, who was coming the next day to see it, from Jersey. I asked, if I could get to him before the other person, and offered him the right money, would he sell? He said yes. First come, first served.

"It was Friday lunchtime. In my lunch break from the surgery, I went to the bank and got a banker's draft. I cancelled my last appointment of the afternoon, and at about four o'clock drove to Penrith and caught a train to Euston, got the Tube to Liverpool Street, then a train to Ipswich, arriving about 11.30 at night.

"He didn't know me from Adam, except that I was a dentist, though I had also said my father was a policeman. Perhaps that helped. Anyway, he invited me, a total stranger, to stay the night, even though they had no room. His two daughters moved in with his wife in her bed and he and I slept in the girls' bunk beds. Next morning he said he hadn't slept a wink, worrying that I would turn out to be an axe-murderer who would kill him in the night.

"Next day I inspected the car, offered him what he wanted, which was £10,000, gave him the banker's

196

order and drove it away. I never saw the man from Jersey. The policeman had won it in a competition run by the *Daily Mail*, and he much preferred the money to keeping the car."

He then went on the trail of the white Volvo P1800 as used in the TV series *The Saint*, starring Roger Moore.

"Someone told me they had once seen it for sale in a garage. They couldn't remember where, just somewhere in the North-East, and the garage was called either Morden or Marden — they couldn't remember that either.

"I went to the main post office and got out all the Yellow Pages for the North-East and started going through them, looking for garages with that sort of name. I listed twenty likely-sounding ones and eventually rang one called Morton Mews Garage in Northumberland. A woman on the phone said yes, they used to own the Saint's car — but one of the directors had taken it when he retired. She said his name was James Smith, but didn't know where he now lived. I think it was James Smith, or it could have been John — anyway, a very common name.

"Once again, I went through all the North-East phone books and made thirty calls to people in the area called J Smith. At last, a man said yes, he owned the Saint's car. He said yes, he might sell, so I jumped in my car and drove over.

"It looked absolutely genuine — but the number plate was wrong. It should have been 77 GYL. In tracking down my cars, I had spent hundreds of hours freeze-framing the cars as they appeared in films and on TV, then examining every detail, so I knew exactly what they should look like. This was very disappointing. I had spent so much time tracking him down, and now I realised it couldn't be the correct car.

"But when he gave me the logbook, it did have Roger Moore's name inside. I then discovered there had been a change of number plate at one stage. One owner had had a wife called Gill and when he sold the car, he kept the number 77 GYL, because of his wife, so the plate had been changed. I could see now it really was the right car, the one which had been in *The Saint*, driven by Simon Templar — or Sir Roger Moore, as he is now."

Listening to Peter's stories of tracking down his cars, I empathised as a collector with his passion, understood his excitement on the hunt, but gee whizz, I have never gone to such effort and extremes when I've been trying to track down my puny little football postcards or Beatles programmes, far less trail across to the other end of the country, just on the off-chance, based on a few clues. Yup, pretty amazing what collectors in the grips will do.

In just under two years, he had tracked down and purchased almost twenty cars. He thinks part of his success, and the excitement, was using the sort of detection methods employed by policemen, which of course he might well have become, had not dentistry beckoned.

And then came the big one, the mega-famous cinema car that he felt he had to have, not just for his collection but to have pride of place, attract publicity and the public, the sort of trophy vehicle any car museum would lust after: a real Chitty Chitty Bang Bang.

There were, apparently, five different versions of Chitty, all of which appeared in the film — one could fly, one go on water and the other three on land. All of them had been expensive, custom-built, one-off cars. But all had long since disappeared, bought by collectors.

Peter heard that one was in Australia, having been bought by an aluminium company that had displayed it for publicity purposes at motor shows, as the bonnet was made of aluminium. He rang them up, checked the provenance, and asked if they might sell. They said yes, but the price was £200,000. Gulp.

Even for a successful dentist, with an entrepreneurial flair, this was a bit too much, but he felt he just had to have it. "We had not been all that long married, and had just moved into this very nice house, but I explained to my wife that this really was a unique chance. I didn't want to miss it, even at that price. I worked out that the only way I could buy it was if we sold our house and moved into the flat above my dental surgery. I took her out for a very nice meal with lots of wine and explained my plan. I did manage to talk her into it, and I sold our house and bought the car."

And so, still scarcely two years after buying his first car, he opened Cars of the Stars in his converted Keswick garage in 1989. His mother and father helped out on the desk, selling tickets, and so did his two brothers, while Peter continued as a dentist. He had to, to keep the cash flowing in.

The museum was an immediate success, attracting fifty thousand in its first year, a figure that has stayed pretty steady ever since. And his family are still helping out. I toured the museum with him, meeting his elderly mum, wearing a jaunty beret, sitting at the reception desk, and his long-haired brother Phil who had recently returned from Hollywood. Both he and Peter have visited Hollywood once a year since the museum began, making contacts, looking at film sets where cars are being featured, making offers for them if the film looks like being a hit, even before the film has come out. From being an entrepreneur manqué, Peter appears to have turned himself into a little industry, covering all the stages in the process — not just tracking down famous cars but identifying them before fame has been thrust upon them.

The first old car to be seen in the museum, once you have passed the shop and a little cafe, is a 1923 Model T Ford as used by Laurel and Hardy. It seemed in good nick, considering the scrapes they got into while driving it, being chased by locomotives, skidding into lamp posts, having wheels fall off. Sitting inside it are life-size models of Laurel and Hardy themselves. With all his cars, he tries to create little displays, setting the scene as it might have been in the film.

Not being a film buff, or having much interest in cars, I found a lot of the technical stuff rather passed over my head, though I did recognise many of the

200

names, such as the Batmobile, Enid Blyton's Noddy car, the Flintstones' car and Lady Penelope's Fab 1 pink Rolls-Royce.

Fab 1 took a great deal of time and detective work to track down, as all he had when he first heard about it was the name Heathfield, somewhere in Sussex. He went through all the Heathfields in the phone book till a Heathfield Garage told him there had been a motor museum locally, which once did have Fab 1, but it had closed seventeen years previously. When he did track it down, it was a wreck and needed rebuilding and repainting.

Chitty Chitty Bang Bang was much bigger than I expected, beautifully painted, luxuriously made and decorated. Harry Potter's Ford Anglia is suitably scruffy and bashed, but that's the point of it. It's an old banger that just happens to be able to do magical things, like fly. This was another example of a famous car being used as a prize in a competition, this time run by the *Sun* in 2002. When he heard about it, Peter immediately approached the winner and bought it from him.

There was a fleet of five modern-looking turbo-charged racing cars, which were meaningless to me, from something called *The Fast and the Furious*. This, apparently, is a very popular series of car-chase films loved by boy-racers, which also appears as a video game.

"They appeal to the younger visitors, who all know the films. They are some of the cars I bought direct from the set, when the films were actually being made.

I paid £10,000 each for the first ones. When the film came out and turned out to be successful, a similar one went to a collector for £100,000."

As I was going round the museum, I was constantly asking him what he had paid for each car, as I'm always interested in prices. Often he couldn't quite remember, which in fact happens to me as well. Or at least I try not to remember, often scribbling what I paid in pencil in code, so my wife never knows how stupid I have been, and then I forget the code. Not that I have ever paid huge amounts. Top whack for a footer programme has been £500 — but keep that secret.

With cars from famous films, the prices do seem astronomical, considering they just sit there, being ogled, not being used or driven. Which does suggest there might be a lot of money to be made from running his sort of car museum?

"Not really. I don't think anyone would open a museum to make money. I did it because it was my hobby, something I was fascinated by. Having done it, the museum has to pay its way, but that's about all it does. Any profit goes into buying new examples."

He hasn't sold very many, unless they were doubles. That second Trotter Robin Reliant he got, the one for nothing, he later sold for £44,000. "I was approached by an auctioneer, desperate to get some of my famous cars in his sale, so I agreed to that one, as it was a spare. I also had a spare Batmobile that went for £110,000. But those are the only two I've sold. And I put the money into cars I didn't have, to keep the museum refreshed and visitors interested.

"Museums have an optimal number, regardless of whether you spend money on advertising or not. Obviously you have to keep adding new items, changing things around, otherwise people would never make a second visit and you wouldn't keep the numbers up, but basically, you quickly hit on your audience. The numbers then hardly change, once you have got there.

"The things that do make a difference are bad weather. Here in Keswick our numbers go up about 15–20 per cent if it rains. People then don't go on the fells but look for indoor attractions. But regardless of the weather, most of our visitors come in July and August, the holiday months.

"I often wonder if we were in London, would we get more visitors? I don't know. All I know is that location is vital, and being in a tourist area is the most important thing of all. It's chance really that brought me to Keswick, because of my dental surgery, but I realise how lucky it was, though I suppose we would have done just as well in Windermere or Ambleside, which are similar honeypots for tourists. Edinburgh has a lot of museums, but I've noticed when I've been there that the ones on the outskirts don't do so well. You have to be in the middle, as we are in Keswick."

When he opened in 1989, his was the first such museum in the world. It is still the only one in Britain and Europe, but a similar one has opened in the USA, in Tennessee. "Naturally I don't think it's as good as mine. They haven't got the quality of cars."

Competition has put prices up since he began, and many multi-millionaires are now bidding at auctions. "I was after one car and the man said I could have it for half a million dollars, which was the price he said Michael Jackson had offered him. He wanted it for his Neverland ranch."

The most he has ever paid for one car was £250,000 for a James Bond car, which he now has in his other museum. Yes, having said what hard work it is, how museums don't really make much money, he had recently, just a few months before, opened another museum, also in Keswick, at the other end of the town.

We walked through the town to the Bond Museum, created like the Cars of the Stars from a disused building, which he converted himself, without the use of architects or designers. He even did his own painting and laying of the carpet tiles.

"What happened was that over the last twenty years, since we first opened, I've bought more and more items, enough to fill another two or three museums, so I've had to put stuff in storage, all over Cumbria, wherever I could find an empty space big enough. For some years I'd been keeping cars in what was an old climbing wall, one of Keswick's tourist attractions which didn't quite succeed.

"Last year I got a call saying that the climbing wall was being put up for sale, so I would have to move my cars somewhere else. I realised I had twenty James Bond cars stored there. It seemed such a shame to disperse them all over the county — so I thought, why not keep them together? So I bought the climbing wall in order to convert it into a James Bond museum.

"I was going to take my time getting it ready, then I realised that it was going to be the centenary of Cubby Broccoli's birth (the producer behind the Bond films). There was bound to be lots of publicity, so I did things in a mad rush, which was why I had to do so much myself."

The entrance is quite impressive, featuring a tall black tower with what looks like a Bond villain with a gun looking down menacingly. The tower was part of the old climbing wall. Inside, the Bond Museum is very much the same as his Cars of the Stars museum, with little display areas, but this time there's a lot more music, from the James Bond films. It was still smelling of fresh paint and newness, but as with the other museum it still has an amateur, home-made feel to it, clearly the work of an obsessive collector rather than a professional museum designer. This after all is the hallmark of Mad Museums, and to me part of the attraction, that they are created by an individual enthusiast and not a focus group. Of all the museums I had visited so far, I suppose only the National Football Museum felt truly professional, but then that is a national museum.

Peter has cars and vehicles on show from twenty-one of the twenty-two Bond films made so far. The missing one is *Licence to Kill*. All the cars are complete with the gadgets, such as guns and flames, and there is also a real helicopter from *The Spy Who Loved Me*. One of the exhibits, a buggy that was driven in *For Your Eyes*

Only, was recently acquired for only £1500, bought on eBay. Since Peter started chasing such vehicles, eBay has made it a bit easier and reduced his travelling. The most expensive is the one that cost £250,000 — the Aston Martin Vanquish driven by Bond in *Die Another Day*.

"That was owned by the Aston Martin company itself, who had built it for the film, complete with guns on the bonnet. It went up for auction at Christie's, which is why I had to pay so much for it."

The Bond Museum also has an area devoted to Bond props, such as guns, golf balls and other gadgets. Although they had only recently opened, Peter was confident visitor numbers would reach around thirty to forty thousand in its first full year, then stabilise at about fifty thousand, like his other museum.

"I have noticed with people going round the Bond Museum that they get very emotional. I have actually come across people crying. The thing about Bond is that it spans the generations. The films have been coming out for so long that young and old alike have seen them. They represent important points in people's personal lives and they spark off memories.

"Many of these cars I have collected over the years were in many respects the stars of their films. Chitty Chitty Bang Bang certainly was. Back in the days of the silent movies, people like Mack Sennett in his two-reelers introduced car-chases and they were what the public loved. Cars have provided big and small screens with metaphors for heroes and for villains. They have stood for symbols of success as well as a representation of escape and freedom. They have contributed to the fantasies of films." Hmm. Not many collectors get so philosophical about their inanimate objects. But not all collectors are as involved and single-minded as Peter has been.

We went back to the flat where he was then living, not far from Cars of the Stars, and he made me some tea. It seemed very untidy for such a meticulous man, a successful dentist-cum-entrepreneur. There were clothes and shoes and paintings scattered all over the floor.

I asked about the future, would his two sons, now aged eighteen and sixteen, take over either or both of his museums? He doubted it, for various reasons.

"In my fantasy world, I would sell both of them tomorrow if an eccentric billionaire from Dubai came along and made me a suitable offer. I would like to see all the items kept together, and displayed properly in a gleaming, purpose-built, modern, glamorous, architect-designed building. As you have seen, I have rather had to make do with old buildings, built for other purposes, and converted them on a shoestring. The objects are unique, part of film history, and I still love them dearly, so they deserve a better setting, to be taken to a higher level.

"But deep down, I know they are just objects, and objects are not as important as people. I am not sentimental about them because they are simply material things. I am proud of what I have done and feel that the museums are genuine creations — and of course I never felt creative as a dentist — but I am not

207

honestly a car fanatic or a film buff. It has just been my hobby, an escape from my professional work.

"In fact the thing I have loved most about creating these museums has been the tracking down of the objects. I love the detective work, the hunt, the chase, then finding the object, checking it out, doing the deal. That has been the best fun of all, rather than the actual possession."

I said I could understand that. With my modest collections, I have felt the same — getting is often more fun than having. In fact once I have acquired certain longed-for things, I have just shoved them in a drawer and hardly looked at them again, which is what happened with my stamps. At least he has done something with his collections.

"Oh, I have enjoyed displaying them, but it's got harder to get good items as there is more competition and prices are getting crazy. I now know there are some objects I will never get. There is an AMC Hornet which did spiral jumps in the *The Man with the Golden Gun*. I would dearly love that, but it belongs to the man who did the actual stunts. Once a stuntman owns something, it rarely comes on the market.

"The collections still give me great pleasure and provide adventure. Every day is different. Someone will ring offering me something, or I get invited to show some of my own items abroad. I was recently in Washington where they have opened a spy museum. It has things like Enigma machines and documents from the Cold War. They wanted to put my James Bond Aston Martin on display. I have also taken cars to Japan and to Korea, for museums or motor shows, and of course they pay me a rent, perhaps a thousand dollars a day for a month, plus my first-class plane trips. I still have just so much more material not on show."

So would he open another museum? It's strange in a way that he didn't start collecting objects associated with his professional life. I, for example, have always collected old newspapers and books. If I had been him, I think I would have been collecting ancient dental instruments.

"Dental objects? But dentistry to me was always just work. I did enjoy it, but twenty years was enough and I wasn't interested in it as a subject. It was just something I happened to be good at. I was always much more interested in art in all its forms, which cars can be."

It was the longing to be involved in something artistic, which he had been deprived of at school, or so he believes, that was at the heart of his desire to create his museums. And this desire to be creative is still there.

"Four years ago I had this strange dream. I'd recently been reading a book about Van Gogh, which perhaps sparked it off. The dream itself was about Picasso. When I woke up I turned to my wife and said, 'I'm going to sell the practice and become an artist.' 'You what?' she replied. She was astonished. I had never before talked about wanting to be an artist. I went into work and wrote out an advert for the *British Dental Journal* and faxed it through.

209

"That evening my wife was at a do at Applethwaite village hall. She happened to be talking to a friend who is also a dentist, over in Whitehaven. 'You'll never believe what Peter says he's going to do — sell up,' she said. Next day, he rang me, made an offer. I sold it to him, all in twenty-four hours from having had the dream. It all happened so quickly I thought, shit, what do I do now . . .?"

What he did was use the money from the sale of his practice to buy another property, not far away in Station Street, which had been a hairdressing salon. He cleared it out, made space for an artist's studio and rang Windsor & Newton to order every form of painting materials and brushes, from acrylic to silk-screen. "They presumed I must be opening a retail shop but I said, no, I'm just doing it for myself, to learn to be an artist."

He took no lessons, went on no courses, apart from a very short one to learn about screen printing, which he then dropped, deciding to concentrate on being a painter and also a sculptor. "I was like a child in a sweet shop, running around, trying out everything to see if I liked it."

After a year he had created enough work — abstracts, landscapes, small pieces of sculpture — to open his own gallery. "One day a director of the Royal Bank of Scotland happened to walk in. He saw all my objects and said he would like some for a new building they were opening in Birmingham. They were looking for some modern art, but not too modern. They were not expensive items, mostly about £100 each, but it boosted my confidence as a painter and sculptor."

He then went on, with the confidence — nay, arrogance — of a totally untaught beginner, to found his own art movement, which he christened Assemblism. He gave me a leaflet that explained the theory, not that I was all that much wiser.

Assemblism is the form of art produced by the use of skill, method, technique and imagination using the Ten Principles of Assemblism to construct and assemble individual components made by the artist. This is in contrast to Collage or Assemblage, where the constituent elements are often found or ready-made objects or pieces . . .

For the last four years, though Peter is still running the museums, working as an artist has become his new passion, taking over most of his life — apart from a six-month gap the previous year when he took time off from his easels to concentrate on his Bond museum.

Six months ago, he said, his marriage collapsed. I supposed it was not too surprising, considering all the upheavals he had gone through. He is now separated from his wife, living in a flat, though he was building a house for himself out in the country and converting a barn into a proper studio where he can work.

"We are still friends. In fact she comes to help in the gallery. And I still see my two boys. I can understand that I have caused all the problems in the marriage by my own turmoil. My wife thought she had married a

211

nice steady rural dentist, not someone who becomes totally obsessed by museums and then throws over his whole life to spend every moment devoted to art. It has caused strains. I have thrown myself into my new love. I tend never to do things by halves.

"Looking back though, I never did expect to be a dentist for life. That was never my aim. On the other hand, I never thought I would end up as an artist."

So is the stage of creating museums over? Possibly, though he intends to keep the two in Keswick, unless of course some Arab sheik comes along and makes a silly offer. "I still have more than enough objects in store for another three museums. If an ideal location presented itself, I might be interested. I've got twenty or so old motorbikes, some of which appeared in films and TV shows, so one day I'd like them to be exhibited, if I had the right space. I've also got two waxwork museums, all in storage."

He bought the first from a man in Morecambe who was closing his own museum. Waxwork museums were very popular many years ago, especially at seaside resorts, but have been overtaken by more modern, sophisticated attractions.

"I was really after his Laurel and Hardy figures, to put inside my Model T Ford, but he wouldn't sell them. He wanted to sell everything. I'd forgotten about it really when he came back and said he had now sold the property, everything had to be cleared out the next week, so if I still wanted the Laurel and Hardy I could have them for £1000 each, on condition that I took everything away as well. So I arranged transport and did the deal, putting most of the stuff into storage. The same thing happened with the Isle of Man wax museum. I bought that as a job lot."

I thought I was pretty daft with my collections, often buying stuff I have no interest in just because I have been offered it or suddenly seen it at a bargain price, such as books on subjects I know nothing about, or collections of coins when I don't collect coins, but they have always been pretty trivial, cheap, small items, easy to store, and forget about.

Were there by any chance any Beatles figures in either waxworks? I said I'd be interested in taking them off his hands. Too late he said. There was a set of the four Beatles, in genuine sixties costumes, but he sold them almost at once. Not slow, our Peter.

"I also sold a group of fifty assorted waxworks to a company working on the *Saving Private Ryan* film. They wanted realistic bodies to blow up. Amongst the ones they bought were D H Lawrence, H G Wells, Picasso. If you watch carefully, you can identify them, if you are quick . . ."

His two mobile phones started ringing, each of them with ringtones from Bond films. I got up and wandered round the room. It had appeared a typical bachelor or student pad, with stuff all over the place, but when I examined the walls, I found to my surprise three Picassos, two Chagalls, a David Hockney and three Damien Hirsts. Blimey, are they real? Oh yes, he said. When he was teaching himself about art, he decided to buy as many examples of good art as possible.

213

I was becoming more and more confused. Having said there was no money in museums, it seemed surprising that he had been able to afford so many valuable paintings. He did of course sell his thriving dental practice for a good sum, and he has made money now and again by selling doubles and spares from his car collection.

And I suppose I was a bit confused by him generally. I had never thought of someone creating a museum as a form of artistic expression, which is what he had done — till now he had realised that art itself is the best form of artistic expression. But at the same time he is clearly an obsessive, who loves collecting objects, letting them take over his life, in his case to the detriment of his marriage. I saw that as a warning, but of course I told myself it could never happen to me. I could also not be as persistent as he has been in tracking stuff down, going to such efforts, travelling so far. Real collectors — well, real obsessive collectors — are always prepared to go to the ends of the earth, or at least of the Northern Line. I don't think I am up to all that. If I began my own museum I would keep it in proportion. Surely. Which he says he is going to do, in future.

"As I get older, I am beginning to realise that less is more. I am going to be a minimalist from now on. To be a collector, as I have always been, is to carry burdens through life. So I am going to try and unburden myself in the future."

Can't see it happening.

Cars of the Stars
Standish Street
Keswick
Cumbria CA12 5LS
Tel 017687 73757
www.carsofthestars.com

The Bond Museum
Southey Hill Trading Estate
Keswick
Cumbria CA12 5NR
Tel 017687 775007
www.thebondmuseum.com

CHAPTER ELEVEN

The Sheep Show, Cockermouth

And then the prize exhibits started to appear on stage, one by one, each of them on their own, unshepherded, emerging from the wings, some in a mad rush, others a bit nervous, some as if taking a gentle stroll, before ascending two rows of wooden tiers arranged like the winners' podium at the Olympic Games.

Each one managed to take its exact place above its appropriate name — most of them to do with places, such as Leicester, Suffolk, Oxford — then sat there preening, looking around, showing off their best points. They could easily have been contestants in a Miss World competition.

"See how they have found their own places," said the master of ceremonies, a Scotsman called Roy in jeans, with rather bandy legs, the legs perhaps of a real thoroughbred countryman or an ex-jockey. "It shows you they can read . . ."

The audience was very quiet, perhaps even stunned, most of them clearly having been unprepared and now rather confused by what was happening before their very eyes. Can sheep read? How had each of them got to its own position, on its own? Beforehand, in the shop, among the fifty or so families milling around, waiting for the doors of the auditorium to open, I could hear kids asking their parents, "What's a sheep show, Mum?" "How should I know?" replied most mums. "I've never been to one before." A lot of the families were foreign, from Germany, Holland, France, but their children were obviously asking the same sort of questions, and getting the same sort of non-answers.

I have to admit I was pretty stunned as well. I don't think I had ever seen such an exhibition before, anywhere, or had ever imagined that anyone could have dreamed up and organised such a bizarre event. The whole thing is strange and weird, amusing and even hilarious, yet, as the Miss World contest — sorry, sheep show — progressed, it was also terribly instructive and informative.

But is it a museum? Well, what is a museum? I find it rather hard to define, but anyway this is my book so I can define it how I like. If a museum is a collection of objects, carefully preserved and open to the public, with the exhibits cared for and explained, and behind it is an enthusiast who feels he has a duty to pass on his knowledge and love for the items, then why have the contents always got to be dead? Why can't they also be living things? After all, every other museum I had visited so far was devoted to inanimate objects. Surely we could do with one bit of real, living, breathing, smelling, active life. For yes, there was a bit of a pong.

217

In turn, the Scotsman introduced nineteen different breeds of sheep, as each took its place, and explained exactly where each breed was from, its strengths, weaknesses and peculiarities.

I tried to make notes as he spoke, though he did rather rattle along. I also took photos, which helped me later to identify the nineteen breeds. So refreshing at a live show, or even in most dead museums, to be actively encouraged to take photos at any time. Museum curators can be a bit fussy and bossy when you want to take shots of their treasures.

We were in an auditorium with seats for about a hundred and eighty, facing a proper stage, as in a theatre. This was the first show of the afternoon — one of four a day that take place five days a week in the season — and there was quite a lot of space to move around and take photos, should you want to, but most people were pretty transfixed by what was going on, sitting still in their seats, even the kids, still wondering how it was all done. Yet it's obviously not a circus, as the sheep don't do tricks. They are there as exhibits, for us to admire and study and learn about.

The nineteen breeds that day were as follows. First on the podium, sitting at the top in pride of place, was a Texel. I think a capital letter is called for, as each sheep was representing a whole breed. Roy the Scotsman seemed pretty biased in favour of the Texel, saying that though it is a relatively new breed to Britain, originating in Holland and introduced here only in 1972, it is now one of our most valuable and popular meat-producing sheep. It also holds the world record as the most expensive sheep sold through an auction market. It did look rather plump, self-satisfied, quite aristocratic, but then he was sitting at the top of the pile, as if on a throne of his own. I say he — imagining him as a king, as opposed to a Miss World — but at this stage, Roy hadn't revealed the gender of any of our star exhibits.

The Cheviot was next, a much rougher, tougher, smaller sheep, a native sheep, bred on the Scottish Borders over hundreds of years. The Blackface didn't have much of a black face, which, despite its name, was black only in patches, while the Suffolk had a definite black face and ears.

The Blue-faced Leicester was, yes, a bit blue-eyed round the eyes, while the Kerry Hill, which comes from Wales, had eyes more like those of a panda. The Leicester Longwool did have very long, curly wool, while the Oxford Down looked large and stocky.

I gave a small clap when the Herdwick appeared, as it is our own breed from Cumbria, where I was brought up and where I live half of each year, an incredibly hardy hill sheep that can survive all year round on its own up on the mountains. No one else clapped, so I felt a bit embarrassed, but it seemed to ease the audience, who began to be more receptive and animated. The Swaledale and the Wensleydale each got a few murmurs of appreciation, probably because they are breeds people have heard of — or perhaps there were some Yorkshire folk in the audience.

The Ryeland is one of the oldest English breeds, dating back eight centuries, originally bred by monks in

219

Leominster, and, according to Roy, the Lord Chancellor when he sits on the Woolsack sits on a sack filled with Ryeland wool.

The Shetland looked small and bony, ready for a fight. Roy told us its wool can come in seventeen different colours and shades and is ideal for Fair Isle sweaters and tweeds. The Whitefaced Woodland sounded more like a flower, white the Mule sounded like a term of abuse.

Castlemilk Moorit was a new name to me, but is apparently Scottish, "moorit" being the Gaelic for brown. Zwartbles, written on its name plate, seemed like a tongue-twister, so I looked forward to hearing how Roy pronounced it when it eventually bounced forward to take its rightful place. It's a Dutch sheep and the name means black with a white blaze.

The Merino sheep got a good poke from Roy, demonstrating what lovely soft wool it has. The Hebridean, when it appeared, arrived with a bang, charging up the ramp to its place and proceeding to knock over a small metal container with a lot of noise and bustle, greatly amusing the children, as it looked as if it was being very naughty. It did look fierce with its three horns — it did originally have four, as nature intended, but had lost one in a fight with another sheep.

"The Hebridean is not daft," said Roy. "He's decided to have a self-service lunch." By this time I had caught on to the fact that before each sheep arrived at its proper post, Roy had taken the lid off a metal container to reveal some sort of food, which the sheep quickly scoffed. While Roy was talking, he also chained up each sheep to its position, which explained why none of them had run away.

Another man appeared from behind the scenes after all nineteen sheep were onstage, having presumably been the one shoving them on in the right order. He then proceeded to give out bits of real wool for us to hold and play with and rub, and keep if we wanted. Roy explained what lanolin is, feel the oil when you rub it, he said, much better for you than any expensive moisturiser. He said wool full of lanolin is fire-resistant, can hold 20 per cent of its own weight in water, and contains no static electricity so it is safe to use and far better than synthetic fibres anytime.

He told us about sheep-shearing, and how the world record was held by an Australian who had sheared 720 sheep by machine in nine hours, a big achievement considering that sheep can weigh up to eight stone and can take some handling. Alas, today no one wants the wool. A British farmer has to spend £1 getting a sheep sheared but gets only 60p for its wool. So sheep-shearing today is for animal welfare, to keep them comfortable, not to make money from the wool.

We then had a demonstration of sheepdogs at work, showing how they round up sheep, obey commands — though in this case they were not working with the sheep, which remained at their posts, looking bored. Instead on to the stage waddled four geese. I suppose sheep might run all over the auditorium, and could cause a nasty shock, and a few bruises, if one of the bigger, heftier ones landed in your lap. The geese on the

221

whole were pretty obedient, giving the odd squawk and flurry of feathers, but moving in the right direction when prodded along by a border collie. One of the geese did fall off the stage, and looked very embarrassed, but bustled on again.

Roy shouted out four different commands to the dog. "Come by" meant move the sheep clockwise, while "Away to me" meant anticlockwise. "Walk on" meant go forward, and "Lie down" meant stop. Roy explained that the dog, having been given his instructions, bossed the sheep by staring at them with his eyes. He had no need to bark.

Then came a Huntaway sheepdog from New Zealand, which did its bossing by barking. In New Zealand and Australia, explained Roy, one dog often has to round up two thousand sheep at a time, so to save barging through the whole flock the Huntaway has developed a smart short cut — running across the backs of the sheep. Which it proceeded to do, running up the ramp and over the top of all the sheep in the back row. It did it three times, to loud cheers and applause from the audience.

Two cows were then brought up, a dairy cow and a beef cow, so we could see the difference, but this was somehow an anticlimax, for they just stood there, doing nothing, whereas the sheep and the sheepdogs had been highly animated, very entertaining and of course tremendously illuminating, as there had been a subtle message behind all of Roy's commentary, which was roughly, hurrah for farmers, hurrah for sheep.

222

He then invited the audience up onstage, to ask him any questions, to see and touch the sheep and take photographs, which everyone did, milling around the sheep, ooh-ing and ahh-ing at their size.

I followed Roy into his office, for he happens to be the big boss of the Lakeland Sheep & Wool Centre, though he was only doing one day a week as the MC of the sheep show.

Roy Campbell was born the youngest of three brothers in Lochgoilhead, in Argyllshire, where his father, Douglas, like his father before him, ran a small hill farm with around a thousand sheep. His mother, Jean, also helped on the farm. Roy went to the local primary school, but as there was no secondary school in his remote area he had to travel away to a state secondary in Dunoon, which meant living in a hostel during the week. He hated school, didn't like any of the lessons, and the teachers didn't like him, so he says, so he stopped going at fifteen, instead of at sixteen as he should have done, in order to help his dad on the farm.

Although Lochgoilhead is remote, at the end of a narrow inlet off the Firth of Clyde, it did get some tourist trade in the season, when steamers landed on trips from Dunoon. One day Roy's father was approached by the Forestry Commission to use one of his fields as a caravan site. His dad agreed, on condition that he ran it. Until then he had shown no entrepreneurial or business instincts, but thought that if they were using his field, he should be involved. "It was from that day onwards he realised that keeping caravans on fields made more money than keeping sheep on fields."

Roy's dad made a success of the caravan park and moved on to acquire a hotel on the same site, gradually expanding into a leisure centre and shops, building up a holiday business in which all three of the sons worked. One of their schemes was to build a curling rink, which of course is a winter activity, so they were wondering how to use it in the summer.

Roy was on holiday in New Zealand when the idea of creating a sheep show came to him. Well, it didn't just come to him — he took the format from a New Zealand sheep show he happened to visit.

They opened a sheep show in Lochgoilhead in 1987, which did well, but they were short of space as they had so many other leisure attractions on the site. "So we looked around to open another sheep show elsewhere, perhaps in a bigger tourist area. I looked at Pitlochry, at Edinburgh, and then I thought of the Lake District. That was the furthest south I was prepared to go, though I'm sure a sheep show would go well in the West Country or Wales, which are great sheep areas. I've nothing against England or the English. I just wanted to stay close to Scotland and my roots.

"I found a good site in the middle of the Lake District at Thirlmere, on the road and beside the lake, and agreed a deal with a local farmer. We had to go through the usual planning board meetings, and in the end our scheme was thrown out. They didn't want a new building going up in such a location. I thought that was it, we'll stick to Scotland, but someone who was on that planning board came back to us and said that in West Cumbria, which had for some time been seen as a deprived area, they were looking for tourist attractions to draw people away from the honeypot areas — and also for an indoor attraction, for people to visit in bad weather. We were encouraged to apply for planning permission, and were also promised grants."

He says he now can't remember the exact figure, as it was a complicated deal involving the West Cumbria tourism people having space on the site (which has now gone), but it did help them to build the Sheep & Wool Centre. It was built on a new, purpose-built site on the A66, just outside Cockermouth, at a total cost of £2.5 million. Apart from the auditorium for the sheep show and a shop selling all manner of sheepy souvenirs and sheep-related objects, they created a thirteen-room hotel, hoping to attract business people visiting West Cumbria.

In the first year the sheep show attracted fifty thousand people. Then it went up to a hundred thousand and in 2000 it was reaching a hundred and twenty thousand — when calamity struck. Foot and mouth disease arrived in 2001 and at a stroke millions of sheep and cattle were being slaughtered, the movement of animals was banned, tourists disappeared.

When you show dead or inanimate exhibits in a conventional sort of museum, you might face many problems — rival attractions, fashion trends changing, tourists going elsewhere, ring roads taking away passing traffic, someone opening up a better museum showing the same sort of stuff — but you don't have to cope with disease and pestilence that starts killing off every one of your objects. For a whole year, they had no sheep to show.

When they reopened, they were forced to abandon one of the highlights of the show, which had delighted visitors in the early years — an exhibition of sheep-shearing. Onstage, live sheep were sheared by a real shearer, so you saw and smelled how it was done, and could touch and feel the wool straight off the sheep's back. To do this, they used around eight hundred different sheep from local farms, as of course the same sheep gets sheared only once a year. So every day they would shear four sheep — one at each show — then return them to the farmer, having done his shearing for nothing. Post-foot and mouth a new rule came in that restricted the movement of all sheep and cattle. They must remain in the same place for at least six days before being moved for any reason. (One of the causes of foot and mouth spreading in 2001 had been the wide-scale and endless movement of animals across the country, with no records or restrictions being enforced.)

The government in its wisdom did not of course reckon on or worry about the possible effect on something like the sheep show, but it meant they stopped shearing. Unless they kept their own flock of around eight hundred sheep in their own fields, they could not shear four new sheep every day. So the sheep-shearing had to go.

One small side effect has been that the pong in the auditorium is now a lot less. When sheep were brought in straight from the fields, they were often wet and muddy, and naturally did a bit of excreting in the excitement and panic of being sheared. Audiences did often remark on the pungent aroma, which they rarely did once the sheep-shearing ceased.

To compensate for the lack of sheep-shearing, Roy introduced the two cows. Normally the dairy cow was milked on stage, which all the children love, but I had been at the two o'clock show which, alas, is not a milking time.

"The point of milking the cow was to show children where milk comes from. Many children really do think that milk comes from a supermarket, along with lemonade and pop, that that's where it originates. They don't realise milk comes from cows. Same with sheep. Everyone knows about sheep, what one looks like, but even adults assume, without thinking about it, that there is probably only one type of sheep. They are not aware that in the UK we have eighty different breeds of sheep, and in the world as a whole there are five hundred different breeds."

The Miss World stars, the different breeds on show each day, are kept on the premises in a field behind the centre. At any one time, he has sixty different sheep, from twenty-four different breeds, nineteen of which are called on to perform each day. All of them are rams, which means they can all be kept in the same field. Any ewes would of course lead to problems, and all the rams are infertile — that is, they have failed on their previous farms to mate successfully with a ewe.

"They are about to be sold off cheaply when I buy them, and are heading straight to the butcher's. So I give them another four years of life, and four meals a day and excellent conditions. They are all happy sheep."

The food in their little metal buckets consists of just a handful of protein nuts, which is mainly dried grass, so they are not exactly living on the hog of the land. Roughly, they perform for up two months each, then they get shorn and can't appear for a while, as the whole point of the sheep show is to show the different sheep with their different types of wool. Naked, newly shorn sheep are pretty creepy. One would not like to stare at them without their normal clothes on.

New ones get trained over the winter when the show is not on, taught what they have to do onstage, so none of them is a total novice when they appear for the first time in front of a live audience.

I later went behind the scenes, where a local farmhand called Eddie has the job of lining up the nineteen sheep before each show — herding them into two narrow corridors on either side of the stage, in the right order, then letting them out one by one. Above his head he has the order written down, as it can change and lead to confusion onstage. I asked Eddie if they were easy to control, or could some get troublesome.

"Only the Scotch ones. But then the Scotch always cause the problems . . ."

"Watch it," said Roy, smiling.

Roy was doing only one day a week presenting, mainly to keep his hand in, to see what's happening. Before foot and mouth they did four shows a day, seven days a week, but since then they have cut down to five days a week. They don't do Friday or Saturday, having observed that local attractions, like the Cockermouth Show and the farmers' markets, tend to be on a Saturday. Saturday also tends to be changeover day in the hotels and bed and breakfasts. On the other four days there are two different presenters, both women.

The Sheep & Wool Centre and its hotel have proved to be a great success so far, despite all the foot and mouth problems, and the family firm back in Scotland has gone from strength to strength. It is still privately owned and run, by Roy and his two brothers, his parents having retired. Altogether they employ 230 staff and have seven holiday parks, two hotels, several shops, a leisure centre and three farms, plus the Shepherds Hotel/Lakeland Sheep & Wool Centre at Cockermouth, still their only business on English soil. The sheep centre itself, including the hotel, employs twenty-four people. Last year the group's turnover was £14 million. Not bad for simple farming folk who came into the leisure industry by accident rather than intent!

"Most farmers, all over the world, have for generations grown up with the feeling that tourists are their enemy, that they get in the way, are hostile, cause problems. A lot still do feel that, but I think in the last ten years their views have begun to change, which is a

229

short period of time in the history of farming. Farmers must be willing to change, to diversify. Luckily the general public like farmers and farming — look at the growth of farmers' markets and the fact that you now see even the biggest supermarkets promoting local produce.

"Farmers have made the countryside the way it looks, and they are the ones who are protecting it. They are the custodians of the countryside. If you got rid of cattle, fields would be full of weeds. Fields can't look after themselves. If you got rid of sheep, the fells would be overrun with bracken and rough heather and scrub. We owe a lot to sheep."

Aren't sheep pretty dopey, stupid, sheep-like animals?

"No more than humans. Humans act like sheep as well, they follow a crowd. A fella goes into a pub and finds it's empty, so he goes to look for one that's busy. Sheep are repetitive, like people. They like doing things at the exact same time each day. All animals get to know the exact time they will be fed. Dogs know it and dairy cows know it. They will stand up and go to the gate when they know it's time to go and get milked. The sheep here now know what time each day they will be going onstage and that they will get something to eat.

"Like humans, there's always some trying to be at the top of the pecking order. A sheep's biggest enemy is another sheep trying to take its grass, its space. You might think they are sheep-like, herding together, but in

230

fact if you watch sheep in a field, they each like their own space.

"The mountain and fell sheep are smaller and thinner but they always have a spring in their step, much more energy, which they have to have out in the wilds in all weathers. The lowland sheep are bigger, fatter, more docile. A wee Shetland or Hebridean or Herdwick is usually looking for a fight. It's the wee man syndrome. Always trying to prove himself."

Roy, despite all his business affairs, still keeps seventy Texel sheep himself, which he breeds and shows all over the country. And of course he does one day a week as the sheep show presenter. "My father always told me that you can't farm from a desk. You have to be out there, seeing what happens on the ground. You have all this modern technology, but you still need to go out and see that the job is being done right. That applies to all industries."

He usually does two days a week in Scotland, back in Argyll, but lives in Cockermouth with his Scottish wife and three children, all of whom now speak with English accents — or at least West Cumbrian, which is not quite the same thing. They love their local schools, both primary and the local comprehensive, which Roy himself never did.

Will one of them take over the sheep centre in due course, or will others in the family firm run it? Ah, there could be a problem there — namely blue tongue, something I had only vaguely heard about and thought had gone away.

"Blue tongue could just wipe out all our sheep — they would just die once they got the disease, not have to be killed, as with foot and mouth. The disease is in Europe at present and might strike at any moment. One of our French visitors could bring the virus in on the wheels of their car. You just don't know. In Scotland, vaccinating against it is compulsory, but in England it is only voluntary at the moment.

"We got completely caught by foot and mouth. We hadn't made any plans, even though we'd had a previous outbreak in 1967. But 2001 was devastating. The sheep centre still hasn't recovered and all the after-effects and restrictions are still upsetting us. Visitor numbers are not yet up to what they were before foot and mouth.

"However, because we got caught last time and had to close the show for that whole year, I am making plans in case blue tongue ever does strike.

"I'm applying for planning permission for another fifteen bedrooms. The hotel side has been doing very well these last few years, more profitable than the sheep show. You win some; you lose some; that's business. I think we are getting more hotel guests because a lot of firms are currently trading down, wanting clean modern rooms but also value for money.

"So, if the worst comes to the worst, we could be forced to turn the sheep show into hotel bedrooms. I don't want to, but you have to plan ahead and be ready.

"We want to keep it going. It's not a gimmick. People have suggested we have voting, with the audience holding up numbers as in a Miss World contest, which would get us a lot of publicity, but we wouldn't do that. It's not a circus, it's a serious show. We're here to tell the truth about sheep and about farming, to help preserve interest in all the different breeds, as the general public is still pretty ignorant."

I had certainly learned a lot and understood a lot, and it didn't seem like a gimmick to me. Nor was it a circus or even a zoo. Because it concentrated on just one species, the sheep, I felt it did fit into my definition of unusual museums. It was being run as a commercial concern, but why shouldn't museums do that? They have to make money, attract the public or sponsors, as the National Football Museum had found, in order to survive. It seemed to have been doing well, despite unforeseen disasters like foot and mouth, and I wished it good luck for the future.

So far, over one million people have been to see Roy's sheep shows. The Lakeland Sheep & Wool Centre in Cockermouth is the only one of its type in the whole of the UK, as their Scottish show has long since closed. It is probably also the only one in Europe. But they are still going in New Zealand.

"The family who ran the New Zealand one I first went to see came to visit us not long ago. I was a bit worried they would be upset I had modelled my show on theirs, though we have different sheep and a different script. But they approved of it. They have opened a sheep centre in Japan as well, but I think that's their only branch so far. They said as long as we stayed twelve thousand miles away, they wouldn't sue . . ."

Lakeland Sheep & Wool Centre
Egremont Road
Cockermouth
Cumbria CA13 0QX[1]
Tel 01900 822673
www.sheep-woolcentre.co.uk

---

[1] The Sheep Show has now closed, see conclusion, pages 382–383.

234

CHAPTER
TWELVE

The Clan Armstrong Museum, Langholm

If you can have a museum devoted to one type of animal, can you have a museum that is devoted to just one name? In this case a family name, the surname that people drag around with them?

In one sense, a name is an abstract concept, a word written on a document such as a birth certificate, rather than an object that you can see and touch, keep and collect, which is how we normally fill museums. So can a family name be turned into a museum? What would there be to show?

Well, as we know, museums in the UK and across the world come in all shapes and sizes, covering many forms of content, though for the purpose of my journey each museum had to be devoted to one subject and, ideally, still have a founder or leading creator around. When I heard about a little museum that was all about one particular family, I was off, well intrigued.

Over the Scottish border and up the A7, a route I hadn't taken for about forty years. When I go to Edinburgh by road these days I always go up the motorway as far as possible towards Glasgow, before turning right at Abington, as opposed to ye olden days when I took the A7 all the way, winding slowly through Langholm, Hawick, Selkirk and Galashiels, ancient and gritty, proud and peculiar Border towns, which look quite near each other on the map but take for ever to reach as you don't realise how big the Borders are — which was of course one of the attractions in the past, when you might have needed somewhere to hide.

Past Longtown and over the Scottish border, the road suddenly widened out, went all modern and smooth, with lush landscaped verges — and yet it was totally empty. How had they got the money? In the West Indies or Africa, you always suspect that an unusually brilliant and pointless piece of road in an empty landscape indicates that the local MP is also the prime minister, keeping his constituents quiet and himself in office. In the UK it's usually the work of some sharp bureaucrat or department that has had the time and energy to understand all the forms and figure out how to apply for grants from Europe, the lottery or some complicated government scheme.

Whatever the reason, the result was wonderful — I was able to glide along an empty, excellent road for about twenty miles, admiring the scenery. I quite forgot how I hate driving.

I arrived early in Langholm. The museum is open only in the afternoons (but not Mondays, except Bank Holidays, or Thursdays), so I parked and wandered round. For a small, isolated country town of only 2300 population it clearly has a self-image above its size, with a very handsome high street, an impressive town hall, a fine bridge over a wide river, a good public library and its own hospital, though when I got near it I saw it said "Welcome to Thomas Hope Hospital — No Accident and Emergency". It even has its own newspaper, the *Eskdale & Liddesdale Advertiser*, founded in May 1848, so it says on the masthead, and known locally as "the Squeak".

Langholm itself is known in Scotland as "the Muckle Toon", which I have always taken to mean a town of many parts — as in "many a mickle maks a muckle", a phrase I learned as a child growing up in Scotland. We finally settled for good in Carlisle when I was eleven and I soon lost my Scottish accent, alas, though we always took the *Sunday Post* and listened to the Scottish Home Service, Scottish Children's Hour with Aunty Kathleen and *Tammy Troot* and *Doon at the Mains*.

In Langholm, apparently, the world "muckle" means big. For a small town, it has been quite muckle in that it has provided two Scottish stars. Hugh MacDiarmid, the poet (real name Christopher Murray Grieve), was born in Langholm in 1892. His father was a postman and his mother was caretaker of the local public library, and they lived in a little house under the library. Thomas Telford started life as an apprentice stonemason in Langholm and went on to become a true Brit star, building roads, bridges, harbours and monuments all over the United Kingdom.

I went into a cafe to read the Squeak, all about the Common Riding coming up. (Too complicated to explain, but all the Border towns have this ancient annual celebration when their boundaries are marked out, horses are ridden, handsome young men get called "cornet" and parades take place.) Around me I could hear some broad local accents. Interesting how they seem immediately to get broad once you are just yards across the border, as if out of defiance, whereas by the time you get to Edinburgh they seem to talk like any member of a Labour cabinet. In the tourist office, where I picked up some leaflets, the woman volunteer was clearly English, from over the border in Cumbria. These days, they do seem to live happily together.

I then drove to the end of the town, left over a bridge, and there was perhaps the prettiest museum building I had seen so far — a twee little wooden log cabin, shaped like a church, which it formerly was, but looking more like a Little House on the Prairie. This is the Clan Armstrong Museum, dedicated to all the people in the world called Armstrong.

Would they have stuffed Armstrongs? Armstrongs hanging around, looking, er, strong-armed and manly? Would they have dead Armstrongs? There were some hints in the garden, where there are plaques to deceased clan members. Armstrongs cannot be buried here, but people do come from across the Atlantic to scatter Armstrong ashes on the roses.

In the porch I noticed an old bike hanging up on the wall. Inside I asked Fiona Armstrong, who was helping out in the museum that day, getting ready for an event in the evening, what the significance of that was. "There's not another museum in the town, so we do tend to get a lot of local things donated to us. I think this bike did belong to an Armstrong — and if it did once have an Armstrong bottom in the saddle, that does make it rather precious to us."

The Clan Armstrong Trust, which runs the museum, and is a registered charity, was set up in 1978 as an educational body, to encourage research into the Armstrongs and to record and care for documents and sites associated with the family over the centuries.

Inside, the museum does have a more academic feel than the bike might suggest, with historic documents and artefacts laid out, and lots of storyboards explaining the history of the Armstrongs. "We hold the world's largest collection of Armstrong records," said Fiona proudly. I wouldn't have imagined there was a lot of competition for this accolade, not having come across an Armstrong museum before, but Fiona said there were Armstrongs everywhere, hundreds and thousands of them, all over the known world, some of them very famous and eminent, and many were very interested in collecting and knowing their heritage and their family history — all of which began here in the Scottish Borders, back in, well, the Dark Ages. No one is quite sure.

Armstrong family records can be traced back to around 1223. They are one of those Border families whose names you still see all over the English/Scottish border today — along with Elliot, Scott, Johnston, Graham, Maxwell, Hume, Kerr, Bell, Douglas, Moffat, Turnbull, Nixon, Jardine, Beattie and several others. Five hundred years ago they were known as "reivers" —

families who were essentially cattle-thieves and sheep-stealers, lawless men who held sway for several centuries, crossing the border and stealing from each other. They were just as likely to fight any other Scottish clan or English authority which tried to control them. It was said that on hunting raids the Armstrongs would carry two flags in their saddlebags, an English and a Scottish one, not knowing which side might capture them.

The Scottish kings, based further north, quite liked having this unruly, wicked, nasty, quarrelsome mob occupying the border-lands to their south — known as the debatable lands, as no one could quite decide who they belonged to. They acted as a buffer state, keeping the English army at bay, or at least making it harder for them to march swiftly towards Edinburgh.

The Armstrongs were the fiercest of these Border clans, able to muster up to three thousand riders, about twice as many as any other family. "Able men," so it was said, "but somewhat unruly and very ill tae tame ... Evil disposed people, thieves, inclined to wildness and disorder ... They have a persuasion that all property is common by the law of nature and is therefore liable to be appropriated by them in their necessity." They got their name supposedly for having strong arms, and there were Armstrong strongholds, with castles, peel towers and fortified farmhouses, right along both sides of the present-day border, in Cumberland and across Northumberland to Newcastle, as well as on the Scottish side.

In 1603, King James VI of Scotland became James I of England and moved south to London. He suddenly wasn't so keen to have these powerful, unruly, thieving clans dominating the centre of his new kingdom, viewing them now in the way we might see gangsters or the Mafia rather than as romantic Robin Hoods. He set about rounding up the reivers. Families like the Scotts and Johnstons chose to work with the crown, laying down their swords and being rewarded with lands and titles. The Armstrongs opted to carry on as before, hoping to cling on to their feudal power, fighting to the death — which is mainly what happened. They were either hunted down and killed, or shipped to Northern Ireland. To survive the persecutions, some of the other expelled clans, such as the Grahams, are said to have changed their names on board ship, turning themselves into Mahargs (which is Graham backwards), but the Armstrongs proudly kept their clan name when they got to Ireland — and it is still widespread there today.

The last Armstrong chief was hanged in 1611. His son and heir fled for his life and was never seen again.

Their brutal extermination became the subject of myths, ballads and legends, kept alive and often embroidered by writers and poets like Sir Walter Scott and, in more recent times, George MacDonald Fraser in his fine book *The Steel Bonnets*. I must admit my eyes have gone glazed over the years when I have come across stories about Lang Sandy, a sixteenth-century Armstrong who was hanged along with his eleven sons, or Johnny Armstrong, who was similarly despatched, or Kinmont Willie Armstrong, who tricked the queen of

England and managed to escape imprisonment in Carlisle Castle. I'm sure all these people and stories are basically true but they seem to have become adorned with such confusing, mad facts and daft legends over the centuries that most now seem fairly nonsensical.

It was to get at the truth of the Armstrongs and sort out fact from fiction that the Clan Armstrong Trust was created, and their little museum opened. It took over a former Church of Scotland church, which it rents for a peppercorn £1 a year from the estate of Duke of Buccleuch, who seems to own everything in the Borders. But the Trust has to maintain it, and recently had to find £4000 for rewiring. One day they would like to install a lavatory.

They attract between eight hundred and a thousand visitors a year, most of whom are Armstrongs or have Armstrong connections, and who come from all over the world, judging by the visitors' book — and they all love it, finding it truly awesome, according to their comments. Visitors don't bring in much money, but the Trust make quite a steady income online, selling Armstrong souvenirs like pens, keyrings, tea towels and books.

The curator is Ann Dalgliesh, a local ex-primary schoolteacher in her fifties. Four years ago, recently widowed, she heard about the job when she was in the Langholm Co-op. A friend asked her what she was doing and she said she was thinking of looking for part-time work. "I didn't know anything about the Armstrongs, but I went along, got interviewed by Fiona, and got the job. I love it. It suits me exactly, as it's just afternoons. It's lovely meeting so many people from all over the world. Yes, almost all are Armstrongs, though you do get people who have just come in out of the rain or happen to be passing through."

Seeing all these Armstrongs, day after day, had she noticed any similarities? "Not really. Fiona tells me there is an Armstrong nose, but I have never noticed it. The thing which amuses all Armstrongs, and I can hear them laughing when they get to that particular board, is a quotation which says, 'Armstrongs can start a fight in a phone box.' They then turn to each other and say, aye, that's verra true . . ."

The storyboards tell the histories of the ancient Armstrong heroes and legends very well, and there's a good display of objects from the time, such as two-handed swords, cannonballs, pistols, uniforms, flags and banners. There's a little research library in one corner, with old books, documents, genealogical tables and facilities for tracing your Armstrong ancestors. It is quite modest and folksy and amateur but they do have a TV corner where you can watch videos about the Armstrong history. Perhaps the most interesting and amusing, as some of it did make me laugh out loud, is one wall devoted to photos and biogs of well-known Armstrongs. Such as, well, Louis Armstrong. I asked Fiona how on earth a black American jazzman could be said to be really a white, Scottish Armstrong?

"We're not saying that," she replies sweetly. "We are simply listing all the famous people with our name. His family must have been brought up on a slave plantation where the owner may have been called Armstrong, which means *he* must have come at one stage from this area. All Armstrongs come originally from the Border lands."

The majority of the famous modern-day Armstrongs do appear genuine enough, with their local roots directly traceable. They included quite a few Victorian worthies I had never heard of, such as Dr John Armstrong who helped found Great Ormond Street Hospital. I had heard of Lord William Armstrong, the great Northumbrian industrialist and arms manufacturer, whose house, Cragside, was the first in the world to be lit by hydroelectricity. He gave his name to Armstrong College, which today has become Newcastle University.

Other worthies include Percy Armstrong, who helped invent stainless steel, and Edwin Howard Armstrong, another inventor, who is credited with creating FM radio. He was American, as were many of the famous modern-ish Amstrongs, and his name was commemorated on a set of US stamps. I discovered that Dame Nellie Melba, the great Australian opera singer — who inspired the peach melba pudding — was really Helen Armstrong, but that was her name by marriage. She was born Helen Mitchell, of Scottish extraction. Dido, a popular singing person of our own times, is a real Armstrong, having been born Dido Florian Cloud de Bounevialle Armstrong (her mother being French and her father Irish).

Lance Armstrong, the cyclist, is clearly a good role model for the traditional image of the tough, fierce, resolute Armstrongs of old, but his inclusion is a little bit of a liberty. It is his real name, but he got it from his stepfather, Terry Keith Armstrong, whom his mother married after his father left when Lance was aged two.

The most famous Armstrong of modern times is of course Neil Armstrong, the first man on the moon. He is a real-born Armstrong, but no one has been able to trace his ancestry further back than Northern Ireland, which is of course where the Armstrongs were shipped when they were chucked out of the Borders. He himself acknowledged he must be a Border Armstrong when he came to south-west Scotland to receive the freedom of Langholm in 1972. During his visit he said he felt he was "now at home".

Unlike some of the other astronauts, Neil Armstrong has not proved keen on personal exposure and fame, becoming a bit of a recluse these last forty years, so Langholm was lucky to get him on one of his rare public outings. An even more interesting outing was the US ceremony, not long after the famous first step for mankind, when he was awarded a medal and received it from President Nixon. Also present was the evangelist Billy Graham and ex-President Lyndon Johnson. Just look at those surnames — Armstrong, Nixon, Graham and Johnson — names to gladden the heart of any old reiver-obsessed romantic. All of them, presumably, must have had Border blood somewhere down the line.

The names live on today and you can see them all over the English-speaking, ex-colonial countries. In the current clan magazine there was a column giving the latest news from the Armstrongs in Barbados, and also about a visit by a clan member to a cemetery in

Georgia, USA, where thirty-four Armstrongs were imprisoned during the civil war and most of them died.

Armstrong tends always to be spelled Armstrong, which makes it easy to spot them, but other Border clan names can have many variations, such as Johnson, Johnston, Johnstone. There are said to be up to seventy different spellings of Elliot — depending on how many l's, t's or e's there are — but all come from the same original source.

The day I visited the museum was 20 July 2009, the fortieth anniversary to the day of that historic moon landing, though I hadn't been aware of its significance till the week before, when I'd rung up, checked they would be open and arranged a visit. It was the reason Fiona Armstrong herself was there. Fiona is not only a genuine Armstrong but for ten years was chairman of the Clan Armstrong Trust — in a sense, their version of a clan chief. She is still a director of the organisation and edits their twice-yearly clan magazine. She lives nearby and is always popping into the museum, helping out.

But she is also one of the more distinguished and recognisable of the living Armstrongs in her own right. That evening, live from the little museum, to mark the anniversary of the moon landing, she was presenting a feature on the Border/ITN news about Neil Armstrong and his Langholm and Borders connections.

Fiona was born a Cumbrian Armstrong, her father and grandparents coming from Maryport, but she spent her childhood in Nigeria, where her father was working for the British Council. They then returned to

Preston, where she went to school and then on to University College London, to read German. She worked for local radio, then moved to Border TV in Carlisle. In 1987 she was invited to London to audition for a vacancy as a reporter-presenter at ITN. They were screen-testing thirty-six different women, as they wanted a woman to replace Pamela Armstrong (no relation) who was retiring. Fiona was the last to be interviewed, but she got the job.

For the next six years she became one of the best-known faces on TV, presenting ITV's *News at Ten*, which got her into all the papers, and attracting the sort of personal publicity she had never sought. "I did have a stalker once, a young man of about eighteen. He followed me all the way home, though I hadn't realised till I was on my doorstep. He tapped me on my shoulder as I was unlocking the door. I dropped my shopping, I was so alarmed. 'Now I know where you live,' he said. He turned out to be harmless, but years later when poor Jill Dando got murdered, it made me realise what a lucky escape I may have had."

Apart from being a newscaster, she did foreign reporting, films about AIDS orphans in Africa, and covered the Lockerbie disaster and two royal tours. She then moved to GMTV, which was just setting up, and hated it. She had been the cool, serious, detached face on ITN but now they wanted her to appeal to the tabloids, wanting her to stand up so the world could see her legs. She was told to wear short skirts and to smile as if she had a coathanger permanently in her mouth. "I do have many fine points, but my legs are not one of them. One paper kindly said I had astronaut's legs — now there's the Armstrong connection!"

After six months she gave it up, left London to return to Carlisle and folksy old Border TV, where immediately she felt at home, not just with the sort of work she had to do but with life generally. She lived in the country and became a keen fisher-woman. She also felt it would give a better childhood to her daughter Natasha, especially after her first marriage collapsed and she became a single mother.

In 2010, she was one of the, er, let's say more experienced female presenters whom the BBC decided to use more often — having been criticised for being obsessed with the youth and looks of their current female presenters, but not of course with their male presenters.

She joined the Clan Armstrong Trust twenty years ago and as chairman helped, with a team of volunteers, to establish the museum, working to get it accredited with the Scottish museums authority — securing two-star status, whatever that means. She has made two dozen videos and films about the Armstrongs and Scottish clans in general, and was responsible for setting up the Reiver Trail. This is a drive round eight historic Border sites associated with the Armstrongs, some of which the Trust looks after. They all have plaques on them and you can look up the history and position of each in a little leaflet. Trails are obviously a big thing in the Borders, as I noticed the Telford Trail and a MacDiarmid Trail in the tourist office.

248

"I am passionate about the Armstrongs and find the whole history of the reivers absolutely fascinating. I do think they have too often been overlooked. In Scottish history books you hardly read much about them, just three or four pages, which is a disgrace when you think what a big part they played in Scottish and English history. Without the Armstrongs and the other Border clans holding the line against the English, Scotland could well have been much smaller, maybe finishing just south of Glasgow.

"I do see the Armstrongs as a personal crusade. I do films and write about them in foreign publications — including the *Scottish Banner*, which is the biggest international Scottish newspaper. You must have heard of it."

The Clan Armstrong Trust has about four hundred paid-up members across the world. The current chairman is Michcil Armstrong of Mungbyhurst, who happens to be a South African businessman. He has done years of painstaking research into the family — and comes over at least twice a year and usually paints the museum's railings while he is here. They are all very proud of their clan motto. *Invictus Maneo* means "I remain unvanquished".

What about their traditional reputation for being quarrelsome? Fiona smiled. "Well, I don't think it's worse than other small groups of amateur enthusiasts who sometimes get a bit carried away. We have had the odd storming out of meetings, but that's about all."

They have their own tartan — in fact they have two. One is called the Ancient, which is greeny with a splash of purple for heather. The other is the Modern. There was at one time an Armstrong Lunar Tartan, to mark the moon landing and Neil Armstrong's visit to Langholm, which sold quite well for a while — but, alas, the firm that made it has packed up.

They are of course proud of having their very own museum. Their old rivals the Elliots have a small museum at the house of their chief, Margaret Eliott of Redheugh. It's just up the road, at Newcastleton, with a collection of Elliot relics, but unlike the Armstrong museum it is open by appointment only.

The matter of not having an hereditary clan chief — unlike most other Scottish clans — is a bit of a sore point. They have been chiefless since that Armstrong was hanged in 1611 and his son and heir did a runner.

Meanwhile, Fiona herself has in effect joined another Scottish clan. In 2005 she got married to Sir Malcolm MacGregor of MacGregor, a tall, dashing, red-haired old Etonian and ex-Scots Guards officer, who is a baronet and the twenty-fourth hereditary chief of Clan Gregor. In his real, day-to-day work he is a well-known landscape photographer who has produced several books — as has Fiona herself, notably on fishing and cooking.

As Lady MacGregor, it would seem she has joined a rival gang — I mean clan — but she says no. Armstrongs are a Border clan, MacGregors are a Highland clan, it's a different kettle of tartan.

"We are in fact quite similar. The MacGregors were also very wild — think of Rob Roy — and for about a hundred and fifty years they were proscribed and no one was allowed to bear the name. Apparently some MacGregors had brutally murdered a load of Colqhouns and the widows took the bloodied shirts of their slain husbands to the king, who happened to be a pretty squeamish man. The image haunted him and he said that's it, these MacGregors are banned from now on. They were the original children of the mist and were hunted down — rather like us in the end. Then a lot of them emigrated, just as we did."

If any Armstrong out there is willing to come back, and is able to reveal himself as having the true blood of the last Armstrong chief, killed in 1611, then would he be welcomed with open arms?

"Oh yes, we would love a clan chief of our own. A clan chief would keep us all in line and sort out any differences, as we would all obey him."

Or her? "Of course, if she could prove the right bloodline, she could become our clan chief.

"We do from time to time put adverts in the Scottish papers, asking anyone to come forward who thinks they have the correct ancestry, and it can be agreed by the Lord Lyon King of Arms in Edinburgh, but so far no one has been able to prove it."

There will be no money or lands or castles, but loads of honour and status and perhaps now and again the odd perk. Her husband, Sir Malcolm MacGregor, does get one nice little gift each year, a complimentary case of whisky from the company who produce Clan MacGregor whisky. They use not just the clan name but his personal coat of arms on the bottle top, so naturally they like to thank him in the appropriate way.

251

I left the little Armstrong museum wanting to wrap it up and take it away, the building itself, as it was so dinky, so sweet and attractive. My stuff would look really good displayed in such nice, homely surroundings. I wonder if the Duke of Buccleuch would be open to offers? I had a look at the foundations and decided it was a bit like a West Indian chattel house — the wooden houses plonked down on slabs, which plantation slaves took with them when they moved. So I could cart it away. It would look great on Hampstead Heath — if I could withstand the campaign that would be instantly mounted against it.

I also took away the notion that museums don't have to be devoted to physical objects. The sheep show illustrated that living animals can be an attraction, and the Armstrong museum shows that a name is enough.

I then headed north — for another of Scotland's well-known preoccupations, though this time a more commercial subject, and one with more topical overtones.

It had been refreshing to come across a museum not really interested in pulling in large numbers, worrying about footfall, drawing attention to itself, or trying to convert outsiders. Most museums, after all, are hoping to interest the rest of the world in their particular passion.

I am like that myself, in that I am eager to show people my treasures, pass on my enthusiasm, even though I very quickly see eyes go glazed, attention wander, and I know visitors would actually prefer a drink to another flick through my albums of suffragette postcards. Perhaps if I had my own museum I should try not to be too eager, just to be. Open up and wait.

In its modest little way, the Armstrong museum is providing a service, a point of reference for those who just happen to have a certain name, preaching to those who have already been converted by the accident of blood or marriage. Oh, and adoption.

Clan Armstrong Trust Museum
Castle Holme
Langholm
Dumfries & Galloway DG13 0ND
Tel 01387 381610
www.armstrongclan.org.uk

CHAPTER
THIRTEEN

The Money Museum, Edinburgh

You don't often come across abuse at museums, and certainly not at the sort of single-issue, unusual, odd museums that I was looking for.

Amusement — I noticed a lot of that on my tour. People arrived at the Laurel and Hardy museum already rather jolly, expecting to enjoy themselves. They were also smiling on arrival at the lawnmower museum — in this case amused and intrigued by the daftness of it all: could there really be a museum totally devoted to lawnmowers? At the pencil museum there was a definite air of excitement, but that was because they had set out to be all action and activity, keen to involve the kiddies from the moment they arrived. At the sheep show, I would say the first reaction was one of bemusement — perplexed, a bit worried about what they were going to experience. I could feel affection as people wandered round the Cars of the Stars, especially when they saw the Trotter three-wheeler.

So, how awful to have a museum where upon arrival some people make catty comments, nasty jokes, critical jibes. Not all of them, and not all of the time, and it has to be admitted it is only a very recent development, since, say, the autumn of 2008 — but it will probably go on for a few more years, till the present crisis, and the present image of bankers as nasty baddies, begins to fade.

At the moment, however, when people enter the utterly splendid, totally wonderful, architecturally magnificent Museum on the Mound at the Bank of Scotland's headquarters in Edinburgh, they do tend to let slip the odd sarky remark.

The bankers don't help their cause, as immediately on arrival, on your right as you enter the first room, there is one million pounds. It's in a glass case, arranged in real cash, neat bundles of it, all in £20 notes, which means — let me see, using the fingers of both hands — there must be 50,000 notes piled up before me.

Well, if you are having a museum revolving round money, you might as well show some, let Joe Public see what one million quid actually looks like close up, as Joe Public is never going to see it in real life. But it is rather asking for comments and reactions, especially in these hard times.

"So whose bonus is this then?" That's one of the more printable reactions.

"I've often wondered what happened to my bank charges."

"Oh look, some banker has left his petty cash behind."

"Wow — a million pounds!"

Was it really real? That was my first reaction. Or just Monopoly money? No, they are genuine Bank of Scotland £20 notes, each with its own individual and correct serial number, properly printed by the official printers — in this case De La Rue, who seem to print most of the world's banknotes.

On closer inspection, I noticed that each note has been overprinted with the word CANCELLED. So don't bother to break in and try to steal them. They won't be worth much — though they will be worth something, as the Bank of Scotland, having ordered these notes for display purposes, had to pay for the cost of the paper and printing, which came to around £4000.

My second thought was, is that all? One million pounds cash didn't seem physically as vast a wodge as I would have imagined. In fact you could cram it all into a large rucksack or one of those outsize wheely suitcases and no one on the Tube would guess what you were carting with you to Heathrow, hoping for a quick getaway. If that's all that one million looks like, I wondered what £19 billion would look like? That figure went through my mind because that was the reported loss that HBOS had run up before it found itself being taken over by, or at least amalgamated with, Lloyds TSB in 2008. At least it had not suffered the ignominy of its deadly rival the Royal Bank of Scotland, which had to be rescued by the government from the gutter or extinction and whose boss, Sir Fred Goodwin, found himself being mocked and ridiculed as "Fred the Shred" and his property daubed and vandalised. Yes, the credit crisis of 2008–9 threw up many dramas and disgraces, collapses and corruptions in the UK and all over the Western, so-called civilised, world.

In some ways, the worst falls from grace, and the most abuse, were experienced by those mighty Scottish bankers, sitting in their Edinburgh strongholds. For three hundred years or so we had so admired them — almost as much as they had admired themselves — pillars of society and industry and the community, people and institutions renowned for integrity, probity, respectability and, above all, security. In Britain, and in the English-speaking world at large, we had particularly looked up to Scottish bankers as representing, so we thought, the very essence of the best traditional Scottish virtues. Scots are supposed to be canny, are they not? Scots like to be prudent, Scots can be trusted with our money. Think of all our Chancellors of the Exchequer in recent years who have been Scots, like Norman Lamont, Gordon Brown, Alistair Darling. And think of all the mess that Scottish banks and bankers have recently helped get us into — sorry, we won't start all that again. Let's give them a break.

Despite being Scottish-born, and spending most of my childhood up to the age of eleven in Scotland, I had never actually known the difference between the Bank of Scotland and the Royal Bank of Scotland, getting them confused when not half-thinking they were the same thing anyway.

I had also never looked properly at Scottish pound notes. On receiving them in my change — in, say, Carlisle or Cockermouth — and knowing I am about to go south, I will always try to change them for real pound notes — I mean, Bank of England notes — feeling rather unpatriotic and ashamed by my behaviour but knowing that if I try to pay with them in some back-street London petrol station, they will be turned over suspiciously by someone who has never seen them before. Or Scotland.

So I have always moved Scottish fivers and tenners on quickly, never properly studying them, assuming they are all from the same bank — which would be, er, that Scottish bank, what's it called? I had never realised that there are in fact three different Scottish banks allowed to produce their own banknotes today — the Bank of Scotland, the Royal Bank of Scotland and the Clydesdale Bank. These three are the only ones left out of around eighty or so different Scottish banks which over the centuries have produced their own notes.

The Bank of Scotland was founded in Edinburgh in 1695 and started producing its own paper currency in 1696, which it continues to do to this day, making it the longest continuous issuer of banknotes in the world. Others have come and gone — particularly long ago in China — but the Bank of Scotland always carried on, taking over many other smaller banks and financial institutions along the way.

By comparison, the Royal Bank of Scotland is an upstart, not being founded till 1727, though over recent centuries it has rather edged ahead, with more capital and more high street outlets than the Bank of Scotland.

The Bank of Scotland's headquarters is on the Mound, on the slopes under Edinburgh Castle, one of the city's most prominent and dominant buildings, its dome roof being seen from all corners of the city. The architects were Robert Reid and Richard Crichton, and it was completed in 1806 to universal admiration. The Mound was in fact mainly man-made, from spoil heaps thrown on to the steep slopes of the castle when they were digging out the foundations for the New Town, and also from the middens and dumps used by the people living above, which were later levelled and built on. The building was extended in the 1870s, attaining the size and stature it is today, with its massive windows and high-ceilinged reception areas and flagstone floors.

It had always kept its archives, as it was proud of its history. Banks, almost by definition, have to keep records and accounts anyway, proof of what it is they have been doing with our money. The Bank of Scotland opened the museum to show its history to the public in 1988, devoting one little room to it — but rather half-heartedly, opening only in the summer months, and then not every day.

This was the case when Helen Redmond-Cooper arrived in 1989. She is Welsh, took a first degree in politics at Swansea, an MA in archive studies at Aberystwyth, and then, after a short spell in the Essex Record Office, landed the job as assistant archivist at the Bank of Scotland. She worked mainly in the archive department but also looked after the museum, such as it was. "It was tiny and very amateurish."

In 2001 she feared the worst, that their little museum would be swept away when a massive reorganisation took place. The Bank of Scotland got into bed with the

259

Halifax plc and emerged as HBOS. Banks seem to be besotted by initials these days. I refused for years to call my bank HSBC and still referred to it as the Midland. I never got my tongue round HBOS either, even though I found they now owned my ISA, which I thought I had taken out with the Halifax. I now know not to worry about bank names. There will be another change along soon, all you have to do is wait.

However, Helen's fears proved groundless. She was made head of archives for the new company, taking over responsibility for the Halifax archives. Then the new chief executive, James Crosby, decreed that the whole building on the Mound was to be upgraded and refurbished. In 2004 it closed for two years and when it reopened in 2006, a brand-new museum was included, with state-of-the-art displays, the latest in design and technology and, most amazing of all, about seven times bigger than it had been.

Now, with its luxurious fittings, gleaming cabinets, spotless displays, space and grandeur, it reeks of affluence and wealth as if no expense has been spared. Is that the case?

"I would get shot if I revealed how much it cost," says Helen. "Halfway through, I realised that three rooms would not do us justice, which was the original plan. I was allowed to expand to seven rooms, or eight if you count our lecture room. The bank was generous in terms of the space they were willing to give me and in providing the budget for museum-quality conditions — temperature, humidity, lighting, secure cases etc.

"The best thing was I had no interference. I was allowed to get on with it as long as I followed two guidelines. The museum had to reflect the whole group — the Halifax's history as well as the Bank of Scotland's — and it had to be accessible and understandable to the general public.

"In fact I did have financial constraints. I didn't have enough money to install any audio facilities, though we have lots of video and interactive stuff. I'm not keen on audio as a rule as it can be disruptive, sound can seep out from one display when you are looking at a different one and be distracting, but on reflection I think earphones might have been useful, with a taped commentary in different languages. To do that was going to cost an extra £40,000 and I had spent my budget — which no, I'm still not going to reveal . . ."

There was enough money though for a grand opening and they hired the well-known Edinburgh writer Ian Rankin to perform the ceremony. He did get a modest fee, but donated it all to the Edinburgh children's hospital, and the bank itself topped it up several times over.

Rankin did the museum proud and came out with a quote that they still use on their website: "The Museum on the Mound is the best new museum to have opened in Edinburgh for ages . . . It's fun. It's free. It's fantastic."

That is its official title, the Museum on the Mound, as if they are perhaps a bit nervous about pushing the notion of a money museum too blatantly — though the title is always followed by the subheading "Money . . .

and so much more", and they usually spell the word MUS£UM with a pound sign.

"It is called the Museum on the Mound," says Helen, "because it is physically located on the Mound in Edinburgh, and its subject matter is not just about money. We deliberately went for a variety of themes and topics, to give the museum broader appeal."

In its first year it attracted over fifty thousand visitors and received a five-star rating from Visit Scotland, though recently it has dropped to around forty-two thousand. Helen puts this down to the traffic chaos in Princes Street caused by the tramway works.

Having survived, and indeed triumphed, as a result of the arrival of the Halifax and the HBOS reincarnation, there was far worse to come in 2008 when the credit crunch and recession struck. Again it did appear cost savings would have to be made, that an eight-room museum — employing a staff of four, with another five behind the scenes in the archives, would be one of the early and easy casualties.

The takeover — or should we say forced amalgamation — with Lloyds TSB, caused by all the debts HBOS had accumulated, was humiliating enough, but at least they retained their independent existence, as opposed to being taken over by the government like the Royal Bank. "Things were a bit hairy when Lloyds arrived. No one knew what was going to happen, what changes would be made. Lloyds had their own excellent archives in London, but I also knew they didn't have their own museum, so I looked upon that as slightly reassuring.

"In the event, the museum has been left largely untouched. I think in the scale of things, with such colossal sums being bandied around, the cost of running the museum was seen as minuscule, hardly worth closing for what it would save.

"But it was also realised that the museum was a real asset to the organisation. It's a proper, genuine museum, not just a marketing gimmick, which the public recognise as such and want to visit — in their thousands. We also cover so many themes, from death and disease to art and architecture. And our schools programme, which focuses on money, has been a huge success. We also happen to be a free museum. No one can hold that against us — say we are trying to take money off people, once again."

In her own personal and social life, it was quite unpleasant for a few months. She says people working in any sort of bank, at any sort of level, did find themselves being attacked and criticised at parties, or when they met strangers and revealed what their job was. "It was a sad time. You would have to be devoid of all emotion not to feel personally affected by it all. The public, quite rightly, felt let down by what happened."

Few could feel let down by the museum itself, and its seven display rooms so lavishly and professionally organised and filled with treasures, even if a lot of them are a bit erudite for someone who has just wandered in off the Mound, attracted by the free entry and wanting to make rude comments about bankers.

The main emphasis is on Scottish banking over the last three hundred years, but they do pause for a while to explain that money has been around a lot longer, and from ancient times onwards came in various forms. Small cowrie shells were one of the earliest forms of currency as they fulfilled the purpose of most forms of money — to be portable, durable, recognisable and divisible. At one time red feathers were used, at least in the Solomon Islands, while in Tibet money was made out of bricks made of tea. In Nigeria bottles of gin were sometimes used as currency — but could also be drunk, which was useful.

There are a lot of ancient documents on display, such as the parchment containing the original act that set up the bank in 1695, banking files and record books — as after all money is only a document, a scrap of paper, so in a museum devoted to the subject there is bound to be a lot of paper.

I happen to like paper, and the more and prettier it is printed the better, so I spent a lot of time studying the development of banknotes, the vignettes and watermarks, lettering and typefaces, and the plates from which they were printed.

Their oldest Bank of Scotland note is from 1716 — earlier ones, back to 1696, have all disappeared, probably burned. As for Scottish coins, I had never consciously realised that they don't exist. Scotland has not had its own coinage since 1707 and the Act of Union, but earlier on the Scottish kings did mint their own coins, back to David I in the 1130s.

Helen would dearly love to discover a 1696 Bank of Scotland note, which would cost a small fortune if one ever did turn up, though probably not as much as some of the classic US banknotes from the 1820s, which have changed hands for up to one million dollars.

In 2007, when some new Bank of Scotland notes were issued, a set of five of them — £5, £10, £20, £50 and £100 — all with the lowest possible serial numbers, were sold for £12,000 at a charity auction held by the bank, despite their face value being only £185.

Old Scottish notes don't fetch enormous prices — the week I was at the museum, an 1878 Clydesdale £1 note had been sold for £4800 at an auction in Carlisle, which was considered a pretty high price. There are banknote collectors all over the world, and the International Bank Note Society, with chapters in most countries, has thousands of members. Collectors of Scottish notes have recently broken away, becoming the Banknote Society of Scotland. They currently have about fifty members.

I was a bit disappointed though by the lack of cheques, which I know is also a keen collecting area. I was going to collect them myself at one time, as in the old days they were so attractive, then I decided no, I'll just collect cheques signed by famous people, though that hasn't got very far either. I only have four — signed by Somerset Maugham, Gladstone, Saul Bellow and Tennyson plus, I think, Charlie Chaplin, which I seem to have misplaced.

265

The object of money is not to keep collectors happy but to make the world go round, especially industry and commerce. Over the years the Bank of Scotland, and all the other banks and institutions it has taken over, such as the British Linen Bank, have served some distinguished firms, like John Brown, the ship-builders, and famous people such as Sir Walter Scott, R L Stevenson and Thomas Carlyle.

In one room there is a display of documents relating to famous customers, which includes Carlyle's spectacles. Seemed to be stretching it a bit, having specs in a museum supposedly about money, but the label wittily says that Carlyle used them "to keep an eye on his money".

There is even a poem by Robert Burns, which turns out to be directly relevant to a museum about money as it was written on the back of a Bank of Scotland banknote in 1786. You could write on the backs at that time, as they were left blank before the need for tighter security. The poem is a furious attack about his lack of money being the cause of all his problems — and could very well have been written by some disgruntled people in the Western world in 2009:

Wae worth thy power, thou cursed leaf
Fell source o a' my woe and grief
For lack o thee I've lost my lass
For lack o thee I scrimp my glass.

The poem continues for another eight lines, ending rather melodramatically:

For lack o thee I leave this much-lov'd shore
Never, perhaps, to greet old Scotland more.

The reason for Burns's fury was to do with the family of Jean Armour, whom he had made pregnant. Her father found out, took her away, and threatened Burns with jail unless he could find a large sum of money, which he didn't have, hence his plan to emigrate. He didn't, as he then met another girl, Highland Mary, and probably made her pregnant as well. Money, or the lack of it, has always been easy to blame for one's woes.

From the beginning of paper money, forgers have been trying to make their own money for nothing, and often succeeded, despite ingenious ways to make it impossible. One of the earliest attempts to diddle the Bank of Scotland occurred in 1700 when a local man, Thomas McGhie, was suspected of a very simple forgery. Because the £5 and £50 notes were at that time the same size and colour, all he did was carefully alter the figure 5 and change it to 50. He was called into the bank one evening for questioning, but because it was late and they were locking up, he was allowed to go home, promising to return in the morning for more questioning. In the morning he was spotted heading south for Newcastle, and was never seen again. A wise move, as up to 1832 the penalty for forgery was hanging.

From the moment the Royal Bank arrived on the scene in 1727 they were in deadly rivalry with the Bank of Scotland, and often up to some pretty dirty tricks to gain an advantage. The theory of all paper money, then and now, is that the bank issuing the paper promises to pay the bearer on demand real money — that is, solid stuff — which of course no one ever asks for. But the Royal Bank of Scotland did. In 1728 they started collecting and keeping as many Bank of Scotland notes as they could. When they had enough, some £900 in notes, they trundled them along in a barrow to the Bank of Scotland and said come on, give us the cash. The bank did not have sufficient supplies and had to close to business for three months, during which time they went back to their subscribers to raise more cash. Even when they reopened, they had only £585 in real hard cash, compared with £70,000 then currently circulating in notes. Banks have always taken a few chances.

It was a rotten trick by the Royal Bank, so why did they do it?

"It was just the name of the game at the time, trying to put the opposition out of business," Helen replied, smiling. "I'm sure we did pretty much the same."

In 1745, when Bonny Prince Charlie and the Jacobites arrived and took over Edinburgh, the bank was frightened that a similar thing would happen — that the Jacobites would appear with Scottish notes and demand gold and silver in return, to take with them to finance their hoped-for conquest of Carlisle and then London.

"In this case, the worry was political. Succouring an enemy by giving them money could have counted as treason, so when the bank heard the Jacobites were on the way, they quickly collected all the money they had and rushed off with it to the Castle where it was locked up and hidden."

On view in the museum is a massive kist, as chests are known in Scotland, which was used by the bank to lock up its money each evening, plus any gold and silver plate or other valuables. It dates from 1701 and is made of wrought iron and has two locks — one at the front and one hidden on the top. You have to press a secret button to reveal the top lock. No bank official would have the key to both locks, so it would take two of them each morning, each with a key, to open up the kist.

Financial scandals and disasters are not new, as bankers and investors tend to get carried away, usually with other people's money, into unwise decisions. One of the biggest in Scottish history was the Darien Company, which, around 1698, was aiming to become a Scottish version of the East India Company, setting up a trading and exploration colony on the isthmus of Panama in Central America where, it was hoped, vast fortunes would be made. Several explorations took place, but it all ended in disaster, with lives lost, families ruined, investors bankrupted. The whole of the Scottish economy suffered — though the Bank of Scotland was not involved.

The Halifax and the history of building societies also gets a bit of space, and I learned something I didn't know, which is why the Leeds Permanent Building Society was so called. Originally, building societies were groups of people who put a certain amount of money each week into a pot, out of which, in turn, they took enough money to build a house. After they had all got their houses, the society was wound up, hence this was called a Terminating Building Society. In Leeds, Halifax and elsewhere, it was soon realised that the society was such a good idea that it should be continued, attracting new depositors, and so the new version was called a Permanent Building Society.

There is also space devoted to life insurance, as one of the elements in the present group is Clerical Medical. You can fill in your own insurance application, stating your name, age, illnesses, where you might be travelling, how much you want to be insured for, and the policy gets printed and given to you when you leave the museum. It's a nice bit of parchment — shame it happens to reflect prices and conditions in 1824, and states that the policy is void if you die by duelling, but it's a neat piece of personal memorabilia all the same.

About the most popular exhibit, enjoyed by children of all ages, is a game called Cracking the Code. You have to reply to certain questions about banking, the answers to which are somewhere on the walls. You then get certain numbers, which have to be arranged in the correct sequence, and if you get them right, and set the combination lock correctly, the door of the safe swings opens and you can get the gold coins inside. I think I've got that right but it looked too complicated for me to attempt. The coins are in fact chocolate, but worth having nonetheless. Every day about ten people manage to crack the code.

These and other interactive displays and computer-generated bits of wizardry were presumably not cheap to create (and they were devised specially for the museum when it reopened) and are extremely popular, but personally I much prefer real objects and genuine relics, such as a brass calculating machine from 1820 known as an "arithmometer", which bank clerks used to count up money. I also liked the photographs and documents showing the social life of bank clerks in the 1930s, their staff magazines, their outings in charabancs, their tennis clubs, their susbidised trips abroad. What fun it must have been to be part of a well-known bank in the old days — what status, what pride. Well, you never know, it might all come back again.

There were so many documents and paper memorabila I would like to have had, as I do like printed stuff, and I did like the way that, as with the pencil museum, they have broadened out the subject into topics and materials connected with the basic theme but not directly obvious. It's a lesson we museum creators — well, possible museum creators — should take on board.

The building of course was stunning, worth seeing for itself, but I don't think I am going to be able to afford such premises. Better stick to the chattel house idea.

Before I left, I went round the museum shop and bought a few exciting presents, such as a Halifax tea towel from the 1950s. It shows a wife in a pinny laying the table while the husband in the foreground is saying he has invested in Halifax paid-up 3½ per cent shares. It appears to be pretty sexist, with the little woman in the background reduced to doing wifely things, but the

271

message from the man reads "My wife agrees we should invest in the security of the Halifax". So they were in it together, even if it would seem to be her agreeing with him.

The Halifax tea towel was reduced to £3.75 as it was not proving as popular as a Bank of Scotland tea towel, priced £5, which features a £20 note. People like the idea of drying their dishes with it. I bought several to give to my wife and daughters. I do spoil them.

All the profits from the shop, so Helen stressed as I left, go not to the bank but to charity — currently the British Heart Foundation. More proof of how caring our modern bankers can be.

Which, in a way, should ensure the museum's future. While other equally specialist if less well-appointed museums might fear for their survival, the Bank of Scotland, now under the wing of the Lloyds group, obviously sees its museum as part of its corporate image.

Of all the mad and unlikely reasons for opening and retaining a museum I had been trying to think of before I set out on my trail, I had never envisaged soft PR as one of them. Museums do have their uses.

Museum on the Mound
The Mound
Edinburgh EH1 1YZ
Tel 0131 243 5464
www.museumonthemound.com

CHAPTER
FOURTEEN

Chantry Bagpipe Museum, Morpeth

So far I hadn't visited a council-owned museum. They tend not to support mad things like a museum devoted to one single, eccentric subject — though in their town museums they often have an assortment of mad things, most of which have been left to them by local worthies, the idea being that they are displaying a variety of items, all lumped together, showing the tremendous range and richness and general wonderfulness of their town's history. Or not, which is more likely the case. A handful of Roman coins, some Victorian costumes, old pop and lemonade bottles and far too many stuffed birds. That was traditionally how town museums presented themselves.

Single-subject museums tend to be the creation of one person who either tries to run it for money, so it funds itself, or else pays for it out of his or her own back pocket, if they are wealthy enough or have another income. Some manage to find a rich backer to help out, as the vintage radios did for a while, or they turn it into a charity with a board of trustees and volunteers who run it for nothing.

Single-subject museums can of course also be the creation of some sort of institution, like the Bank of Scotland, or an industry, like the pencil museum, or a society, like the Clan Armstrong Trust. Then there are interesting museums attached to a university, or to a scientific or medical foundation. I did consider quite a few of them, such as the Pitt Rivers in Oxford, which is a truly amazing museum and was the work of one collector, or the Wellcome Institute, with its marvellous medical relics, but they cover too much and are too big, too rich, too broad in scope to be classified as either single-subject or truly, deeply mad and eccentric.

The bagpipe museum in Morpeth — that sounded genuinely unusual and strange, though I was a bit worried when I heard it was in the same building as the town's tourist information centre, fearing it would just be a couple of cases in a corner, along with the leaflets for town trails, guest houses, animal farms, kiddies' adventure playgrounds — but I was assured on the phone that it was a proper museum, separate from the tourist stuff, with its own curator.

Morpeth today is an affluent, country town in rural Northumberland, not far from the coast, which serves as one of the more desirable commuter towns, along with Hexham, for the better-off professional types who work in Newcastle, about fifteen miles to the south.

As with Langholm and Ulverston, little country towns that I had never been to till I first stumbled upon their museums, I was surprised by Morpeth's architecture, the historic connections, ancient buildings carefully preserved, a bustling little market in the middle of the town, giving a sense of prosperity and well-being. It may be all a mirage, and there were slums and deprivation and drug dens I missed, but it made me wonder why I ever go abroad when there are clearly so many attractive small towns in Britain I have yet to visit.

Shame about the second-hand and antique shops. I found only one antique shop, which looked interesting enough through the window, but it was closed. One good-sized bookshop, Appleby's, but I couldn't see any old books. I was directed to what I was told was a bric-a-brac shop above a butcher's, which I eventually found, but it had been empty for six months. I had hoped that with its middle-class residents and nearness to Newcastle I would find loads for my collections, but no luck. In Cockermouth, which with a population of seven thousand is only half the size of Morpeth and is much more remote, after I had done the sheep show, I found eight different places selling second-hand treasures. Oh bliss.

The bagpipe museum's location, however, was a treasure in itself — a medieval building called the Chantry, beside the river as you cross the bridge into the town centre. The earliest records date back to 1296, when it was a chapel where chants were sung and travellers were blessed on the way north to Scotland. The priest in charge would also take a small fee for letting them cross the bridge. Over the centuries, it changed hands and purposes many times, housing a boys' grammar school, a cholera hospital and then in more modern times, it was a pop factory, bottling mineral waters and lemonades. Then it lay derelict, allowed to fall into disrepair, until 1974 when Castle Morpeth Borough Council bought the whole building and began to restore it, installing an information centre and a shop selling local crafts and gifts. But it still had space, in fact the whole of the upstairs, to house something else. But what?

Enter the sound of pipes, which until then had been droning away, hardly listened to or seen by anybody, some fifteen miles distant in the centre of Newcastle. A collection of Northumbrian pipes had been left to the Society of Antiquaries of Newcastle upon Tyne, one of the oldest such bodies in the land, founded in 1813. For fifteen years, the pipes had been kept in a room in the Black Gate of Newcastle Castle. Despite all the times I must have been to Newcastle over the decades, I couldn't quite remember where the castle was — or even whether they had one or not.

"Precisely," says Anne Moore, curator of the bagpipe museum. "That was the problem. Even people who passed the front door every day never knew we were there. We were up three flights of a narrow and steep spiral staircase as well, which didn't help, and it was always freezing. People were puffing and shivering as they came up the stairs, then when they got to our door, they were met by a notice saying entrance 15p. I could then hear them say 'I'm not paying that,' and walk all the way downstairs again."

Anne was born in Blyth, and read English at Hull. She worked at the Laing Art Gallery in Newcastle before getting a job at the bagpipe museum on a temporary contract. "It's how museum curators got a bit of work experience in those days, the 1980s. There was massive unemployment. We seem to be going back to that sort of situation now."

The Society of Antiquaries had decided they could no longer afford to look after the pipes. They were being moved to Morpeth, and Anne, who had originally come in to catalogue them, presumed she would be out of a job, but she moved with them. After a year, she was appointed curator, a job she still has.

Anne had had no formal training in museums or curating, which back in the 1980s was not always required anyway, but she did a diploma in museum studies at Leicester part-time. Today there are loads of places where you can take a first degree in museum work — and you won't get far unless you have one, at least if you are working for a council-owned or government-funded museum. The do-it-yourself museums of course do not have the same requirements. Anyone can open a museum. You don't even need Latin.

Once the pipes arrived at the Chantry they were properly displayed, a professional designer hired, storyboards printed, and they soon expanded from one half of the top floor to take over the whole floor, and a sound system was installed. When they were in Newcastle they attracted only a couple of thousand visitors every year, though of course people were being charged a hefty 15p a time. Now they have up to ten thousand visitors, from all over the world. Entrance is free, so the figures are estimates. Such are the joys of being properly funded, professionally run.

But ah, what goes up on the wall can come down. Being tied to a council means you are also tied to their fortunes, vagaries, fashions, whims, political infighting. At one time councils appeared as safe and secure as, well, er, banks — but not any more. They are just as likely to go bust as any other business.

"Six years ago, we thought we were about to close as the council had to save money. We are not a statutory service, like emptying dustbins. They don't have to keep museums going. Their finances were about to be officially investigated by central government, and we thought that was it, we would be the first to go, but then a massive worldwide campaign started, with appeals and petitions and emails flooding in to Save the Pipes."

Anne thinks it was because musicians, as a breed, can very quickly get steamed up and become very active. Perhaps it's because they tend to spend half of their time unemployed, and like a good fight. But it was mainly the nature of the pipes — Northumbrian pipes, not your run-of-the-mill Scottish type — which stirred up all the emotions. Exiled Geordies in the far corners of the English-speaking world decided they were not just saving some old bagpipes but their own heritage. So phew, at the last moment, the museum was saved.

Then came drama number two. In September 2008, Anne had been on holiday for a week. She came in on

278

Saturday morning, not normally a day she is at the museum, to catch up on some paperwork.

"Out of the corner of my eye, through the windows, I noticed that the river was quite high, but I wasn't worried. The river often is quite high. After all, we've been here for eight hundred years, so you presume we must be safe enough."

Next time she looked, a couple of hours later, the river had burst its banks, come across the little stretch of garden and was flooding into the Chantry building — straight through the 800-year-old stone. There was apparently no damp-proof course, or deep foundations. They thought at first it was seeping under the doors, so they closed them — then opened them again to let the water out when they realised how it was getting in.

"When I got downstairs, the water was up to my ankles. Outside the door it was up to my knees. I quickly found help and began rescuing all the pipes."

Although the museum proper is upstairs, they had a small display downstairs as well, plus a storage room with around sixty instruments, and all their archives.

"A piper who was coming to play that evening offered to come and help. She brought her daughter and her brother too, and on their way down the street they managed to rope in another friend who happened to be passing. It took us four hours — but we managed to carry everything upstairs to safety, by which time the emergency services ordered us all to evacuate the building."

The whole building was closed for six months, during which the pipes were moved to another museum six miles away. The building was then totally refurbished, refitted and redecorated.

When I arrived in August 2009, it had just officially reopened, with Princess Anne doing the ceremony. It was all gleaming, the new paint and display cases sparkling — but alas, the sound system was still not yet working upstairs in the museum. In normal times, you put on earphones and as you go round each display case you can hear the exact music made by the pipes you are looking at. What they hadn't realised was that the flood water, which had ruined all the plaster on the downstairs walls, had also upset their sound system. (However, it was all working not long after my visit.)

Fortunately, as Anne Moore was about to take me round the museum, a real piper arrived, Maureen Davison. She had recently retired from working in the graphics department at Northumbria University, and she had also lost her house after a vehicle smashed into it, so she was spending a lot of time practising her pipes in the museum, to amuse herself and the visitors.

She had first heard the Northumbrian pipes as a child when they were used as a jingle on Radio Newcastle. "I fell in love with them then, but it was about thirty years before I decided to learn how to play them." She now plays semi-professionally, when she can, at weddings, funerals and parties.

Like most people, at least outside the North-East, I had no idea what Northumbrian bagpipes were and assumed, as most people do, that all bagpipes look much like Scottish bagpipes, so it was interesting to see her open her case and assemble her set. They call it a

280

set of small pipes and it does come in a set — of four different pieces. The strangest part was the bellows, which looked exactly like fireside bellows, which she strapped on under her right arm. I asked if left-armers put it under their left arm. She paused and thought. No, she had never seen people do that. The bellows always goes under the right arm, as you can see in the ancient illustrations.

The wind from the bellows then goes into a bag held under the left arm, which is made of leather with a cloth cover, and from there the wind goes into the chanter, on which the tune is played, and also the drones, all of which extend from the bag. The drones, as the name implies, drone on, giving a background harmony hum. Maureen had four of them sticking out, which she adjusted slightly before she began.

The big technical difference between Northumbrian and Scottish bagpipes is that in the former the air comes from the bellows, as opposed to the mouth. The chanter also works on a slightly different principle — having the end closed, so the fingers have to be lifted and replaced individually to make notes, giving the characteristic peas-popping sound. The Northumbrian pipes also have keys, which give them a wider range.

Finally, the Northumbrian pipes are smaller, quieter, sweeter, and are meant to be played indoors, for dancing or festive occasions. The Scottish pipes are louder and were used for marching, going into battle, and for sending signals and conveying emotions across long distances, from hill to hill. There is an old Scottish

281

proverb which says that twelve Highlanders and a bagpipe make a rebellion.

So who invented bagpipes? Ah, said Anne, as she took me round, if only we knew. Surely the ancient Chinese, the Egyptians, or the Greeks and Romans, they must have had them, as one of them always seems to have got to everything first, from central heating to football.

Strangely enough, bagpipes as we know them — and as I went round, I found more variations of bagpipes than I had ever imagined — are mainly restricted to Europe and North Africa. In these regions, almost every little country or area had at one time its own form of bagpipes, and played its own traditional bagpipe music.

Bagpipes have been made and played in England for eight hundred years, though they were originally a bit simpler, and every region, every county, had their own types. Not all of them used bellows as the Northumbrian pipes do — this seems to have come in around the late fifteenth century. There is a piece of sculpture from 1480 Hexham Abbey that shows the pipes being blown from the mouth. The change to using bellows was probably pinched from France where bagpipes were seen as a court instrument, favoured by the king. They were very popular under Louis XIV, during a period when rustic, peasant music was all the vogue. Vivaldi and Handel composed music that imitated the sound of pipes, though not many famous composers created music directly for the bagpipes. Pipe music was not written down till the late seventeenth century, and pipers had to learn tunes from other pipers. Quite a few well-known artists, like Watteau, Brueghel and Dürer, have featured bagpipers in their works. In England, in the sixteenth century pipes became the instrument of the common people, while the toffs favoured lutes and virginals. It was considered a bit vulgar to have bellows under your arm and bagpipers generally were thought of as drunks, rogues and disreputable travelling players who would get up to anything dodgy unless you watched them carefully.

One of the earliest English descriptions of a bagpiper occurs in Chaucer's *Canterbury Tales*, which dates back to the fourteenth century, where Robin the Miller, usually depicted on his horse playing the pipes, gets drunk and frequents whores and harlots.

When Maureen had finished playing, and I politely clapped, I asked her what the tune was. It was called "Jamie Allen", named after one of the more colourful characters in the history of the Northumbrian pipes. He was born in Hepple, Northumberland, in 1734, his father a piper and his mother a gypsy. In his early days he seems to have been quite respectable, invited to play at Alnwick Castle, home of the Duke of Northumberland, who traditionally has always had his own personal piper — and still does. Jamie Allen took the king's shilling and joined the army, but ran away after he had got it. He then rejoined the same regiment — which wasn't very cunning — to get another shilling, and went on the run again, becoming a travelling piper, usually with a gang of cronies who picked pockets while the crowds listened to Jamie playing. He was convicted of

283

horse-stealing and landed up in Durham jail. His many fans, admirers of his piping, petitioned for his pardon. The Prince Regent finally agreed to a free pardon in 1810, but it arrived after Jamie had died in jail. In 1817 a book was published about his life story and legends, entitled *James Allen — the Celebrated Northumbrian Piper, Containing his Travels, Adventures and Wonderful Escapes in England, Scotland, Ireland, France, Holland, Arabia*, etc. His Arabian adventure sounds more like legend than reality.

Today, Northumbrian pipes are the last remaining regional pipes in England, still actively played, listened to and studied. In places like Worcester and Cornwall, once well known for their local pipes and pipers, the art has died out. Anne thinks one reason they have remained and flourished in Northumberland is because of the region's remoteness.

There was a great revival of interest in them that began in the late 1920s and 1930s, and local Boy Scouts and school cadet corps were encouraged to take up the instrument and use it when marching. The Northumbrian Pipers" Society, first established in 1928, has eight hundred members today, and there are probably the same number again who are piping fans — hence the avalanche of letters when the piping museum seemed doomed. There is also the Alnwick Pipers" Society, formed in 1977, and Northumbrian pipers" societies in North America and in New Zealand, so the instrument is now global.

Scottish bagpipes come in three forms — Highland, small and half-long — and are of course still more popular and better known around the world than the Northumbrian pipes — but the Northumbrian ones are all hand-made, so there. Some Scottish bagpipes, said Anne with a slight shudder, are now being mass-produced in factories, in places like Pakistan. Northumbrian pipes are individually hand-made by local craftsmen and are not cheap. Maureen said her set would cost about £1800, but you can get a set for £500. Because they are individually made, they are all slightly different, which makes it harder for Northumbrian — unlike Scottish — pipers to play in groups, though Northumbrian pipe bands do exist.

There are about six full-time makers of Northumbrian pipes, one of the best known being David Burleigh who set up in business in 1972. There are also three full-time professional players — Kathryn Tickell, Andy May and Pauline Cato, all of whom have recorded a lot of their music. Kathryn Tickell, who has recorded with Sting, is the best known and has built up a national name and reputation.

The exhibition starts off chronologically, from the time of Chaucer, though Anne has a theory that they could have started with the Romans, as she believes that Nero played the bagpipes. "Traditionally he played the fiddle but I think *tibia utricularis* suggests a kind of chanter." Shakespeare has a reference to bagpipes in *Twelfth Night*, but doesn't give details of their type.

When we came to the French display, which shows a *musette de cour* from the court of Louis XIV, she insisted that it probably, possibly, maybe, was one that

285

the Sun King played himself. There is a painting in Versailles that shows him playing a very similar set, and at the end of the chanter in the museum's set there is indeed an image of the Sun King. Most sets of bagpipes have their maker's name, so they can be identified and dated. The museum also has a set that was decorated in 1806 by Thomas Bewick, the great Northumbrian engraver, whose son Robert played the Northumbrian smallpipes.

The whole museum has been updated and improved since the flood, a new glass lift and disabled lavatories installed, thanks to the council having proper insurance — which a single-person, privately owned museum might never have been able to afford.

In the second room they now have what appears to be a large embroidered rug, showing three stained-glass windows. I carefully walked round it, but Anne said no, I had to walk on it. That was the point. As I did so, stepping on each window, bagpipe music started playing — not any particular tune, just different bits of bagpipe music, interspersed with the chime of the original Chantry bell.

The image of the window turned out to be projected from a camera above while the music was triggered by some unseen sensor — all dead clever, very high-tech and arty, and no doubt pretty expensive, but it seemed a bit out of place and unnecessary. I like museums that have solid, genuinely fascinating objects and stick to showing and explaining them, not dazzling us with technology as if they fear our attention span will last only ten seconds.

The headphones for listening to the bagpipe music as you wander round, though I didn't have them that day, would seem perfectly sufficient, plus the occasional real live piper. However, they don't appear to have paid for what they call the "Cantaria", as it was part of some project that began at Sunderland Cathedral.

The museum was also given, anonymously, £7000 to spend on some modern, brand-new bagpipes, specially commissioned, of different types, which are in cases at the top of the stairs, so you can compare the old pipes with the new. These new ones are all playable — all you have to do is ask and convince Anne that yes, you know how they work. Now that does sound like a useful hands-on addition.

Anne herself can play, but is self-taught. She felt she had to learn if she was going to be pontificating to other people on the wonders of the Northumbrian pipes. She does think they are wonderful, a sweeter sound than any other form of bagpipes. She obviously gets a bit jealous when Scottish bagpipes appear to be get more publicity and reverence. She noticed recently on the soundtrack to the film *Rob Roy* that they had not used a Scottish pipe. "On one soundtrack I could clearly hear Irish pipes being played. Oh yes, I know the difference and can recognise each one by ear. Rather sad, I suppose. Even sadder, I can often recognise the player as well." Some modern British composers, such as Peter Maxwell Davies, have written music specially for the Northumbrian pipes.

I was surprised to find just how thriving all bagpipe music has become, all over Europe. In their excellent

287

souvenir guide, they have a map of Europe and North Africa that shows all the countries where bagpipes are played today, and their local names. They get many foreign visitors to the museum and very often they turn up with their own set of pipes, from France, Germany, Italy and Holland. They like to compare them with the Northumbrian versions, and give Anne a bit of a blow.

France appears to be the most bagpipe-conscious country, with many regional types still being played, and lots of regular festivals and competitions held every year, but every country has at least one variety left. Anne is particularly fond of the *dudy* from the Czech Republic and the *gaida* from the Balkans.

The museum also has a small display in honour of the man who created the collection in the first place, William Alfred Cocks. He left it to the Society of Antiquaries on his death in 1971, on condition that the pipes were put on display for at least fifteen years. He must have known, or feared, what might happen, as it was exactly fifteen years later that they began to look for a new home for them.

Anne says little is known about him, though he died so relatively recently. He was a bachelor, a bit of a recluse, who avoided publicity. He was a keen member of the Antiquaries and when he had written a learned paper for the society, he got another member to read it out. He collected many other things, mostly of an antiquarian nature, as well as old documents, photographs and memorabilia to do with bagpipes. In 1924, according to a letter from Buckingham Palace, he made a miniature set of Northumbrian pipes, just one inch long, but perfect in all details, which were presented to Queen Mary for her doll's house.

He was a master clock-maker by profession, but Anne suspects he must have had private means to have been able to afford to buy several hundred bagpipes and related objects, many of them rare. I suggested that being a bachelor, with no family to support, he was in quite a good position to indulge himself, if he didn't otherwise spend a lot of money. I know quite a lot of collectors of modest means who have managed over the decades to build up pretty valuable collections by having the time, energy and a good eye, yet only a small purse.

The collection has been added to in the last forty or so years, with donations and the occasional purchase, and now consists of a hundred and fifty sets, with around sixty of them on show at any one time. They once bought a set at Sotheby's — the set engraved by Thomas Bewick, which was made by John Dunn, a famous pipe-maker of the late eighteenth century. They paid £3500 for it, the money coming from the Society of Antiquaries and the V&A.

Mr Cocks would no doubt be very pleased that despite a dodgy moment or two in the 1980s when the collection could have disappeared from public view, and later when it might have been ruined by floods, the museum is now one of the most thriving musical museums in all Britain and wins awards and gets rave notices. There is even a website set up by Friends of the Bagpipe Museum.

I'd like to have Friends of My Museum, whenever I get round to it. Like the Tate or the National Gallery. Wouldn't that be useful? Sort of reassuring, bestowing status and indicating that it wasn't all just a personal indulgence. It obviously helps if your museum has cultural overtones, preserving something that local people value, and you have enthusiasts for the object itself, in this case the bagpipe, which people like Maureen are more than willing to come along and demonstrate.

Anne herself would be a useful addition to any museum. Very calm and quiet, but keen and organised. I wonder if I could persuade her to be my first curator. I'm not going to do it all on my own, am I? Got books to write.

Anne, after over twenty years running the museum, is still quite young and clearly committed to the cause, but council-run museums can always come a cropper for reasons outside the museum's control, despite their fame and renown.

More changes are in the offing. There is a plan to move the museum out of council hands and into the care of a new body, which will run all the museums in Northumberland. That would bring it under museum people and perhaps keep the Northumbrian pipes piping for another few hundred years.

Around the country, there are lots of town museums where they have old instruments lying around in cabinets, mixed up with other objects. Or house museums — by which I mean an historic old house, owned by some worthy from the past, where their

290

collections of clothes, furniture, toys, books, games have been carefully preserved, amongst which you can often come across an old piano, fiddle or flute. But there aren't many devoted entirely to one old ethnic instrument. Or many museums of any sort that are three-dimensional — where you can see, touch and hear the objects, one of the purposes of which is to inspire others to listen and play. Or municipal museums that are looking after their inherited treasures so lovingly.

Right, I think that covers everything. I can't see myself ever visiting it again, but as I came away, I did feel I should give it a little clap, write 9/10 on its report, say well done, keep up the good work, chaps. Museums can make you feel good, made virtuous by their virtuousness. Now for something soppy, as we head south again.

Morpeth Chantry Bagpipe Museum
Bridge Street
Morpeth
Northumberland NE61 1PJ
Tel 01670 500717
www.morpethnet.co.uk/chantry/bpmus

CHAPTER
FIFTEEN

Teddy Bears of Witney

Witney is a small, prosperous country town in Oxfordshire, about fourteen miles west of Oxford, famous for centuries for its woollen blankets. The high street is long, broad and imposing, the sort of high street I used to consider very Southern, because of its handsome buildings, prettily coloured stone, affluent air, lots of space and flashes of greenery, as opposed to the meaner, narrower, darker high streets of the North. I suppose it counts as the Cotswolds, though I'm not sure where the Cotswolds begin and end, or if it's just a state of mind, not geography.

Naturally, I went first to look for the charity shops. All this affluence was bound to conceal some unconsidered treasures. They seemed a bit cleaner than the normal run, but disappointing, full of the usual modern tat, plastic toys, cheap clothes. Anything old — that is, earlier than the 1980s — seems to have disappeared completely from all charity shops. Flown to eBay, perhaps? I don't think I've actually bought anything in a charity shop for about three years, though I live in hope, and they are always my first points of call in any strange town.

I spotted an Oxfam bookshop, one of those dedicated ones that have become more popular in recent years, though their prices are not all that remarkable, considering they get their books for free and don't pay their staff or council tax. Real second-hand bookshops hate them of course, as they compete unfairly for the same market.

This, too, turned out to be disappointing — no old books at all, just cheap, modernish rubbish. Clean and tidy, but characterless. Nothing like the wonderfully crammed, untidy, atmospheric little treasure trove which is my local Oxfam bookshop in scruffy old Kentish Town.

Opposite the church and the green, I came upon a real secondhand bookshop, Church Green Books, which was open — surprisingly, it being a Monday. I asked for Lakeland books, as I always do, especially when I am far from Lakeland, as you can often buy first editions of Wainwright that have been lounging at the back of their shelves for decades. They did have two volumes of a 1777 guide to Westmorland and Cumberland, but I couldn't find the price. I asked the lady assistant, busy-looking but doing nothing in particular at the front desk. She couldn't see the price either. She said the boss was not here, she could ring him on his mobile but didn't want to disturb him again. Oh no, poor thing, how awful to be rung up by people wanting to give you money. But she eventually did agree to ring him. The price was £275, so she reported back, but he could drop it to £250. I said I'd think about it. Still am. But I did buy a little 1920s booklet on Coniston, price £5. So I hadn't totally wasted her time. Poking round the shop, I came across two special sections — one on bell-ringing, another on morris dancing. "It's what we are known for," said the woman, rather proudly. How wonderful, I thought, to have so many books on such esoteric subjects. Is there any subject which is not being collected by somebody? I do hope not. We are now in an age of niches. The smallest specialist magazine, shop, dealer, blogger, tweeter, twitterer, if they can somehow raise a small flag, put themselves on the map, can let their existence be known to others of a like mind out there in the big wide world.

I was in Witney looking for one particular niche — teddy bears. And there it was on the High Street, at No. 99, Teddy Bears of Witney, known to teddy bear lovers all over the world, a mecca for worshippers to come to and gaze longingly and dewy-eyed at their priceless collection of famous and historic teddy bears. I'd started at the wrong end of the High Street, so had to work back to the other end, the quieter (north) end of the town.

It's in a twee, sweet-looking, double-fronted Beatrix Potter drawing of a building. Primarily it is a shop, dating back to the seventeenth century, selling teddy bears in order to survive, but the most important and most interesting part of the premises is a museum, containing over a hundred and fifty old teddy bears, which you can look at for free, for there is no admission charge to the museum part.

294

How did they come to be here, in Witney? Something to do with blankets? Were the earliest teddies made of wool perhaps? Or is it simply because the creator, the collector of the teddy bears, happened to have been born and brought up here in Witney? Neither theory turned out to be correct.

The owner and creator is Ian Pout, a rather distinguished-looking gentleman of about sixty, a little plummy, definitely officer class, who could easily be running a high-class Chelsea antique shop, used to putting cheapskates in their place — the sort who poke around his premises for ages, ask the prices of his best bits, then spend only £5 on a cheap booklet.

He led me through the shop part, past rows and rows of simpering, ever-so-appealing teddies. There are over a thousand different ones in all in the main shop, which extends into a long back addition, unseen from the street. We went upstairs to his little office, crammed with packages, books and files. He had to clear a space before we could both sit down at the same time.

Pout, that's an unusual surname? Never come across it before. He said it was a corruption of Dupont. Some Duponts had come across from France during the Huguenot times but didn't get much further than Dover, which is why today you find most Pouts, if you find any at all, still living in Kent.

He was educated in Kent, at King's School, Canterbury, the son of an accountant who worked for BOAC. Ian left school at eighteen and went into the City to train as a stockbroker. "It seemed exhilarating and as good a way of earning a living as any. There was

295

a stockbroker in our road, who was conspicuously well-heeled. Maybe he gave me the impetus, I can't remember, but join the Stock Exchange I did and became what was known as a 'blue button', the lowest form of life allowed on the old stock-market floor. I was really just a clerk, learning the trade. I loved the buzz, but always saw it as a way of building up some money prior to doing something else I really wanted to do, on my own — my fantasy being to move to the country and open my own antique shop.

"There was a financial slump in 1973–4. I was only twenty-eight and hadn't made a lot of money but had no family commitments so decided to make the break then. I opened a small antique shop in Charlbury, not too far from here. It is an attractive village close to Woodstock and Burford, so drew quite a few tourists. I sold country furniture, nothing too specialised, and soon became a dealer's dealer. I did a brisk trade, with small profits but a high turnover, selling mainly to other dealers.

"Business went quite well. I married and by 1981, with our second child on the way, I began to think I needed a more secure income — not dependent on travelling hundreds of miles every week scouring the country for stock. I had expanded to a second shop, here in Witney, where we had a lot of space. I decided to devote some of this to selling Crabtree & Evelyn products — then not as widely available as they are now — and stylish stationery. It was a steady enough business, but little that we sold cost more than £5 and we could not sell enough to make a living on that alone.

We began to sell a few soft toys, and, with vintage toys and teddy bears also being for sale with the antiques, the beginnings of a new niche business dawned on me."

It was in 1985 that he decided to clear the stationery and toiletries, and concentrate instead on just one item — teddy bears. He could, in theory, have gone for any number of other items. Like a good many of the other museum creators and curators I had met so far, he had not been before then a passionate collector of the subject that was to dominate his life. He freely admits it was a calculated business decision: he needed to make a living. Selling teddies to collectors was an original concept, which he felt would be interesting, unusual, fun and, hopefully, profitable.

"It was a time when lots of niche shops and businesses were setting up — Tie Rack, Body Shop and many others. Selling something specific seemed to be a good way to draw people to the workaday town where I was — as long as we made the right choice of what to specialise in. I had some experience of selling teddy bears in the shop and knew that one or two such specialist shops had been established for a few years in the USA. My family and friends, not unreasonably, thought I had gone mental."

From the beginning, he saw his shop, and museum, as being aimed at adult teddy bear lovers and collectors, not at the children's toy market. He knew of the famous firm of Steiff, the world's leading manufacturer of teddy bears, and approached them with a view to stocking their replicas of classic teddy bears. As an antique dealer, he knew about buying at auctions and fairs, and from other dealers. So he set out to source as many old teddy bears as he could. His main aim was to resell them in his store, but, from the beginning, he found he couldn't part with some he really liked, so found himself keeping these for display in the shop, eventually giving over one room to create his own teddy bear museum.

I had assumed, without ever really thinking about it, that teddy bears have always been with us, since children first had cuddly toys, back in the, er, not sure which century — but surely a long time ago, possibly medieval?

Rag dolls are in fact pretty ancient, hand-made long before any were manufactured, while images of animals such as bears had appeared in children's books and had been used in toys and games, such as skittles since the early nineteenth century. But the cuddly, soft toys we know today as "teddy bears" are a relatively modern invention, scarcely more than a hundred years old.

Both the Americans and the Germans have claims to have first thought of them, but Ian prefers the German version and believes it was the Steiff company that first manufactured them, in 1902. Margarete Steiff had founded her eponymous soft toy firm in Giengen in southern Germany in 1880. Her nephew, Richard Steiff, was the company's chief designer and thought that boys should have a masculine equivalent of a girl's doll. Like a doll it should be jointed — i.e. the head, arms and legs should move. The two animals he thought would be best to model the toys on were an ape and a bear. Using drawings he had made of these animals at Stuttgart zoo when he was an art student, he made samples from mohair. His aunt, Margarete, thought that this material would be too expensive, as the company had become famous for products made of felt, which was cheaper. Richard persisted, believing that mohair would be more durable and sympathetic to the character of the animals.

He took samples of his two new toys to the Leipzig Toy Fair in February 1903. He displayed them on his stall, but failed to get any orders. He was packing them up and about to leave the hall when an American buyer, arriving late, stopped and asked him if he had any new toys. He showed him the ape and the bear. The buyer immediately said the bear was just the novelty he was looking for — and, there and then, ordered three thousand. They did so well he soon increased the order to twelve thousand.

They were made in the Steiff factory in Germany and despatched in crates to the USA. While the American Ideal Novelty and Toy Company also has a claim to have made the world's first jointed teddy bear, Ian has studied the factory records and believes the claim by Steiff in Germany is better documented.

The rival story involves the American president Theodore Roosevelt. In October 1902 he had gone south to settle a border dispute between two states, Mississippi and Louisiana. After various political meetings, his hosts took him out hunting, as they knew Roosevelt was a keen game-hunter. They promised him bears, but after several days' hunting they found none, except a baby cub, which they captured and tied to a post. They invited the president to take a pop at him. The story goes that President Roosevelt refused, saying he could never look his sons in the eye if he shot a tethered bear cub. This incident made all the American papers next day and Clifford Berryman, an illustrator for the *Washington Post*, drew a cartoon of Roosevelt refusing to shoot the cub, with the caption "Drawing the Line in Mississippi", thus bringing the two stories together with one headline, as all good cartoonists try to do. Very smart.

In New York, Morris Michtom, the owner of a Brooklyn shop selling novelties and candies, decided to get his wife to do some quick needlework and create a soft toy based on the cartoon bear. She did so and he put it in his shop window, calling it "Teddy's Bear", Theodore Roosevelt being universally known as "Teddy". He wrote to the president, asking permission to use his name, and the president is reputed to have written back saying that it was fine, that he had no objection but "did not know what good his name would do in the toy bear cub business". This actual letter has been lost, although Ian believes it did exist.

The New York shop owner may therefore have inspired the name "teddy bear" for that particular sort of toy bear. A year later he started manufacturing them, setting up the Ideal Novelty and Toy Company.

Ian, however, is convinced that the Steiff company was the first to produce them — if only by a few months. Either way, it seems that teddy bears were created at around the same time and independently on each side of the Atlantic. The success of the teddy bear was immediate, with the craze particularly strong in the USA. Society women carried them around, lovers gave them to each other on Valentine's Day, popular songs were written about them, and hundreds of different manufacturers in the USA, Germany and, later, England, started making them.

The Steiff company still makes a wide range of teddy bears and other soft toys, for both collectors and children. Steiff teddy bears are still the most coveted, particularly by collectors of old bears. So when he began his museum, Ian sought to collect the rarest Steiffs he could afford.

In 1989 he received a postcard from Christie's in South Kensington. This showed a photograph of a red teddy bear in a Cossack outfit on the front and, on the back, a teasing riddle, which read "When is a red teddy bear white?" The answer, written upside down, was "When it belonged to a Russian princess". This drew his attention to an upcoming sale of vintage dolls, containing this old Steiff teddy bear called Alfonzo. When the catalogue arrived a few weeks later Ian was pleased to see that the cover featured a seventeenth-century doll and not the red bear he coveted. Inside, a brief description said the bear dated from between 1906 and 1909 and had once belonged to a Russian princess, given to her by her father, the Grand Duke of Russia. It was the first red Steiff bear ever seen at auction and his Cossack costume added to his aura.

"I could see that he was in what we called loved condition — i.e. worn — but I was immediately smitten by him. He had it all — rarity, provenance and an extraordinary magnetism. I just had to have him! He would be the ideal star for our museum and I felt his association with imperial Russia would be something teddy bear collectors around the world would want to share."

The estimate was £2000–3000. Ian set off by car early on the morning of the sale on 18 May 1989. Over breakfast in a hotel near the South Kensington saleroom he opened that morning's *Independent* newspaper — to find the teddy bear looking at him. He subsequently discovered Alfonzo had also been featured on breakfast TV that day. By the time he got to Christie's to have his first look at the teddy in the fur, the estimate had jumped to £6000. He had hoped that only a few teddy bear collectors would attend the sale, as there were only fifteen teddy bears (compared with over a hundred dolls) in it. The bears were not due to be auctioned until the afternoon, so Ian went off to the West End. "I was so excited and preoccupied by thoughts of Alfonzo that I returned to find I had left all my shopping in the taxi!"

There were in fact only fifteen or so people in the room when the teddy bears came up, but bidding quickly jumped to £6000. After that, there seemed to be just one other bidder, whom Ian didn't recognise. They fought it out, with Ian eventually winning, paying £12,100 to secure Alfonzo. This broke the world record for a teddy bear, the previous record being £8800.

His purchase received worldwide press attention, but with it came rumours that he might have been done, that the teddy bear was a fraud. Christie's had not revealed who had sold the bear. So Ian wrote a letter to the vendor, c/o Christie's, asking them to forward it. For months he heard nothing.

"The silence was puzzling but, fortunately, within a week of the sale, I received a visit from Jorg Junginger, the head of Steiff's design department. He knew about the sale but had never seen Alfonzo and could find no record of him in their archives. He had heard the rumours as well, but the moment he saw Alfonzo, he confirmed that he was undoubtedly a Steiff from around 1908. He even found a thread in his left ear, a tiny remnant of a cotton label, which would once have been attached under the button in his left ear. Since 1904 all Steiff teddy bears have had this mark. So I was happily reassured.

"Then out of the blue, six months after I had written my letter, I got a reply from the USA from a Mrs Nancy Leeds Wynkoop. She confirmed that it was she who had sold Alfonzo, and that he had belonged to her mother, the original owner, Princess Xenia. Her father, the Grand Duke of Russia, a first cousin of the tsar, had given him to her in 1908 when she was five years old. She christened him Alfonzo and it was her English nanny, Miss Ball, who made his Cossack costume, turning him into a truly Russian teddy bear. Princess Xenia loved Alfonzo and took him everywhere with her. In 1914 he accompanied her for a holiday in London, staying in Buckingham Palace with her mother, who was a cousin of King George V. War broke out during their stay and so they were unable to get back to Russia till it was over.

"Then the Russian Revolution came and the Romanov family were executed. Her father was one of those who were killed. She eventually ended up in exile in the USA, still with Alfonzo. He was the only present she always kept with her until her death, as he had been given to her by her beloved father.

"Her daughter, Mrs Nancy Wynkoop, had inherited him, but in 1988 decided to sell him. She took Alfonzo to Christie's in New York to be valued. They suggested that he should be sold in their London saleroom, as this was where their specialist toy sales were held and, with a teddy bear expert there, he would fetch a better price."

As for why he is red, no one is quite sure of the reason, although red was a fashionable colour in Russian society at that time. Ian thinks only a limited number were made, perhaps as samples, and that the duke may have bought him from Harrods in London on one of his visits.

"We think of red as the colour of the Russian Revolution, but I was in St Petersburg recently and learned that red has always been a distinctive and much-loved colour in Russia, long before the revolution. It signifies beauty."

After Alfonzo was purchased, Ian took him on his own world tour, visiting the USA, Japan, Monaco, Germany and other countries, starring at teddy bear conventions and gatherings. Mostly he now lives at home in Witney, safely inside a bulletproof glass case above the reception desk. Getting him through customs and security these days is much harder than it used to be.

Ian admits his business has benefited greatly from Alfonzo, in attracting customers and collectors, which was part of the object. He's also made quite a bit of money on the back of Alfonzo. Steiff in Germany agreed to manufacture five thousand exact models of Alfonzo, which Ian sold for £150 each. All of them were sold by 1993. Now the replicas are collector's items in themselves, as no more will be made, though he has for sale replicas of other well-known teddy bears, by Steiff and other manufacturers. Ian has gone on since to pay other big prices to secure choice teddies for his museum. In 1990 he sent his wife Jane along to a Phillips sale to bid for a black Steiff bear, deciding that if he was seen to be there, the price might go up. She bought Othello for £8800.

The most he has paid so far is £55,000 in 1995 for Aloysius, the teddy that appeared in the Granada TV adaptation of *Brideshead Revisted*. After the series, which took twenty-one months to film, had finished, the producer, Derek Granger, said that Aloysius had been an exemplary actor. "He was never late, never bumped into other actors and was never drunk. He continued to work while he was quite ill. He once bled a little straw and had to be rushed for treatment. Not the first time that an actor has come apart at the seams . . ."

Aloysius was a very old American bear which had been loaned to Granada by Peter Bull, the actor and famous collector of teddy bears. It had been returned to him after the filming. On Peter Bull's death, his partner sold Aloysius to an American couple, the Volpps, who were at the time the world's greatest private collectors of teddy bears. In 1995 they were downsizing and offered it first to Ian. "I did have to pay a lot for him, considering he had seen better days, and suffered from a lot of loving, but I wanted Aloysius to come back to England, where he had earned his fame. I was willing to pay what they wanted."

In 1994, the world record was smashed when a Japanese businessman paid £110,000 at Christie's for a teddy bear. Like Ian, the businessman was planning to make this bear the centrepiece of his soon-to-be-opened teddy bear museum in Japan. This particular bear had a good story, as it had been owned by Colonel Bob Henderson, who as an officer in the Royal Scots had carried his bear into battle in his uniform pocket. Many photographs exist showing him at the front with the bear. Colonel Bob, who died in 1990, went on to become a leading light in teddy bear collecting and did a lot of work for charity. His daughter had once dressed the bear in girl's clothes, and teddy boy became teddy girl.

The all-time record price for a teddy bear has since been broken yet again. It currently stands at £135,000, for a teddy sold in a Christie's charity auction of twenty one-off, customised teddies made by leading design firms and couture houses. The record breaker had been customised by Louis Vuitton and was bought by the owner of a Korean museum.

"I've not seen his museum but know that it has a fine collection of modern bears. The price was a result of a lot of publicity plus the important charity element. I don't expect another teddy bear to reach that price again in the near future."

While we were talking, Jan, one of his five staff, had been popping into his office from time to time to say that someone had arrived with a teddy for him to see. Most times he gave a sigh, for, in his experience, most people imagine their bears to be older and worth more than they usually are.

He went down on one occasion to see a lady who had arrived with two teddies. "I don't really want them," he said on his return, "but I've offered her £50. They're not interesting enough for the museum, but I might get £75 for them from a collector, if I'm lucky, but they are not worth more. She's turned me down. She says she will only accept £75. So that's it. She's gone."

He picked up a box from the floor, which had arrived by post that morning, and took out a small bear wearing a home-made knitted black woollen jacket and trousers. "It's from a lady in Scotland. I told her just to send a photo but she's sent the actual teddy, which is very trusting of her. It's early German, although not by a recognisable maker. I love him and will offer her £150, which is a fair offer, which I hope she will happily accept. The most I have paid to someone just arriving off the street, or contacting me out of the blue, has been £5000.

"It's age, combined with charm, a certain look in their eyes, that can do it for me, but often what attracts me most is their story. Obviously, if you have a provenance like those of Alfonzo or Aloysius, that is extra special, but I am touched by ordinary people's stories. The other day a lady donated one to the museum, asking me to take care of it. She had had it throughout the whole of the war and it kept up her spirits in dark times. She didn't really want to part with it but she was now very old and had no one to leave it to. It wasn't a very attractive or valuable bear, but my feelings towards it changed when I heard her story."

We then went down to look at the museum. It's in a small side room, to the left as you enter the shop, with the exhibits in glass cases, well presented, clearly and informatively labelled. I duly admired Aloysius and also Theodore, which had been Peter Bull's personal teddy bear, a very small one, which he carried everywhere with him in his pocket, for which Ian had paid £14,300.

One of the special displays is of Winnie-the-Pooh memorabilia, which he collected at various auctions. Of the many literary teddy bears, Winnie-the-Pooh, who featured in A A Milne's stories, first published in 1926, is almost certainly the most famous. Milne wrote the stories for his son Christopher Robin, to whom he had given a bear on his first birthday. It had been bought at Harrods and was made by the English firm of Farnell. This was known as Edward Bear, as they decided to give it its Sunday-best name instead of run-of-the-mill Teddy (in England, Edwards have always been shortened to Teddy, but in the USA, Roosevelt got his nickname from a contraction of Theodore), but became known as Winnie-the-Pooh. Christopher Milne bought other soft toys at later birthdays till they had a whole family of animals — including Piglet, Eeyore and Tigger.

The displays have some original 1920s Farnell teddies of the appropriate type, but not Christopher Robin's actual teddy, the one that was the original Winnie-the-Pooh. That is today in the New York City Library. But the display includes the original "Hunny" pot, made by Christopher himself and labelled "Pooh Bear", and a letter from Christopher Robin aged six. There are other letters and telegrams from family and friends, in one of which Piglet is spelled Biglet, which appears to have been an alternative name used in the family.

There is also a letter and drawing by Ernest Shepard, the artist who drew the original illustrations. In this letter, written in 1971, he explains that he based Winnie-the-Pooh on his own son's teddy bear, who was known as Growler. "When the Second World War came, my son and his wife decided that they should go to Canada for safety. There in Montreal poor Growler was savaged by a dog and died."

Reading the labels as I went round the museum, and the stories attached, it is remarkable how loyal people were to their teddies throughout the whole of their lives. During the First World War it was quite common for ordinary soldiers, not just sensitive officers, to take little teddy bears with them into the trenches — special

309

little souvenir teddies, manufactured for this purpose, probably given to them as good-luck tokens, which they carried in their pockets. On their deaths, the teddies were returned to their families and kept as family memorabilia.

In 1912, after the sinking of the *Titanic*, Steiff created a limited run of 494 black bears to commemorate the tragedy. Sounds a pretty cynical bit of merchandising, but I suppose no worse than many touching souvenirs that have since been produced on tragic occasions. Today they are greatly prized and rarely appear on the market. Ian has only one.

According to Ian, showing me a copy of an old children's story published many years ago in Canada, the term "punk", which became popular in the 1970s for a certain style of pop star, and haircut, came from this book. Its hero is called Punkinhead Bear — and on the cover his hair does stick up in that spiky way favoured by Johnny Rotten. That's Ian's story anyway. However, looking up the word "punk" I learned that it was used in the sixteenthth century for a harlot, later it referred to a gay boy, then in the 1900s it was used in North America for a worthless youth. I suppose though that the sticky-out hair element could well have come from that Canadian children's book about a punky-looking teddy bear.

At one time, in the 1920s, novelty teddy bears were very popular, especially those made by a firm called Schuco in Germany. They included bears that contained vanity sets or scent bottles, or teddies holding violins that played when you wound them up,

310

or driving cars. These are now greatly desired by arctophiles, as teddy bear collectors are called (taken from the Greek for "lover of bears").

At one time, there were several notable teddy bear collectors in Britain, such as Gyles Brandreth, who with his wife ran a teddy bear museum in Stratford-upon-Avon, but that is now closed, with Ian having bought some of the choicer items.

In recent years, Peter Bull was perhaps the collector best known to the general public. He was born in 1912, son of Sir William Bull, MP, educated at Winchester, and became a successful and much-loved character actor on stage and in films. He died of a heart attack in 1984. In the world of teddy bears, no one has quite taken his place. Ian failed to think of any celeb collectors today; celebs of course always help to put any unusual collecting subject on the map.

"Peter Bull was the first person in England to write seriously about teddy bears. His books were bestsellers and he acquired a huge following. Now that he and Colonel Bob, another huge character, have gone, we haven't got anyone at the moment in England whom the general public associates with teddy bears. A shame, but maybe one will come along soon."

Ian has no idea how many collectors there are in Britain or in the world at large, but he says these days they are pretty equally divided between men and women. This surprised me. Until about thirty years ago, most collectors were women. He thinks the subsequent rise in prices, with world records being smashed at auctions, by people like himself, brought in many men who bought with a view to investment. In Britain alone, Ian reckons there are now more than fifty dealers who sell old teddies. Prices have remained very high for top quality, but second-eleven examples have gone down in value.

Although some manufacturers and shops have clubs, there is no generic teddy bear society, which I found surprising, as most collectors, however esoteric their passion, usually manage to join together in a club, have meetings, issue a magazine, elect officials — before they all fall out. However, there are lots of teddy bear conventions and exhibitions held at regular intervals around the world.

Each year, Ian has a big teddy bear event in Witney, hiring a local hall, as his museum and shop could not cope with the crowds. This normally attracts around four hundred teddy bear collectors. In 2008, to celebrate the hundredth birthday of Alfonzo, over five hundred fans turned up for the two days of celebrations

His museum and shop, so he says, is still primarily a business, not simply a labour of love or a self-imposed duty, as it is with many people who have created their own museums. In a way his interest is academic rather than a mad obsession. Ian is highly knowledgeable, but yet he is still devoted to his teddies. So what will happen to them in the future?

His three children, now all grown up, are building careers in other fields. "Naturally I would like it all to stay together, as a going concern, with the museum kept open and available to anyone who wants to visit. Teddy bears have an uncanny ability to make people smile. They have had a place in the childhoods of millions of people all over the world for over a hundred years. But I don't know what will happen to my collection. At the moment though, I have no intention of retiring. There is one famous bear I would still love to own, but which one is something I prefer to keep to myself."

I tried to guess, suggesting the original Teddy's Bear, the one the New York shopkeeper made in honour of Teddy Roosevelt and stuck in his window? Too late, he said. That no longer exists although a replica is now in the Smithsonian Institution in Washington, which shows how seriously some countries do take their teddy bear history.

In that case, what about some of our famous British bears, such as Rupert Bear? I used to read about him in the *Daily Express* when I was a boy and his stories go back to the 1920s. Or what about Paddington Bear, or Sooty? Originals of them presumably exist? Perhaps something do with the "Teddy Bears" Picnic', the song made famous in the 1930s by the Henry Hall Orchestra?

Ian refused to be drawn. But I do hope he eventually acquires it, whichever elusive teddy bear it is he is so keen to get his hands on one day, and that his museum continues to grow and expand.

There are lots of museums that contain toys and games, dolls and teddies, showing us how they are part of our heritage, of our life and cultural history, but very few that restrict themselves just to one particular toy. Or is it a doll. I still wasn't sure.

Anyway, I learned a great deal I didn't know about teddies — but perhaps not much about museums. It is an unusual situation, with a museum as part of a shop, and each clearly helps the other, but it is not the sort of thing I would envisage running. My wife would go bonkers if I came home and said I was opening a shop as well as a museum.

But I came away inspired to keep an eye out for old teddies. Trouble is, I am already looking out for old wirelesses, ancient pencil sets, baked bean advertisements, lawnmowers, Laurel and Hardy memorabilia, and even Northumbrian bagpipes. Over and above all the stuff I'd been collecting before I started on my travels. I'm not sure how I will cope. Unless of course I do open my own museum . . .

Teddy Bears of Witney
99 High Street
Witney
Oxfordshire OX28 6HY
Tel 01993 706616
www.teddybears.co.uk

CHAPTER
SIXTEEN

The Kelvedon Hatch Secret Nuclear Bunker, Essex

I was beginning to wonder if I had made a mistake, or misunderstood the words, written them down wrongly. Perhaps it was bunker as in golf — and I hate golf, wouldn't want to visit a museum devoted to golf. Or should it be banker, not bunker. I'd done a money museum, so didn't want another museum on a similar topic. I do have rules.

The whole idea of a secret bunker did sound bizarre and unlikely, especially in such an ordinary, nondescript, featureless stretch of rural landscape deep in the heart of Essex, the rolling, changeless countryside bit, not the suburban chunks where the chavs are supposed to live.

I'd got out at the end of the line, at Epping station, and then went to look for a taxi. I asked the driver how much to the secret bunker and he said £20, which sounded reasonable enough, as on the map it looked about ten miles away but didn't seem to be near anywhere and I knew I would never find it on my own.

Anyway, I hate driving. Done more than enough of it this last year.

As we left Epping, the driver told me that Rod Stewart lived not far away, and also Aaron Lennon, the footballer, and I said how fascinating. Then once out in the country he insisted on stopping at a place called Greensted outside what he said was the oldest wooden church in England. "And I suppose that means it must be the oldest in the world," he added as an afterthought. Possibly so, I replied. He asked if I'd like to go in, look at the spyholes in the wooden tower where the lepers were forced to sit and watch services. He'd wait for me. No extra charge. I said how kind, but really, I had to get on, I'd only come for one thing, the secret bunker. "It is thirteenth-century," he said. Another time, I said.

Fortunately, he did know where he was going, as he'd once taken a German film crew there. We wound in and out, through country lanes, quiet villages. Then on to a mainish-looking road between Chipping Ongar and Brentwood, near a place called Kelvedon Hatch, where a signpost with a red arrow informed the world "Secret Nuclear Bunker"!

Obviously it's not secret any more, or the arrow would not have been there, but I would still not have found it without the helpful driver.

We turned off the road, down a little lane, worked our way round several fields where stuff was growing, wheat by the look of it, and came to — well, nowhere in particular. The driver let me out and said walk through that wood.

I followed various signs, convinced I was lost, as there was no one else around, till I could see what looked like a 1950s bungalow. I went inside and came to an iron grille and behind it a counter and various notices and warnings, such as "Decontamination Unit — Dirty Area".

Ahead of me stretched a long, menacing tunnel, for at least a hundred and twenty yards, then it seemed to bend and disappear. Was this the entrance? Or a trap? Or was I in totally the wrong place? I walked gingerly along it till I came to a steel-caged door, then came back to what I had taken to be the entrance. There was still no sign of life. Had the bomb gone off and humanity done a runner?

From my huge experience of museums, the first thing you always come to is someone taking money. The second thing is the museum shop, which is also there to take your money, usually manned by the same person. I always think it's a bit of a liberty, trying to sell you souvenirs of your visit when you haven't done any bleedin' visiting yet. The exit to most museums is also where you came in, so they aim to catch you twice. This bunker was proving a right puzzler. Nothing seemed to be obvious.

There was a sort of counter and grille at the entrance, so perhaps there were people crouching, watching me on hidden monitors. Yet it felt abandoned, with dusty files and tatty notices and back along the tunnel I could see a couple of ancient 1950s bikes parked against the wall.

I then realised that behind the counter were neat rows of what looked like large red mobile phones. There was an instruction I had missed, saying please take one as you enter and make sure to leave it behind when you go. These were described as "wands", these red things. You had to hold one against your ear and then press various buttons. It turned out to be a most ingenious audio system. As I progressed down the tunnel, I pressed appropriate buttons and could then hear a very informative and amusing commentary explaining everything as I went along.

All the same, it did still feel very eerie and confusing as I made my way down the long tunnel. I could hear echoes, bleeps and far-off messages, instructions and warnings in the distance, round corners and in rooms ahead. I wasn't frightened, as the commentator's voice was comforting, but it was still very spooky. I felt displaced and vulnerable, yet presumably the point of a bunker is to make you safe.

I went round bends and eventually came to another set of massive blast gates. Once through them, I appeared to have come to the heart of the bunker — a three-storey underground building, with staircases rising up above my head. I'd expected, having come in on the flat, that I would have to go down, into the bunker. But it was all above my head. The tunnel had already taken me a hundred feet below the earth, for the bunker had been cunningly built into a hill.

This long tunnel, so the commentary informed me, served to keep the bunker secret and to reduce the effects of any nuclear blast. It would also have been a good place to pick off any locals daring or stupid enough to have ventured inside. They would have been slaughtered once they got into the tunnel, as the bunker was not for the likes of them. It was for the likes of our prime minister and cabinet members, military and civil defence leaders, who would take refuge inside at the first warning of a nuclear attack. Or so they hoped. Bolt-holes for the privileged, so the cynical would assert, or a secret centre from whence our leaders would continue to run the country, according to the official line.

When fully operational, this particular bunker would have accommodated six hundred fortunate people, the great and the good, along with experts and boffins and support staff. As it's just twenty-five miles from central London as the crow flies, and the nearest of its size and amenities to Downing Street and Whitehall, it would have probably been the chosen bunker for our dear leader in the event of a nuclear explosion.

A nuclear bomb never did land on Britain — at least not up to the time of writing — but for almost four decades there was a real threat, a bomb seemed imminent. Any responsible government had to take measures, and so this monster bunker, about the biggest ever built in Britain, was kept on full alert for nearly forty years — and of course in total secrecy.

It was all to do with the Cold War of the early fifties. It came after the real war, against the Germans, and the strong possibility that our new enemies, the Russians, would send over a nuclear bomb. A nuclear bomb had been exploded at Hiroshima in 1945 by the Americans.

Then in 1952 they exploded a hydrogen bomb in the Pacific — just testing, just flexing their muscles. Stalin had ordered his top scientists to catch up and they had their own hydrogen bomb by 1953. The danger, everyone agreed, on both sides, was real and deadly.

In 1952, when this monster bunker was built, there were hundreds, if not thousands, of smaller versions going up, or should I say down, all over Britain. Every county council had one, every local borough, even parish councils, even if it was just one large room a few feet under the earth where the local bigwigs would retreat once the early-warning sirens had sounded. An organisation called the Royal Observer Corps had their own chain of small, three-person bunkers in which they would hunker down with emergency supplies and send secret signals to their HQ and the other ROC bunkers. In all, there were probably about twenty thousand people — councillors, builders, boffins, ROC members — who knew where at least one bunker was, so they were never exactly dead secret.

It's hard to believe that the local population here in rural Essex, or in downtown Chipping Ongar, did not suspect something was up. Over forty thousand tons of concrete were poured into the hole inside this hill, lorries going back and forth twenty-four hours a day for seven months. Tanks containing twenty-four thousand gallons of water were stored. Some thirty-five thousand square feet of living and working space was created underground, with forty-odd rooms in the three-storey building. Surely to goodness there were people who said cor blimey, stone the crows, somefink going on

320

here, or do I need my eyes testing. The official explanation, that it was a water reservoir, appears to have been accepted.

For the first few years the bunker was run by the Air Ministry as part of their early-warning systems, then the Home Office took it over directly and it became in effect the government bunker. I followed, as instructed, the directions on my wand, going into all the rooms, down endless corridors, and then upstairs and into more rooms, all of them equipped with government notices, desks, tables, files, documents, typewriters, radios, teleprinters, Geiger counters. Now and again I did a double-take, seeing secretaries sitting at their desks, waiting silently for instructions, in their 1950s frocks and hairdos. Blimey, not doing much work, I thought, till I realised they were shop-window mannequins.

Communications were vital, as it was from here that the government would be in touch with all the other bunkers, big and small, all over the country, and also with the public at large, broadcasting to the nation the final warnings and instructions when the bomb was about to fall. The bunker had its own enormous telephone exchange, a large radio room and a huge plotting room, the sort you see in war films, with a massive map on the floor, counters being moved around, incidents and troops plotted, with the top brass, eyes narrowed, looking grim but brave, watching from a balcony or barking orders.

The bunker even has its own radio studio, fully equipped, from where the prime minister of the day would have broadcast to the nation. He — or it could have been she, as Mrs Thatcher was in power while the bunker was still in operation — would doubtless have told us to keep calm and carry on. It is in fact a real BBC studio, equipped as it was at the time, and through a glass panel, sitting at a desk with headphones on, broadcasting away at the microphone, I could clearly see Mrs Thatcher. Only a mock-up, obviously, but pretty scary all the same.

Once the final warning had been broadcast to the nation, which they hoped would be three days before an actual attack, a government booklet called *Protect and Survive* would have been issued to every household, telling us to turn off the water, gas and electricity, fill the bath with water, ensure there was enough tinned food to last fourteen days, take down the net curtains (in case of fire), paint the inside of the windows (to reflect away heat flashes), and make sure you had candles, toilet paper, notebooks, pencils and a calendar, then finally take cover under the kitchen table or in a cellar or wherever the head of the household had created a safe place. Where of course you would have instantly died. Well, the vast majority would have done. It was estimated that only three to four million out of the fifty million of us would have survived the initial blast, and most of those would then have died a slower, lingering death, perhaps taking to the streets in wild hordes, searching for food and water, no doubt furious that our leaders were safely inside their hidden bunkers, scoffing dried food and listening to the BBC.

I think I managed to go into most of the forty or so rooms, but I lost count. It was easily the biggest museum I had visited so far, and with easily the most objects, even though most of them were government documents, files and papers. But there are also several thousand bits of technical equipment, big and small, the largest being two complete sewage systems. They had to have two of everything, just in case one packed up. No chance of popping out to B&Q — OK, it hadn't been invented then — or to your local hardware store to get another washer, not after the bomb had gone off. The idea was that the six hundred people inside would be able to survive for up to three months, and be totally self-reliant.

One of the many weird things about living underground, so I discovered as I wandered around, is that there is no need for heating. Once you get a hundred feet or so below ground, it remains at the same temperature, around 60°F, all the year round. This is not because of their ten-feet-thick concrete walls, or the iron doors and steel grates, but because the earth's natural body heat stays constant. It means in a hot summer you come inside and it feels nice and cool, while in a freezing winter it feels warm.

However, this was dependent on the bunker being virtually empty. Once you fill it with people, the temperature soars, the air gets a bit fetid, not to say pongy, so to offset this they had their own an air-conditioning system. Energy was provided by diesel oil, thousands of gallons of it, stored underground, which would run generators to supply electricity. There

323

was also a fully equipped sickbay and operating theatre, with cardboard coffins lined up, ready for any casualties.

I went into the room where the prime minister would have stayed. Unlike all the other rooms, it had a carpet — just to show his status — as opposed to polished concrete or lino. Lying in a bed with a grey blanket over him was John Major. I got quite a shock. He had an inane smile on his face, as I suppose you would, finding yourself a hundred feet underground. He was the last possible PM who could have used the bunker, before it was decommissioned — and he did in fact make a secret visit there, as did Mrs Thatcher.

Beside Mr Major, on the bedside table, just to give it the authentic period touch, was a copy of the *Daily Mirror*, which had a photo of him on the front and the headline "Hanging On". I got as near as I could, just to check it was a genuine copy of the *Mirror*, as I am a collector of old newspapers, and I saw it was dated 10 April 1992. The headline referred to the fact that Major had won the general election, but with a reduced majority. I then noticed the byline on the story — the *Mirror*'s then political editor, Alastair Campbell. I made a note to tell him next time I meet him out walking on Hampstead Heath.

As I made my way to the canteen, following the signs, I could hear regular announcements coming over the tannoy, giving what sounded like genuine messages: "Squadron Leader Parrish please attend the ROC room", or "PBX calling Flying Officer McPhail". Then some really scary ones: "Severe fallout reported over

324

Chipping Ongar", and "Five megaton bomb dropped over North London". They were accompanied by lots of crackly peep-peep-peeps, mysterious bleeps, and were all spoken in a period accent that sounded genuine to me, though I did think one of the voices sounded exactly like Peter Donaldson, the veteran BBC announcer, whom I used to meet in the days when I presented a BBC Radio 4 programme. I didn't know he was that old, or had been doing secret government work.

It did turn out to be the Mr Donaldson, but he had recorded the messages only recently, as a favour to Michael Parrish, the owner of the secret bunker. The reference to a Squadron Leader Parrish is one of his little jokes.

I met Michael Parrish in the canteen, an avuncular-looking gentleman in his sixties. He must be worth a bob or two as he farms two and a half thousand acres and lives in an ancient manor house on a site mentioned in the Domesday Book, with a lake created by Capability Brown. That day, however, while we were talking, he suddenly rushed off into the kitchen where he donned an apron and proceeded to get the lunch ready. The cook had not come, but Michael has always worked on the principle that if you want something done quickly, do it yourself.

The Parrish family had been farming in Essex for at least five generations, growing wheat, rape and other stuff, when one day in 1952 a government official approached Michael's father and said they would like to buy twenty-five acres of his land. It was clear that if

325

he didn't agree, a compulsory purchase order would be put in place, so he sold the twenty-five acres for the then market price of £100 an acre. (Today, the average price in that part of Essex is between £4000 and £5000 per acre.)

When work started, digging into the hill, moving thousands of tons of soil, Michael says that of course local people could not help noticing, or being aware of the fleet of buses bringing in RAF personnel all day and night. "But we just accepted it. You have to remember that the war had not long finished, rationing was still going on, it was normal to see servicemen in uniform all over the place, strange constructions going up and government buildings with armed guards. No one questioned it.

"Today of course there would have been action groups demanding an explanation, holding protest meetings, wanting assurance there would be no pollution, the environment would be protected, bird-life saved. In 1952 we were all pretty docile, after a long, hard war. My grandfather had served in both wars and accepted what our government said.

"But my father, he was more inquisitive. He arranged with one of our farmhands who was doing some ploughing to send him a signal when the armed guards were on the other side of the hill. There were always one or two, guarding the outer compound around the bunker. When the guards" backs were turned, my father ran up the hill and looked down into this massive hole — and could see hundreds of ant-like figures scurrying round, and lots of stairs and rooms. It

326

clearly wasn't a reservoir, but all the same, he wasn't bothered.

"As a schoolboy I would sometimes trespass on the site, just to see what was happening. Often an RAF guard would catch me and then call the police. Not exactly terrifying, as the police consisted of the village bobby who had known me all my life. 'Hello, Michael,' he would say, then he would have to go through the farce of asking me to produce documents proving my identity, then he would let me off with a caution, telling me not to trespass again."

The guards, who worked in shifts round the clock, were based in the bungalow at the entrance to the bunker, which, though it looks fragile and flimsy from the outside, like a post-war prefab, was in fact bulletproof, with massive walls and steel ceilings. Officials and workers came and went all the time, going into the bunker to test equipment, check and repair, keeping everything in full working order, decade after decade. It was never fully occupied, but there were regular exercises, lasting up to two weeks, when sixty or a hundred people would lock themselves inside and live as if the bomb had gone off, broadcasting away, sending signals to other secret bunkers, which were also on manoeuvres. Sometimes there would be a mock attack on the bunker by the Territorial Army.

"We also knew when a big exercise was going on. It wasn't just all the activity, we could smell them. Even with just sixty people living underground for three weeks, the pong would build up. When you passed the air vents, it would smell like rotten cabbage."

The original cost in 1952 had been about £1.5 million. In the sixties another £10 million was spent to make it suitable for the government team. In 1990 another £19 million had been earmarked for repairs and improvement, including any extra works. Even just keeping it empty but ready and waiting was costing £3 million a year.

In 1992, the government finally decided it was all a nonsense, though naturally those words were not used. The Soviet Union had collapsed, the threat of nuclear attack from that source had therefore ceased, and it was announced they were decommissioning the Kelvedon Hatch bunker, and all the others.

Under the original agreement when the initial purchase of the twenty-five acres had been made, they had to offer the land back to the Parrish family, still farming away, at the market price. They bought it, but all the structures underneath were not included. That was being put out to tender — a secret tender.

"We were determined, as the family farming all the land, that we could not let it go to someone else, who would perhaps allow the public in to trample over our fields and paths. We had to control it."

They bid as much for the bunker as they thought it would go for. He says now he can't remember how much they had to pay, but it was a lot, for the time. They later heard that other bidders had included people who wanted to use it as a warehouse, for electronic testing, to turn into a pistol range and, perhaps scariest of all, at least three religious organisations who were interested in using it for their own purposes as a retreat. "We honestly didn't know what we were going to do with it when we first bought it, but there was such a great deal of media interest and public attention that we decided to open it up for a weekend, let people visit. Loads and loads came to it. We did it again another weekend and thought, this is great, why don't we charge people for conducted tours."

So that was what they did, with Michael blithely taking round groups of twenty at a time, giving them a personal tour and commentary, though at the time he knew very little about the purpose or contents of the bunker. Almost immediately, being only a simple farmer, as he still likes to call himself, he fell foul of every possible health and safety law, building control, fire regulations. The endless bureaucracy almost made him wish he had never started, but he was determined to succeed, despite having to close for six months while awaiting the results of various applications.

He had one long row with the council, who would not let them use the existing country lane and made them form a new, private, mile-long road to the bunker, built at their own expense. The biggest and most expensive alteration they had to make was when the fire brigade ordered them to install a new exit, for safety reasons in the event of an emergency. They therefore had to knock through the ten-feet-thick concrete walls. It took eleven weeks, using diamond cutters, just to create a hole.

They got their initial planning consents in stages, six months at a time, and it was seven years before they

329

had all the full planning agreements, but from 1994 they began opening to the public.

Michael quickly tired of the idea of guided tours, as he personally found it exhausting, while still trying to run the farm and wrestle with all the planning problems, so to save money and labour he hit on the idea of letting the public enter on their own, without any charge — until they reached the end. There would be no tickets, entry barriers or human contact. "We farmers are very practical people. When I worked out that we needed to pay someone £60 a day to sit at the entrance to the tunnel and sell tickets, I realised it was a waste of money."

It does of course, he now realises, create a perfect atmosphere of mystery and suspense, as it does feel as if you are really entering a secret bunker. In the early days they provided little tape machines and earpieces, but they were not very efficient or handy. Then around ten years ago, when he heard the Millennium Dome was going bust, and selling off their state-of-the-art technology, he bought three hundred of their wands, the very latest in audio guidance, which is what they use today.

But, ah ha, the bunker is not exactly free. At the very end of the tour, which on average takes between two and four hours, you hand in your wand at the canteen and are then encouraged to put £6.50 per adult, or £4.50 for children, into an honesty box. It just lies there on a little table, a scruffy wooden box, unsupervised, totally dependent on people being honest and coughing up.

As you go round, there is another little honesty box in which you are supposed to put £2 if you want to take photographs. In the box I noticed there were three £1 coins, with a little handwritten scrawl saying this will be your change if you pay with a £5 note. The day I was there a party of Americans were busy taking photos of the honesty box — unable to believe such a system could work. Surely it gets abused?

"In the early years we did get a few Essex wide-boys who heard about the open honesty box, and they did come in and nick quite a bit, but that doesn't seem to happen any more. We don't know exactly what percentage of people are honest and pay up, but I believe the vast majority do. We even have an honesty box for soft drinks, where people help themselves, and that seems to work OK as well. The fact that we now have proper surveillance cameras, for safety's sake really, and to help people who are lost, probably encourages people to be more honest than they might otherwise be. I like to think most people are fair and honest. But from our point of view, the object is still the same, to save us money and manpower so we can devote ourselves to more important things."

The second most important thing, after getting all the planning permissions, was stocking the bunker. When they finally took it over, they found the government had cleared out almost all the contents, selling some stuff, but dumping most of it as scrap. "I don't know why they did this. When I heard, I tried to stop them, but we hadn't at that time legally taken everything over, so we could do nothing about it."

Fortunately, he realised that the government was doing the same thing with all the bunkers, all over the country, so he rushed round and made clearance deals, either with the government or with the new owners. "There were quite a few legal firms who bought some of the smaller bunkers, and they wanted all the old contents cleared at once, so they could store their own documents. In most cases we got the stuff for free. We also got given a lot of artefacts, equipment, historical documents when people heard what we were doing, and we eventually managed to track down a lot of stuff which had been here, in this bunker."

Being a farmer helped as well, as he always had lorries and tractors and trailers and strong men at his disposal, able to rush off and collect stuff at a moment's notice.

He also managed to contact many of the RAF guards and government officials who had worked in the bunker over the forty years or so when it was still operational. They had signed the Official Secrets Act, so in theory could not spill the beans. He invited about a hundred of them to lunch and asked them to write down their personal memories. Almost all of them, on first returning, exclaimed about the smell. They said the polish on the floor was exactly as they had remembered it, yet they had never smelled that same smell since.

This is because it is exactly the same polish, special government issue, which Michael managed to track down. He has a huge supply of it, which will last many decades ahead, as vast supplies were left in the bunker.

One of the ex-Home Office guards was hired for a while to go with them on their tours of other bunkers, advising them on what stuff to buy. "He didn't reveal any infomation, because of the Secrets Act, but when asked if this would be a good item for us, he would nod or shake his head."

No professional historians were employed, or expert designers or graphic artists to help them recreate the bunker as it was. They worked things out as they went along, researching items and notices as they acquired them.

Today, they have about sixty thousand visitors a year, a figure that goes up gradually most years. Michael's son James, having read agriculture at Reading University, is now mainly responsible for the farm, while Michael is still occupied with the bunker. "I still do seven days a week, in the summer months anyway. As a farmer, that is how you are brought up."

Some ten years ago, when he was still trying to put the bunker on the map, he announced that for £30,000 anyone could be guaranteed to use the bunker for up to ten years in the event of a nuclear bomb or attack. "It got a lot of coverage, but nobody actually took up the offer. I just did it for publicity anyway. But after 9/11, the threat of some attack became much more real and I suddenly got about two hundred enquiries. Nothing came of any of them, but people had got worried again, as in the Cold War. I then found myself receiving death threats, accused of trying to cash in on a tragedy like 9/11. I hadn't of course, as the offer had been made long before 9/11. I had really forgotten all about it, but some paper had dug out the old story. I discovered later that the people making the death threats were firemen."

He now does corporate events, hires out some of the rooms for conferences, which I found hard to believe — who would want their fun day out to be in an underground bunker? — but that day there was a party of twenty NHS workers having a private lunch, a tour of the bunker and a bit of paintballing, one of the new activities he has set up in his woods.

He says yes, the bunker does make a bit of money, but can't offhand give figures. Better than farming? "You can't compare the two. Obviously the farm, as it's two and a half thousand acres, makes more money in a year, but in farming you only have one big cash day. With the bunker, I have a cash flow every day."

He has still not taken a penny in grants or funding to open or run the bunker, even though they are now one of the main attractions of the local tourist economy in Essex. "We have once, and only once, received some public money. It was during foot and mouth. They gave us £3000 as compensation for loss of income when school parties were not allowed on visits. Other than that, we have never received, nor applied for, any grants or financial help. I prefer to be in control of our own destiny and not be beholden to others. We are not a trust because with a trust you will have trustees, some of whom will think they know what's best. We are not even a company. I refuse to hide anything behind a company name. We are still just a farming family, doing things our way, on our own."

He has a daughter as well as a son, and four grandchildren, and he hopes one day perhaps they will take over the running of the bunker. But whatever happens, he wants it to stay in the family, for ever. "I see it in many ways as like owning an ancient castle, the sort of building many landed families have inherited and have had to look after over the centuries. Castles were originally defensive, to protect against enemies. This bunker is a modern version, only it happens to have been built underground. But I still feel the same pride in ownership, of owning an historic monument, caring for it, working out ways of making it pay its way. Like an upside-down Norman castle, it was built to last . . ."

But as a Briton, is he proud of it? Did our dear government do a good job in creating this and all the other hundreds of bunkers?

"All governments are cynical. If you look at the instructions on that ancient copy of *Protect and Survive*, it is clear they wanted you to stay in your house, knowing you would probably perish. And afterwards, they would know where you were. They weren't actually interested in you personally, or your greater good. What they didn't want was you out in the street and rioting. On the other hand, it had to be done. They couldn't have lawless gangs roaming around.

"Where I do take real exception to what the government did is that they wasted so much money. They were forever starting new policies and systems, at vast expense, when the existing ones were perfectly OK. That old *Protect and Survive* leaflet, which they printed in millions, was redone again quite recently, yet basically the advice was the same as it had been forty years earlier. They did this all the time, bureaucracy gone mad, changing things every three months, keeping themselves occupied and important — throwing our money around.

"I assume today they have a modern version of these bunkers, in fact I know they have, where the prime minister and his main officials will retreat to if and when there is a massive terrorist attack, ready in case the suicide bombers land in Whitehall and planes start crashing into Downing Street.

"Governments have always operated by fear — our fear that something awful is about to happen, whether it is a nuclear bomb, terrorism or global warming. They need us to be frightened so we will pay our taxes, but of course they take it to extremes. I mean, they are still making every airline passenger take off their shoes when they enter any airport. That's ridiculous, bureaucracy gone mad. But they need us to feel fear, to believe they are doing things for our good, even when the risks are totally minuscule."

Would he rush into his own bunker if he thought a terrorist attack was on its way, heading straight for Essex?

"I would be very stupid not too, wouldn't I, if I didn't take advantage of my very own nuclear bunker? I'd never forgive myself. So yes, I always do make sure there is fresh water in the bunker and lots of dried fruit we could live on."

Who is we?

"My own family of course. We own it. Naturally, there would have to be a list of those who qualified as family. Would I, for example, invite my granddaughter's current boyfriend into the bunker, and if so, would we also invite his parents?

"I often lie awake thinking of it, amusing myself, working it out, for it changes all the time. But it could be done, when the time came. After all, it would be no harder than working out a wedding list. They can of course cause problems, and people missed out get upset. This time, it could well be a matter of life and death, for those not on the list . . ."

I also found myself lying awake at night, for days after I had visited the secret bunker. It is so unusual, in fact unique, that there are not really any lessons to be learned for a would-be museum creator. It is totally a one-off. The bunker came first, was already there. The museum had to be created round it. Not the sort of place that a diploma or a degree or a master's in modern museum studies prepares you for. Entering without having to pay, and without the need for any staff at the entrance, that is an idea I could pinch. But would it work with an ordinary building, and create the same sort of atmosphere? It really was the most extraordinary museum that I had visited so far. I kept on dreaming I was trapped inside, wandering round the forty rooms, lost and locked in for ever, the only human left alive on the planet.

It was so strange, eerie, scary, and yet I found myself raving about it, telling everyone that they must go and see it. If you are ever anywhere near that part of Essex, don't miss it, it's amazing.

Perhaps bizarre is a better word. It was bizarre to build it in the first place, at a time when the world was pretty bizarre, and then equally bizarre to think of turning into a museum, a museum of our times.

The Kelvedon Hatch Secret Nuclear Bunker
Crown Buildings
Kelvedon Hall Lane
Kelvedon Hatch
Essex CM 14 5TL
Tel 01277 364883
www.secretnuclearbunker.com

CHAPTER
SEVENTEEN

The Old Operating Theatre, London Bridge

Having gone underground, time to go up in the world. Setting off to find my highest museum meant, alas, going on the Tube, now that I was back in horrible, marvellous old London town.

By going on the Tube I was breaking all my rules, which I have stuck to for ten years. My only ambition in life, I used to tell myself, was never to go on the Tube again. Modest enough and easily achievable. But looking at the map, seeing that this museum was right next to London Bridge, which is on the Northern Line, direct from Kentish Town, my local station, and reading that morning's newspaper which announced a series of marches and demonstrations in central London to do with the G20 meetings and President Obama's first visit to London, I decided that going by Tube would be easiest and quickest.

The smell was the same — nasty — the atmosphere spooky and oppressive, the people looked un-human and un-present, refusing to admit the presence of other un-humans. At least on London buses people do sometimes speak to each other.

The biggest change in ten years was — nothing. The platform clock, the carriages, the upholstery of the seats had not only remained the same, they seemed to have gone backwards in time, so the experience of being on the Northern Line had somehow taken on a period charm. Quite a neat way, I thought, of coming towards the end of a book about museums — using a form of transport that is itself a museum piece.

I got out at London Bridge station, and was immediately lost. I used to go regularly to this station on Saturdays about twenty years ago, in the days when the whole forecourt was taken over by a massive if shambolic collectors' fair, searching for treasures for my various collections. It was one of the cheapest such markets in London. The nearest to it now, on a Saturday, is underneath the arches at Charing Cross station. It's mainly stamps and coins, but beautifully scruffy and atmospheric. Covent Garden on a Monday is quite good, while Spitalfields on a Thursday can be excellent.

It's a confusing station anyway, as it's built on several levels. I walked round the block a few times, unable to work out which direction I was facing or even where the Thames might be, which seems daft, as I knew it must be only yards away. I do have a poor sense of direction. In strange hotels it takes me several nights to remember where the lavatory is, unless I leave chalk marks on the ground.

I found myself back at the station forecourt and so asked a taxi driver which was St Thomas Street. On the map it appeared right beside the station, and seemed a major road, but it turned out to be more of a side street, a little Georgian enclave, so quiet and sedate, so hidden away.

The address I was looking for was No. 9a St Thomas Street, which told me nothing, gave me few clues. The full title of the museum, now I looked at my notes again, was the Old Operating Theatre Museum & Herb Garret. Very confusing. I had worked out that the "theatre" bit was medical, not theatrical, but who was "Herb Garret" — a famous surgeon perhaps, from the nineteenth century? Would I see a mock-up of his gory operations, with fake blood and plastic limbs all over the place? Not the sort of exhibit I would normally want to see, being of a squeamish disposition, but I know there are those who do find operations interesting. Such as Noël Coward.

In 1969 to celebrate his seventieth birthday, Coward agreed to give one interview, which was to the *Sunday Times*, where I was chief feature writer. He invited me to dinner at his house in Switzerland. I booked into a local hotel, the Montreux Palace Hotel, and awaited his call. When it came it was to cancel. "The Master is indisposed," so I was informed by his secretary, Cole Leslie — born Leslie Cole, but Coward had changed it. However, I could join the Master the next evening.

It meant I had twenty-four hours to put in, with nothing to do. Hanging around an empty reception area next morning, my eye caught a directory of names and room numbers. The hotel appeared totally empty, as it was out of season, but I realised there was a wing containing permanent residents. I read the names upside down and saw that one was called Nabokov. Could it be Vladimir? I went back to my room, rang his number, and talked him into seeing me. We met at a coffee bar in the town and he chatted away for over an hour — but on one condition. I wasn't to write anything about our conversation.

Next night, I reported to Coward's house, where I enjoyed an excellent dinner during which Coward performed, telling lots of funny stories, mostly of a theatrical nature. Many I'd heard before, or read in the cuttings, so, to get him off the subject, I asked him what sorts of things he did locally, at home in Switzerland. He said, well, the previous week he'd been to watch an operation. I tried not to express not too much surprise, asking if he did this regularly. Oh yes, he had friends who were surgeons in many cities and they often let him observe them at work. He'd seen hysterectomies, childbirth, death. By now I could hardly contain my amazement, perhaps appearing too fascinated by what he was telling me, wanting to know precisely what pleasure he got out of it. He suddenly changed the subject, refused to discuss it any further.

I've often wondered since what it revealed about his true character, and why people who are not medics would want to witness other humans being cut up. I suppose remembering that incident was one reason I was here, wanting to see a real operating theatre for myself. But not in use, of course. Or so I presumed.

No. 9a is a small, modest doorway, leading into a small entrance hall. Ahead there was a glass door, leading into what appeared to have been a church, but was now some sort of classy offices. To the side, an arrow pointed to the Old Operating Theatre Museum. It led upstairs, via a narrow and winding stone spiral staircase, which I started to ascend, squeezing myself up. I'm quite thin, if not quite as thin as I was, but a person of hefty proportions, which of course two thirds of the British population are these days, could easily find these narrow, bendy stairs hard to negotiate. Some people must get stuck, jammed on the staircase.

I went up and up and eventually came to a wooden door, barring my way. There was nothing on it except the words "Open this Door". I felt I'd stumbled into an upside-down Alice in Wonderland world. Instead of falling down though a hole in the ground, I feared I had fallen up, into the air.

How could it possibly lead to a hospital operating theatre? Obviously it wasn't in operation today, or I would have seen the ambulances and stretchers and bodies, that would have been a clue, but even in ye olden days, when it was a working operating theatre, how and why did they have it in such a high, awkward place, all the way up these narrow stone spiral steps, which led, well, wherever they might lead?

I opened the door — and it was a wonderland, one of the most remarkable little museums I'd ever seen. But it did take me some time to work it all out and discover how and why it came to be here.

343

The site was once St Thomas's Hospital, hence the name of the street outside. Originally, in the twelfth century, it was part of a priory, the monks and nuns doing the nursing, such as it was, but mainly offering hospitality — from which the term hospital comes — to poor and sick travellers, many of them pilgrims on their way to Canterbury. In 1215, after a fire, the hospital was rebuilt, and it continued to operate as a hospital for the next six hundred and fifty years. It was a charitable hospital, for poor people, catering for all ages, including children, who were lumped in with the older patients, but from the beginning there were always separate male and female wards.

During the 1720s, another hospital was built alongside St Thomas's, catering for the "incurables", those patients St Thomas's refused to admit. It was funded by a wealthy City printer and publisher called Sir Thomas Guy. He had made a killing on the stock market during the South Sea Bubble and donated some of his winnings towards a new hospital. It was named after him — Guy's Hospital. Thus we have two of London's most famous hospitals sitting there side by side for the next hundred and fifty years.

St Thomas's church was part of St Thomas's hospital, originally the hospital's chapel, but the present building went up in 1703, in the style of Sir Christopher Wren, who was a governor of the hospital, though the architect was Thomas Cartwright, Wren's master mason. It seems to have operated both as a proper church, open to all, and a hospital chapel.

In 1859, Florence Nightingale became involved with St Thomas's, hoping to establish a nursing school as part of the hospital. After her return from the Crimea in 1856, she had been working on the Nightingale Fund, raising money to create the first proper training school for nurses. Nursing had traditionally been a low-grade occupation, on a level with domestic service, and nurses were not trained but just picked up skills while working on the job. Surgeons and physicians and male assistant dressers, who assisted surgeons during operations, were considered quite sufficient, and the medical profession resisted any moves to create another layer of medics, who might well challenge their power and positions.

Florence Nightingale managed to get the money together, some £50,000, and her famous nursing school opened at St Thomas's in June 1860, with fifteen pupils. And then it moved out again, two years later.

One of the reasons she was keen to move into St Thomas's was that she knew its days were numbered — the whole hospital was likely to have to move to a new site, and she therefore reckoned that by moving with them she would end up with brandnew premises, as opposed to the sprawling, decaying collection of ancient buildings that St Thomas's had become.

All the old hospital buildings soon disappeared, knocked down and rebuilt as part of the railway premises or as a new post office — all except the church of St Thomas. That is the only part remaining today of what was originally the medieval hospital.

345

So how come the old operating theatre exists today, if the hospital itself disappeared? Ah, the answer to that is that the theatre, when it was rebuilt in 1822, had been built into the roof of the church itself, under the rafters. The reason for building it there was that it backed on to the female ward, which was at the top of the hospital building next door. They were therefore able to knock through and give easy access from the female ward right into the operating theatre. The other advantage was that by being in the roof of the church, they could give themselves lots of excellent natural light by installing fanlights in the roof.

I think I've got all that correct, more or less. Anyway, the upshot was that when the whole hospital was moved, the old operating theatre part was left stranded, still in the roof, but of no more use or interest. It was blocked off, ignored, and pretty much forgotten for the next hundred years.

Of interest to nobody, except of course anyone who happened to be a medical historian, especially one researching the history of Guy's and St Thomas's Hospitals.

A gentleman called Raymond Russell, after some research, discovered — or at least rediscovered — the theatre in 1956. A restoration campaign was set up with as its figurehead, Lord Brock of Wimbledon. Russell Claude Brock, later Lord Brock of Wimbledon, had been a student at Guy's and went on to become one of the pioneers of cardiac surgery and president of the Royal College of Surgeons. He was known as being pretty fierce and a stickler for correct medical usage. A

346

woman patient once asked him, "Do I need surgery, sir?" and he replied, "Everyone needs surgery, madam. What you need is an operation." This story is still told in medical circles, but personally I can't see why he corrected her. He must have known what the woman meant.

Brock was also a keen medical historian and writer, and in his retirement spent a lot of time researching the history of medicine. In the 1950s, along with several others, he started looking into the history of Guy's and St Thomas's.

In 1956 it was decided to make a proper investigation of the old operating theatre. Someone climbed up into the rafters to see what, if anything, was still there. It was discovered that most of the shell was intact, including the original plasterwork walls and the greater part of the floor. By clever detective work, examining the different ways the wood had discoloured, it was possible to work out where the original steps and cupboards of the theatre had been. They were also able to locate an old inventory of the theatre that had been made in 1862, before the contents had been dispersed and the attic closed.

Lord Brock led a campaign to raise interest and funds, and with the help of a grant from the Wolfson Foundation they opened the attic to the public in 1962. Since then they have collected hundreds of ancient medical instruments and artefacts, turning the whole attic into a medical museum.

The first thing that strikes you is yes, this really is still a church attic. The beams and rafters are

347

enormous, looming over your head, leading into every corner. In fact the building is itself a museum, quite apart from its contents and the part it played in medical history. So many museums often have to make do with a rough conversion, taking over premises meant for other purposes.

The second impression is that it's just the sort of museum I like — full of real objects, not audio stuff and computer visuals, and all of it in apparent clutter and chaos, with exhibits and cases and displays scattered everywhere, on ledges and shelves and tables, nooks and crannies. On closer inspection though, you can soon see that all of it has been beautifully and carefully arranged with excellent labels and explanations, neatly and artistically written, by the curator, Karen Howell.

The third impression, which hits you in the nose the minute you have finally scaled the heights, is the delicious, herby, pungent smell. This attic, as well as containing the female operating theatre, was also the hospital's storage room for its medical herbs and natural potions — hence the word "herb" in its title.

I didn't know where to start, which usually annoys curators in modern, professionally designed museums. They have bossily organised it in a certain way, with lots of arrows and numbers and plans, forcing you to proceed in a certain order, or so they hope. It always confuses me and I find myself going in the wrong direction. Sometimes deliberately, in order not to trail round with the herd. In this case it didn't matter. The cases and displays didn't appear to be laid out in any order. You are just left to wander round, gaping.

My eyes alighted first on some leech jars — big, old glass jars in which leeches were kept. I could see scratches inside the glass where perhaps the leeches tried to get out, or maybe the marks were made by the instruments used to take them from the jars. You clearly didn't want to take them out with your bare hands, as leeches, so a note informed me, have three jaws and hundreds of tiny, sharp teeth. If you got bitten by one, the wound would be trifoliate, with three sides. You could bleed for up to twelve hours, which of course was the point. The theory of blood-letting was that it drained away the bad humours in a sick person.

On the other hand, you could give them snail water to make them better. Ordinary garden snails were soaked in water for twenty-four hours, the liquid mixed with herbs such as juniper berries, aniseed and cloves, then the patient drank it. Said to be good as a treatment for venereal diseases, according to a pharmacy book dated 1718.

The nursing equipment included a fiendish-looking stomach pump, a metal nipple shield, and a female and a male urine bottle from the 1800s, each made of pewter. They looked like large hip flasks. The female version had a larger, flared spout, while the male spout was smaller. In a case marked "Obstetrics" there were some forceps from the eighteenth century, which looked pretty much as they are today in shape, if a little heavier. Perhaps the eeriest displays were the human specimens, parts of long-gone bodies preserved in ancient jars of formaldehyde, including a section of a child's brain, a heart cut in half, a kidney and a uterus. I wondered why Damien Hirst hadn't thought of trying to use humans instead of animal bodies. Much more dramatic.

The so-called Herb Garret was in one corner, under the eaves, but of course its fragrances were everywhere. It looked like a rather high-class farmers' market, with all the herbs laid out in ever-so-sweet straw baskets. The earliest reference to this area of the church attic being used as a herb store for the hospital dates from 1821, but it is assumed it was in use much earlier. It is clearly a good, dry, safe place, with plenty of air, where the herbs were cured, dried and then made it into medical compounds for use on the hospital patients. When the attic was opened up in 1956, dried opium poppy heads were found amongst cracks in the rafters.

The hospital itself would have had its own herb garden outside, for growing the herbs, but would also have bought supplies from herb women who travelled round hospitals and clinics with their baskets. Until the development of the chemical and pharmaceutical industries in the late nineteenth century, virtually all medicinal compounds were made out of natural plants. Today, it is estimated that 70 per cent of our medicines still originate from plant sources.

There is a record dated 1605 of a woman in the female ward at St Thomas's having a bath that contained herbs and a sheep's head. I'm sure Prince Charles would have approved of that.

350

I could see other visitors sniffing the herbs, like Bisto kids, breathing in and out and exclaiming, while some of the cheekier ones were picking up handfuls, running them through their fingers, lifting them up and smelling them. In most ordinary museums of course you are not allowed to touch or handle any of the objects. There seemed to be no notice on the herb baskets saying "Don't Touch", so I did the same.

The herbs included many I had never seen before in the flesh, such as marshmallow — which is not the soft sweet loved by children but a form of twig that grows in marshes. It was used to aid digestion. There were baskets of frankincense and myrrh which I never even knew were herbs. There were bits of willow bark, from which, I learned, an early forerunner of aspirin was extracted and used to cure pains and headaches. The bark contains salicin from which aspirin was later synthesised. I had heard of comfrey, which I'd come across in lots of nineteenth-century letters, but never knew that it was a herb. It was renowned for its healing power.

The old operating theatre itself is entered from a corner, and then up some more stairs, so you look down into it. It reminded me of Mitchells' auction ring in Cockermouth, where cattle have for centuries been auctioned. It is circular in shape, like a small amphitheatre, with tiers of wooden steps and railings where spectators could watch, looking down into the centre where the beast for sale would be paraded — or, in this case, some poor woman was going to be

351

operated on. The actual operating table, made of wood, did look like a butcher's block.

You can see why it was called a theatre — the setting was theatrical, the construction very like a real theatre, the audience looking down on to the stage, all eyes focused on the drama before them.

This theatre ceased to be in operation after 1860, when the hospital moved, and it did not use anaesthetics until its last few years. Reliable anaesthetics did not come in till 1846, when experiments with chloroform began, and St Thomas's itself did not have its first anaesthetist on the staff till 1878. As for antiseptic procedures, they came in long after this operating theatre had closed, thanks to the work of Sir Joseph Lister published in 1867.

So for almost all its history, this operating theatre was a bit like a butcher's — with limbs chopped off, parts of bodies removed, without the poor patient having any recourse to any sort of painkiller. Below the operating table the floor was covered in sawdust, to soak up the blood and gore. The patient was usually blindfolded, led into the theatre from the adjoining ward, not quite knowing what was going to happen or where she was, or aware that so many people were now staring at her. It then all depended on the speed of the surgeon, a cool head, the sharpness of his tools and his knowledge of anatomy to extract the offending organ in the quickest time with the least pain.

And yet for centuries surgeons did manage successfully to do amputations, the removal of bladder stones and trepanation (operations on the skull), with quite a lot of the patients living to tell the tale. There was of course a high risk of infection, as the causes of it were not then properly realised. Surgeons usually operated in their frock coats, "stiff and stinking with pus and blood". If they did wash their hands, it was usually after rather than before an operation.

St Thomas's, along with Guy's next door, became an important teaching hospital from the eighteenth century onwards and the operating theatre provided an opportunity for students to watch their masters at work. There is a graphic description of an operation at St Thomas's, which was written by a medical student in 1814:

The first few rows . . . were occupied by other dressers and behind a second partition stood the pupils, packed like herrings in a barrel. Those behind were continually pressing on those before and not infrequently had to be got out exhausted. There was also a continual calling out of "Heads, Heads" to those about the table whose heads interfered with the sightseers. After our operations were over, the students rushed down two flights of stairs and across the street to Guy's to rush up as many stairs and repeat the same scrabbling for places as before. The importance of the operation and the reputation of the operator had a large influence on the number of spectators and their violent scrambling to gain entrance. It often led to severe contests and even fighting with the hospital servants.

That day I was alone in the theatre, but it was easy to imagine the atmosphere when a star surgeon was at work. Beside his operating table were cupboards filled with his tools for amputations. I could see a strange-looking machine like a mangle, which apparently was a bandage winder, for quickly bandaging up people who were bleeding heavily after their op. I couldn't think of a comparable instrument today, although for many of the old tools on display there are modern equivalents.

The museum has at its entrance a set of 1821 Theatre Regulations painted on a wall, which were applied in the theatre in its operating days:

> Apprentices and Dressers of the Surgeon who operates are to stand round the table. The Dressers of the other surgeons are to occupy the three front rows. The Surgeon's Pupils are take their places in the Rows above. Visitors are admitted by permission of the Surgeon who operates.

So even in the old days, visitors were allowed to watch. I wondered if they would have been the Noël Cowards of their day, celeb actors and impresarios, or rich City merchants.

I then noticed one of the museum staff, who had come to replace a light bulb in one of the display cabinets that had been flickering off and on. She said she was in fact the assistant curator, Kirsty Chilton, and she also gave medical lectures. In a hospital, I asked? No, here in the theatre, she explained. Most Saturdays there is a lecture in the theatre at two o'clock, in which she describes what the procedure used to be like. I asked her which of the many exhibits she personally liked best, and she took me to a large case filled with knives. I'd hardly looked at them as they looked like, well, knives, if very big and frightening ones. Surgeons must have been pretty big and strong to use them properly. She pointed out the ones that were used for trepanation, for opening up the brain.

I said I'd been particularly struck by the human specimens in the bottles, wondering if Damien Hirst might use them. No chance, she said. "We now have to get a licence for them. A human tissue act has come in which prohibits the display of human body parts without permission. I think about the only other place in London you will see them is the Royal College of Surgeons."

She was clearly very proud of their museum, especially the operating theatre, and said it was the only old operating theatre in the world that can be seen in situ. "Padua and Leiden do have theatres that can be seen, but they were dissecting theatres, not operating ones. Most old operating theatres were brought up to date, converted and altered over the years, but because this closed in 1862 it was never modernised.

I told her my Noël Coward story and asked if she imagined that celebs in the old days were allowed in. She looked quite aghast at the very idea. "I suppose it might have been done, but I've never seen it listed. I

355

have always assumed that by visitors it meant VIP visitors connected with the hospital, like one of the governors, not total outsiders."

The museum has a total staff of six — director, curator and four assistants — who all muck in, helping to keep the place clean and tidy as well as working on the research and educational side. They are always on the lookout for medical equipment and items they might not have, as long as they are of the right period.

Yes, it was true, they didn't mind people picking up the herbs and smelling them, as people enjoyed it. And very few of the herbs get stolen. But every year or so they have to renew them when the scents fade, just as they had to in the old days.

It was so pleasant to find a museum with a nice smell. I'd heard lots of interesting sounds and noises on my travels, from the Northumbrian pipes to scratchy soundtracks from old Laurel and Hardy films, but had not done a lot of smelling. I suppose there must be museums somewhere that are all smells, for I have heard of museums in Europe that are devoted to perfume. I wonder why more museums don't feature interesting smells, perhaps a different aroma for every room, instead of being obsessed by computer things for the kiddies.

I wondered if in my museum I could drag in and incorporate some smells. Such a useful and unusual addition to any museum, and an attraction in its own right. My collection of old football programmes do have their own, er, particular aroma, which I personally find so resonant and romantic, but I have to admit that most people go, ugh, what's that damp smell?

It was also pleasant to visit such a personal, human, cluttered, ad hoc sort of museum. Not the type of presentation I had expected from something so scientific. I had considered several medical-related museums, as there are quite a few around the country, but they all sound institutional, dry and ascetic. As opposed to fun. It had been such fun that I went round all the objects and displays again, in case I had missed anything. Not hard to do, for, as museums go, it is pretty small but awfully crowded.

As I was leaving, the girl on the counter at the little shop, an Italian called Valentina Lari, asked me if I'd seen any signs of a ghost. "We are supposed to have the ghost of Florence Nightingale. I've not seen her myself, nor has any of the staff, but we have members of supernatural societies who come here, looking for her, and swear to her existence. They often hold their meetings here, just to get close to her ghost. Some of them are clubs who stay the night here, soak up the atmosphere, measure their own temperatures to see if there are ghosts around."

I later talked to the museum's director, Kevin Flude. He is an archaeologist by training, who used to lead walks round London and give lectures. In 1989 he found the museum had closed, for no apparent reason, and remained closed for some time. "I made enquiries and found that the old curator had left and they couldn't find anyone to run it, so a partner and I offered to take it over. We've been running it ever since.

357

I think we are probably the only museum in London that is virtually self-supporting. We get between twenty-five and thirty thousand visitors a year and rely on them for our income. We are a charity of course, but we are not part of a bigger body, or supported by a professional organisation like most medical museums, so we don't get any funding, apart from the odd grant of a thousand or two. Naturally we'd like more, if we could, but at the moment we are surviving, even in these hard times.

"We have had clever young designers coming in and offering us plans to revamp and redesign it and make our displays more modern and edgy, but I have one basic rule — Don't fuck it up, stupid. I am resisting all attempts at updating, but there is a chance I might agree in the near future to include a small audio-visual display . . ."

Kevin, don't do it.

The Old Operating Theatre Museum & Herb Garret
9a St Thomas Street
London SE1 9RY
Tel 020 7188 2679
www.thegarret.org.uk

CHAPTER
EIGHTEEN

The Packaging Museum, Notting Hill

For twenty years, watching and wondering from afar, I have intended to visit the Museum of Brands, Packaging and Advertising, to give it its present, rather formal and offputting mouthful of a title. It is basically just a load of old packets, boxes and tins, or so it seemed when I first saw a feature on it in the *Sunday Times* colour supplement many years ago. The colours, the images, the graphics, the memories conjured up were so striking that I remember thinking, how utterly brilliant. Wish I'd thought of that. It seemed to be the ultimate in collecting, landing upon a subject that no one seemed to have thought of before, doing it so marvellously, then creating your own museum, on your own chosen topic. Ah, bliss.

So why didn't I go and visit it, if I considered it so unusual? Hmm. Not sure. Mainly because it was in Gloucester and life and work and circumstances never took me anywhere near Gloucester.

When I was in Bath earlier, on postal duty, and then heading for baked beans in Wales, I did think this would be the chance, the perfect occasion, to visit and properly investigate the packaging museum, now I was in the West Country, more or less — only to find that it was no longer in Gloucester, had not been for some time. Behind my back, it had migrated to London and was on my doorstep, more or less.

Instead, I have been able to save it up for my final destination, once I was back in London after my round tour. And a chance at long last to meet Robert Opie, who had long been my hero from afar, and find out how it all began.

Cue music, bit of crunching, paper rustling, tins dropping, perhaps some nice smells of old digestive biscuits . . .

The moment of epiphany occurred in 1963 when Robert was sixteen. He had gone to Scotland with his parents, who were attending a meeting of the British Association for the Advancement of Science in Aberdeen. His father was president of the anthropological section and was giving a paper. After it was over, young Robert decided to go further up to the north of Scotland to visit a schoolfriend. He had to overnight in Inverness and found as he wandered around that there was nowhere to eat, which was typical of most places in Scotland on a Sunday in those days — or of most of provincial Britain for that matter. He ended up back at the railway station where he found a vending machine and purchased a packet of Rowntree's Munchies and some McVitie & Price's ginger nuts. Back in his hotel room, he opened the packet of Munchies, "And it suddenly dawned on me that were I to throw away the wrapper, a small fragment of history would be discarded."

Today he still has those packets. But more importantly, he realised that here was a vast subject that was disappearing unrecorded. And so began a lifetime's passion.

Now why did he do that, as a young lad of sixteen? What made him have those thoughts? Why was his passion not revolving round, say, football, which is what I was thinking about aged sixteen?

According to the poet Philip Larkin, your parents don't necessarily always help you out. In the case of Robert Opie, and I suspect the majority of people, you do in fact owe a great deal to your parents, most of it positive, although you might not be aware of it or feel grateful at the time.

His parents, Peter and Iona Opie, were pioneers in the field of folklore, studying nursery rhymes, singing games and children's verse, and became experts known in social and academic circles around the world. They were keen collectors — because of course you don't just have to gather physical objects to be a collector, you can collect oral history, songs or, in the case of Sigmund Freud, jokes.

As a small boy Robert had started collecting the usual sort of things that children do, such as stamps, coins and stones. The Matchbox die-cast toy models from Lesney were another collection, and his father encouraged him to date each box as it was acquired. "Collecting is an instinctive thing within our human psyche. In my case, that instinct was helped by my surroundings — I thought every home had its own little museum."

Most people who collect in childhood, as I did, give up in their teenage years, distracted by other foolish things, but Robert kept on. He never stopped. At boarding school, at Ardingly in Sussex, he gradually moved on from adhesive stamps to the Cinderella world of philately that included postal stationery, stamp booklets and greetings telegrams. Instinctively, he wanted to collect something that others didn't.

"Stamp collectors tend to begin by saving everything, because it's all new to you. Then gradually they realise that the task is overwhelming, so the obvious thing to do is concentrate on one country, then one reign and then finally specialise on one scarce issue. They end up narrowing it down so much that only one other person has the same interest — and they live in Australia.

"My thinking has always been the opposite. As my interest in our consumer world developed, I wanted to put everything into context, which meant looking at an increasingly bigger picture. To begin with, it was all about saving the contemporary material around me. It was a few years before I realised it was even possible to discover earlier items — after all, why would anyone have saved a Birds Eye fish finger pack from the 1950s or a Force cereal box from the 1920s?"

Robert did his A levels and at eighteen went to Portsmouth to do an HND in business studies. Why not a proper university, studying some traditional subject? After all, he'd gone to a well-known public school, the sort that sent its pupils to the better-class universities?

"I really don't know," he said, pausing, staring at me through his spectacles. His accent is clipped middle-class, very fluent, with a great flow, a good way with words and images, and most people would take him for a product of Oxbridge, not a provincial poly. "I can't remember now how it happened. Business studies was a new thing in the sixties. I just decided I wanted to try it and someone suggested Portsmouth."

While at Portsmouth, he discovered the exciting world of CTNs — confectioners, tobacconists and newsagents. He visited as many as possible every fortnight, asking them for any dummy packages, posters or point-of-sale items that they might be chucking out. As it turned out, this was the last era of the much-admired shop-window display, with its intricate displays of boxes of chocolates with contents that looked like the real thing.

After he finished his diploma he started work with a market research company in London, and stayed in market research, fulltime, for the next sixteen years. But that was not his passion, that was work. Now he was aware that at antique markets and in places like the Portobello Road it was possible to find earlier examples of packaging and advertising. He still saved every piece of contemporary packaging that came his way, but now he was seeking out earlier examples, going back to Victorian times.

"The term 'collector' tends to be a rather nebulous description. I see myself as a recorder of the recent

363

past, a consumer historian. I am gathering the evidence of how society has been transformed by this extraordinary consumer revolution. To do that properly, I have to save enough material to put that massive story into order — and it seems that this task will go on for ever."

Gradually he acquired thousands, then tens of thousands, of packages and wrappings, tins and boxes, till they were taking over his whole house, his whole life. "I remember when I was still a keen philatelist and had joined the Royal Philatelic Society, I gave a lecture to the members called 'A Load of Rubbish'. The idea was to show how packaging and other ephemera was just as important and as relevant to save as stamps. They all have a design and social history and are equally part of our throwaway society. So I made comparisons between my varieties of postal stationery and the 57 varieties of Heinz baked beans labels. Indeed, they were all throwaway items, as are stamps. They are part of our history, with fascinating designs and graphics and artwork. These labels are just as worthy of collecting as stamps. Not better, not worse, just as important."

Robert Opie and his passion for packaging received national recognition in 1975 when he exhibited some three thousand items at the V&A in London. The Pack Age — A Century of Wrapping It Up was open for seven weeks. "Actually, it received international attention. There was coverage in magazines, TV and radio all over the world. Some eighty thousand people came to see the exhibition. At one time there were so many in the museum that they had to close the front doors. Mind you, there happened to be a Wombles exhibition on at the same time. Even so, the reaction was amazing. I did much of the PR myself, sitting in a cubicle at the V&A and ringing the newspapers.

"The public loved it, including the museum guards on duty, who became animated and were reminiscing along with everyone else. Visitors made lots of animated comments about how it should be on permanent display." That of course was his end goal. And he hoped the V&A attention would help make it happen. Alas, it didn't.

For almost the next ten years he carried on with his day job, hoping someone or some organisation would come forward and offer to finance or sponsor some sort of permanent exhibition. "I gave a talk at a J Walter Thompson client evening, created a display for NatWest bank at their Port Talbot branch, and presented a museum proposal to senior management at MetalBox, one of the biggest packaging manufacturers at the time. As expected, everyone expressed interest, but no support was forthcoming."

Eventually the time came to go it alone, and with two others and a bank loan, the Museum of Advertising and Packaging opened in 1984. British Waterways allowed him to have the ground floor of a disused warehouse in the inland docks of Gloucester.

In the first year, he attracted crowds of twenty-nine thousand, which grew to fifty-seven thousand within six years. In 1993 some of his collection went on tour in Japan as The Treasures and Pleasures of Childhood.

From 1999, for six years, the Museum of Memories was open, funded by Wigan Council.

"Visitor numbers began to decline in 1991. There was a credit squeeze and then Sunday trading meant people went to Tesco instead of a museum visit. National museums stopped charging in 1997 and the lottery took a lot of loose change out of the economy. But perhaps the biggest difference was that during the 1990s the number of attractions doubled. Despite all of this, our museum attendance held up at around thirty thousand."

However, in 2001 the lease was up and the search was on for a new venue. By now they were pretty well known, and had offers of new sites from Cumbria to Cornwall. Several bodies offered free premises, promised to pay start-up costs, but they were never quite in viable locations. "A place like Bath already has enough museums, and visitors from London would often say we should be there, and I would say no way, there are already enough attractions there. As it happened, the best offer with the chance of backing came from London, thanks to the design and branding company PI Global. They were moving out of their premises to ones next door and were able to help with fund-raising and a support network."

Having failed to gain start-up funding from the Heritage Lottery Fund, the next step was to approach possible brand owners for support, and fortunately some big names came forward in the form of Cadbury's, Kellogg's, Twinings, McVitie's, Vodaphone and Diageo (makers of Guinness and Johnnie Walker).

The Museum of Brands, Packaging and Advertising opened in Notting Hill in December 2005. How could I have missed it? Well, I suppose London is a big place, with so many competing museums. In Gloucester it had been a star attraction, attracting attention and publicity out of proportion to its size. Also, the thing with time is that it gets concertinaed. I could have sworn I read an article about the packaging museum in Gloucester only the other month, or could it have been last year? Anyway, not all that long ago, surely, so it had become imprinted on my brain that it must still be there.

So what's it like? Well, it is a bit hard to find. I don't know Notting Hill, apart from Portobello Road, which I have been visiting for over forty years, looking for treasures — rarely with much success in recent years, as it seems to be full of rich Italians being ripped off with repro antiques.

I found Colville Terrace but Colville Mews, where the museum is situated, is actually off Lonsdale Road. I entered Lonsdale Road halfway down, not knowing whether to turn right or left into it, so asked a council worker, cleaning a lamp post. "What museum? Never seen no museum round here." I said it was in a mews and he said oh try that way, there is a mews down there.

When I eventually found Colville Mews, there was a little gaily coloured sign on the corner indicating the right direction. Outside what I assumed was the entrance, there was a crowd of about twenty or thirty young people, standing around chattering — students by the look of them, international sort by the sound of their voices. London is full of language schools these days, so perhaps there is one next door. But no, when the doors of the museum opened, all the students made a mad rush forward.

The entrance was a delightful surprise, all new and gleaming, very slick and well appointed, with a pine-tabled coffee bar, interesting-looking bookstall and of course lots of attractive displays of vintage boxes and packaging. I'm not sure why, but I thought it might be dusty and decaying, which is how you tend to think of old packaging. But it is in a brand-new building, recently and rather lavishly equipped.

The girl on the till said just start here, to the left of the till, wander round, it's all in chronological order, you won't get lost.

I have been in too many museums where they have said that and even when I've finished, I'm still not clear which was the right way round, but this was totally clear, with rooms in order, the periods clear and all beautifully laid out.

It was the neat arrangement of everything that rather stunned me. How on earth did he do it? My own modest twenty or so little collections are in a permanent mess, however much I try to organise some sort of cataloguing system. It often starts with some sort of logic, then goes potty. For example, my football postcards. Originally I had one album with named teams and players, followed by unnamed teams. Then I started collecting single footballers, pairs of footballers, teams in unusual formations — lined up in the goalmouth as opposed to in three rows, as nature and football photographers have ordained. Then came comic football cards, birthday cards, plus of course foreign teams. They are now at a stage when I can never find what I am looking for, yet I probably have only five hundred football postcards in all.

But dear God, Robert Opie has over half a million items in his collection. Only twelve and a half thousand of them are currently on show in his museum. Only! How did he cope with creating any sort of order?

The answer, as I soon found, is that for two thirds of the museum, everything is in strict chronological order, starting with the Victorian age, then Edwardian, First World War, twenties, thirties, Second World War, forties, fifties, sixties, and so on, in decades right up to the present day.

The museum tells the extraordinary story of culture and the consumer revolution, the changing styles of packaging and promotion, the ceaseless arrival of new brands and the constant innovation and inventiveness that have catapulted our lifestyles into the comparative ease of leisure time (time enough to visit a museum or two). It is a story of mass manufacture and mass communication, which have changed every detail of daily living.

As visitors travel through the 150-year time tunnel, each comes to that point where history leaps worryingly into nostalgia, toys become childhood memories, and a bag of Rancheros crisps triggers a schoolday vision from the dim and distant past. Suddenly your personal moments are on display, and you join the story of the consumer revolution from that moment on.

Each period is in its own gallery, clearly labelled, but instead of just lumping all his Victorian items into rows of glass cases, any old how, he has attempted to create separate tableaux, such as the Great Exhibition of 1851, which has a case of its own. There are special displays showing fashion items, such as knitting patterns, advertisements for women's clothes, and including some genuine 1920s flapper dresses draped over mannequins. Naturally, most of the stuff does consist of packaging — boxes, tins, containers, wrappers, everything from biscuits to boot polish.

Each period follows a similar style, with special displays containing real objects, such as a fifties fridge and cooker, along with contemporary boxes of soap powder or washing-up liquid.

Throughout, I was astounded by the condition of every single item. You could believe they were all fakes or mock-ups as the colours are so strong, everything is so uncreased, untorn, unmarked. I have always told myself that I don't actually care much about the condition of my stuff, as long as I can read the writing. But I could see there's a lot to be said for always having the best example you can find, or afford. The trouble he must have gone to, demoting his poorer examples to the ranks when he got a genuine officer-class example worthy of display.

Around 90 per cent of the items were new to me, in that I had never seen them in the flesh before, only in books. Even when I got on to the two world wars, periods I think I do know something about, and have lots of items in my collections, he still had masses of stuff I'd never seen, let alone acquired. In his Second World War gallery there was a poster, totally new to me, reading "Hitler Will Send No Warning — So Always Carry Your Gas Mask".

As I was walked round I got more and more depressed. I began thinking, why do I bother? I am just messing about, faffing around. I've got nothing worth keeping, far less displaying, might as well give up now.

There was a girl behind me, going as slowly as me, examining every display, who turned out to be Italian. I asked her to take my photo standing in front of the Hitler poster. I do have an original wartime gas mask, so it would look good beside it. She then asked me to take her photo in front of various objects she particularly liked.

She was one of the students who had arrived at the same time as me. Most had zoomed ahead, probably in the cafe by now, or outside having a fag, but several had lingered in each room, as I had done. I later met up with the group's leader, who said they were all from the Istituto Marangoni, Italy's oldest fashion college, founded 1930. You've come a long way, I replied, but it turned out they have a campus in London's East End — in Fashion Street.

When I got to the sixties I came to two cases devoted to subjects I do know very well — the 1966 World Cup and the Beatles. Each display was quite modest and he didn't have as much as I have on either subject —

thank God for that. But how could he? He is trying to cover several hundred topics.

He had a Beatles cloth I'd never seen before, and his Yellow Submarine toy was in gleaming condition, and in its original box, whereas mine is bashed and the conning tower is missing. In his Wembley case, he only had a semi-final ticket, not the final, and his programme was the souvenir one, very easy to get, not the programme for the final between England and West Germany. That did cheer me up.

In the final third of the museum, the remaining galleries dispense with strict chronology and are devoted to individual brands, such as Cadbury's Milk Tray or Guinness, over the last hundred-plus years, so you have old and new items together and can see the progression and advances. It's a good way to end, pointing up that it's not just a gallery of old rubbish — packets normally thrown away — but a gallery of history, of social and economic change and development through the ages.

Robert had been busy all morning, so it was only after I had finished my tour on my own that I was able to sit down and talk to him about what I had seen. We sat in the coffee bar first, but behind us was a vintage TV which was showing old commercials from the fifties, amusing first time round, but the noise was getting on my nerves, so I asked if he had a quieter place. So we went upstairs to their conference room and had our talk.

The museum is now registered as a charity and they are self-supporting, living on admission fees and a percentage of the books and items sold in their shop. The annual number of visitors is much the same as it was in Gloucester, at around thirty thousand a year. "We didn't have the same competition as we now have in London, but nevertheless our visitor numbers continue to grow."

I raved about his museum, the items, the arrangement, and said how it struck me that in the early periods, especially the Victorian and Edwardian, the packaging was so much more artistic, decorative, the design and lettering better and of higher quality. As the decades have gone on, it seems to have got worse, cheaper, thinner, poorer.

Or perhaps I was looking through rose-coloured specs, nostalgic for decades I never knew, never experienced, but found attractive partly because they were old. This always does tend to lend a patina, making items seem better and more interesting than the recent or modern. But everyone must agree that Victorian biscuit boxes are miles more attractive than those boring packets of Surf washing powder from the seventies with their crude colours and lettering.

Robert did not quite agree. He rather likes 1970s soap powders, especially the own brands produced for the supermarkets.

He has written about twenty books, all related to product packaging or social history, many of which are on sale in the shop, but, like his parents, he hasn't made a lot of money from his writing.

Like me, he is a member of the Ephemera Society and goes to their fairs, and also to the Bloomsbury

373

postcard fairs, but he does not attend football programme fairs, as he has no specific interest in football, except when it crosses over into packaging, like World Cup Willie sweets and toys.

So what's the most he's ever spent? He had to think. It probably wasn't a piece of packaging, but a poster, which can sometimes go for over a thousand pounds, particularly those art deco ones from the 1920s. They can be a huge expense for him. Mostly he has not paid more than £100 for things, and often just a few pounds. He doesn't sell things, despite often being hard up. He would rather just keep the duplicates because quite often they are needed for other exhibitions or for recreating period shop windows, when a number of the same objects helps to give the right effect.

"I still get a great buzz from an item coming in that I didn't know existed, particularly if it helps me to understand something better. The collection is rather like some limitless jigsaw and all the time I'm trying to see the picture, endlessly fitting the pieces together until the picture becomes clearer and makes more sense. And there seems to be no limit to the material.

"When people go round the exhibition, many visitors say to me afterwards, "You must be so proud, having done all this," and I guess that's so, but actually I'm looking around at the things that need to be improved, or where something should be added to make the story work better.

"People used to think I was nuts, and some may still think that — but once they have actually been to the museum, then they understand. I feel the need to explain and celebrate the packaging and marketing story, and raise the status of a much-misunderstood industry. I see what I'm doing almost as a duty. No one ever says thank you to the packaging industry, and yet this museum is as important as any art gallery, science museum or natural history museum."

But why should they? OK, the material might be pretty and attractive, and reflect our social and economic history, but basically it is just rubbish, stuff made to be chucked away. And in this age, we are being encouraged all the time to avoid waste, to save resources so we can save the planet. Packaging is now seen as one of the public enemies in environmental and green circles.

"Yes, I now hear that argument a lot, which makes me even more determined to help the understanding. What people don't realise is how much we owe to packaging. Packaging saves waste. In the old days, half of fresh items that travelled any distance had to be chucked away, as they'd gone bad or got bashed. Now that was a terrible waste. Packaging preserves the contents, keeps them safe and fresh, helps you use the product wisely, tells you what's inside and so on. To give you one simple example, a cucumber will have an extended shelf-life of fourteen days just by using 1.5 grams of plastic film."

But why do certain items, like, say, those posh Belgian dark chocolate biscuits whose name escapes me, have to come in three layers of heavy-duty plastic, which takes for ever to open and puts up the price?

"Surely you wouldn't want your biscuits to be broken," he said.

Oh, I wouldn't mind the odd one, I replied, if the price was a lot lower. Anyway, I've personally now stopped buying those biscuits, much though I liked them, purely on principle, as they really annoy me.

However, I do enjoy the pleasure of having raspberries and blueberries all the year round, which I buy from street markets, which I realise come thousands of miles and have to be encased in little plastic boxes, otherwise they wouldn't make it. On the other hand, my wife refuses to buy items out of season, such as daffs and tulips at Christmas time. She says there's no need for it. She prefers to wait for things in season, as we all had to in the olden days, before the age of cheap transport and clever packaging.

Even now, when he has already assembled more than enough stuff to fill several museums, Robert is still on the lookout. When he goes to the supermarket for his weekly shopping, he always looks for interesting new products, whether he himself needs them or not. "Obviously I have to make instant choices. A supermarket might have thirty thousand different items, with new ones coming in all the time, but with wisdom and knowledge based on hindsight, I now tend to know what is worth saving. For example, yesterday I bought a packet of Ariel, even though I have more than enough soap powder to last me a lifetime. It was the first time I'd seen a claim for 'save up to 40p in energy with this pack by turning to cool wash'. This is an example of the environmentally aware, save-the-planet world in which we now live, so that was interesting.

"I now look back over forty-five years and realise there were innovations I missed or was not aware of. Hopefully, most of the time I've got things right, like buying the first plastic milk bottle, which arrived in 1971 when milk was 6½p a pint."

Sometimes he gets to the checkout before realising he has not bought anything for himself to eat, so he has to go back and think, what's for dinner?

As yet Robert has not married. Although some of his girlfriends have understood his collecting passion, he's never taken the leap. Perhaps there has been that concern that the time might arrive when a wife might say, "either your collection goes, or I do."

Did he feel fulfilled, then, not having a family? "Doing something so different from most other people has meant that plan A was not necessarily going to work out. But I've been incredibly fortunate to have found something so utterly absorbing, and something that has been needed as a resource for the nation. It's just taken a lot longer than I ever thought it would.

"Yes, I do feel fulfilled. I'm always busy, never bored. There are enough books to write to last me another three lifetimes. I'm always travelling to different places, meeting new people, talking to groups and associations, being interviewed on radio or television. But then I'm thinking, I must press on, there's so much more to be done."

So, with no children to inherit his museum, what will happen in the future?

Having made the museum itself into a charity, he is now working on turning over all the contents, as well as his own, into the care of a charitable trust. This will ensure the museum continues.

His museum certainly deserves to succeed. It's not just a collection of old tat, gathered willy-nilly, shoved into any old order, as with many museums and collections around the country. He has a clear, cold logical mind, rather scientific. I don't see him as at all potty or crazy for devoting his life to packaging, though personally I would never think of sacrificing my marital or family life for my collections.

All the museum creators and curators I met on my travels had different reasons for doing what they do, from the commercial to the cultural, from escapism to self-promotion, but Robert Opie was about the only person who was inspired by a sense of duty, who seemed to see himself as almost on a religious crusade, with talk of principles and sacrifices.

Has he had self-doubts? Not, apparently, since the age of sixteen, when he first saw the light and settled on his path.

How could I ever compete, identify an area no one else had bothered with, build up such an extraordinary collection, then create a unique museum? I found his museum totally wonderful, fascinating, awe-inspiring. And he himself is a remarkable man. I felt humbled in his presence.

The Museum of Brands, Packaging and Advertising
2 Colville Mews
Lonsdale Road
Notting Hill
London W11 2AR
Tel 020 7908 0880
www.museumofbrands.com

Conclusion

So am I going to open my own museum? And if so, where and when and how and most of all, why?

Talking to all those people made me realise that there are many and varied reasons why people open museums. It's not just simply the obvious motivation — they have collected some quite nice stuff that they would like others to see and enjoy. That's vanity museum-ing, a little-known branch of vanity publishing.

Some do it, like Robert Opie, as a cause, almost as if it were a religious calling, showing the zeal and devotion of a true worshipper, not for their own ego and glory but for the greater good of humanity. They feel it has to be done. Even at the cost of their own relationships. Or lack of them. I am not saying that Robert has not married because of his passion for packaging, as it would be impudent to presume such a thing, but there must surely be a connection.

Some do it to express themselves, as an art form, a piece of creativity they find unable to achieve in their normal working lives, such as Peter Nelson, the dentist who collected all those Cars of the Stars.

Others use it as an escape, to distract themselves from something upsetting or tragic that has happened in their lives, such as the death of two babies in the case of Helene and the fan museum.

Some have fallen into museums by chance, like the Bests at the Casbah, inheriting a house that had interesting connections, or Mike Parrish and his secret bunker, which just happened to get built on his land.

But some people are true obsessives, who from their earliest childhood consciousness have been fascinated by the insides of old wirelesses or old chocolate wrappers, and the obsession never leaves them.

With a few of them, it is clear that there is a commercial motive, that a product is in some way being pushed, as in the pencil museum, which is not to suggest it is just a money-grabbing operation — but it is a spin-off from the pencil factory and is seen as a source of income and also publicity. The Bank of Scotland's excellent money museum is not at all money-making, as entrance is free, but it is clearly image-making, raising the profile of the bank, making us all feel good about them.

The money museum is unusual in that it doesn't have to make money, which all the others have got to do, to a greater or lesser extent, regardless of how big and famous and successful they appear to have become, as with the National Football Museum. There is some good news there since I visited. Not only is the move to Manchester assured but it looks as if there is a good chance they could keep some sort of presence in Preston after all. They would then have two museums

381

in different locations, a football version of the Tate Modern in London and Tate Liverpool.

But there is some bad news about the sheep centre at Cockermouth. Roy Campbell, the owner, did hint at the end that he had begun to realise that commercially he would be much better off with hotel bedrooms than sheep onstage, hence he had applied for planning permission to extend his hotel. Not long after I visited, there was a disaster, but not another animal one, like foot and mouth, which he had been dreading.

In November 2009, Cumbria was devastated by the worst floods for a thousand years and the little town of Cockermouth suffered some of the worst damage, with flood water up to eight feet deep along the main street, which happens to be called Main Street, much to the confusion of the TV reporters when they first landed, most of them not knowing where they were.

The sheep centre, being just outside the town, well away from the river, immediately became a place of refuge. Around a hundred people, including some of their own staff, who had been rescued by the police, fire, ambulance and other services, many from the roofs of their homes by helicopters, found themselves camping there. Good job it was there, a modern, warm, spacious structure, just minutes from the devastated town. Mattresses were laid out in what was normally the souvenir shop while the theatre next door, where the sheep show was staged, was filled with clothes. From all over the country, and abroad, people had sent clothes, many of them brand-new, to help the flood victims. People slept and lived in the sheep centre for up to six days before they were found other accommodation. For most of them, it will be up to a year before they can return to their normal homes.

Roy decided not to reopen the sheep show in the spring, as he had been doing for all those years. This decision was not connected with the floods, though of course attendance would have been badly affected, with so many bridges down, and roads still closed. His planning permission had come through. In 2010 work was due to begin on converting the sheep centre into hotel bedrooms. So that chapter has now to be read as a record, an account of what once was an unusual and fascinating live museum. You never know, someone might attempt a similar venture once they read about it. Anyway, please don't go there hoping to see sheep on a stage — only if you want a bed for the night.

Let's hope all of my other museums survive, at least for a good many more years. I know Cockermouth well because for the last twenty-four years we have spent half of each year at Loweswater, seven miles away. There was flooding there as well and our house was left isolated, an island in a sea of flood water, but as we are on a slight hillock we were not directly affected. But our next-door neighbours got flooded out. As I write, they are living in our house. It will take up to six months before their house is habitable again.

Because I know Cockermouth so well, it suddenly came to me during my journey that that would be the perfect place to have my own little museum. I had realised by then that museums could be anything — big and important and purpose-built or small and situated in the bedroom of your council house. Most of all, they can be anywhere. Cockermouth already has many antique and second-hand shops, book places and galleries. Premises are quite cheap, compared with London. And then what seemed to clinch it was telling my brother about my plan. Instead of saying how daft, how stupid, how can you contemplate such a thing when you live half of each year in London? He said great, I'll run it for you.

He lives in Carlisle, his own family is grown up, and he has recently retired. A little toddle out to Cockermouth each day would quite suit him. "I've always fancied being a museum curator." Which was news to me.

In my mind's eye, I saw all my collections being given their own little space and display, perhaps even their own room, if I could find a place big enough. It would go against one of the principles of my Mad Museums, which is a museum devoted to just one topic, but it would be the collections of just one person, like a workingman's version of the wonderful Sir John Soane's Museum.

But would people come? Cockermouth, for all its attractions, is not a tourist-trap town, like Keswick or Grasmere, or anything like the size of Bath or Edinburgh, which are museum magnets.

When local people or the odd passing tourist had visited my museum once, why would they want to come back? What's so special about my stuff anyway? Would the world and his wife really want to trail to Cockermouth to see my suffragette postcards, my used tax discs, wartime ration books, lottery tickets, old newspapers, ancient children's books. I say I have twenty or so different collections, at least, which is true, but if pressed, I have to admit there are only two areas where my stuff is better than half-decent.

Then I thought — why do I want to do this anyway? What are my reasons? I don't fit any of the types or patterns I have listed. It wouldn't be for commercial reasons, as a crusade, or an escape from some tragedy.

I would be doing it partly for vanity, showing off, which would surely rebound when people saw how pathetic most of my stuff is.

On the other hand, why can't ordinary collectors have their chance in the sun? I had already been thinking, lying awake at night, that when I came to do the marketing and publicity, I would stress the ordinary, Mr Pooterish nature of my treasures.

There is in fact nothing wrong with vanity, not when it comes to creating a museum. It is always an important element. You have to believe that your stuff, which you have personally collected, is worthy of display, because after all you have spent such time and thought and energy acquiring it.

More than vanity, was it also an attempt at immortality? Possibly, but then isn't that the nature of all museums, all collections? You collect in order to conserve, protect, and you hope that what you have gathered will be kept together, proof of who you were, your legacy to posterity. Collecting is the ultimate vanity, believing you can instil order, create something that will last for ever.

I know in my case this is pure foolish fantasy. When I pop it, the first thing my wife will say is "Off to the skip." Neither she nor any of my children has any interest in my treasures, so they will dump any stuff still left in my room, get rid of it however they can.

Multimillionaires with proper collections are of course different and their treasures are desired. When they donate items to our famous galleries and museums, they are very keen to have them displayed in the Joe Bloggs Wing or the Joe Bloggs Gallery — not for themselves, they say, but it will please Mrs Joe Bloggs and all the little Bloggses to come.

Opening my own little museum would be a form of vanity, ensuring my stuff got its own little show, but most of all it would have to be fun. That would really be my main and only real motivation.

As I lay awake, planning the opening, I began to try to analyse where the fun would actually be. After the first few months, I would grow bored — I always do, after the first flush of most excitements.

I have so many other things in my life, such as work — oh yes, I hope I have a few more years turning out the old words. Then there's my lovely family, four grandchildren, and all that football to watch and, gawd, I almost forgot, this museum idea has come out of my collecting — but I want my collecting to go on, and on and on. I need as much time for that as possible. The hunt is the best fun for me, not the displaying. In fact, in my own house I have drawers full of stuff I haven't looked at since I bought it.

So, after about a week turning it all over, I decided I was being mad, self-deluded, potty. I had allowed my brother Johnny to get quite keen, which I should not have done. When I told him I had changed my mind, he was a bit disappointed.

In thinking seriously about what I might have to show, it's really only my Beatles stuff that is of any interest, plus a bit of the football stuff. And many years ago, I had already made plans for my best Beatles stuff.

This consists of ten or so original lyrics of some of their songs, written by Paul and John. When I was doing their biography all those years ago, I would be sitting in Abbey Road at the end of the evening session and see scraps of paper lying around, on which they had drafted their songs. They were being left for the cleaners to burn. Now and again, if I wanted to use the exact words in a chapter I was doing, I would ask if I could have them. They said yes, of course, take them. They had recorded the song. Why would they want to keep these scraps of paper?

I shoved them in a drawer at home for about ten years, when suddenly places like Sotheby's started selling Beatles memorabilia. I woke up one day in 1978 and realised that the ten scraps I had were worth more than my house. I offered them to the British Museum, and in turn they went into the manuscript room of the British Library when it opened. They are classified as being on permanent loan, as I was never quite sure what I might eventually do with them. Not put them in my own museum is the answer, which is why I have now written my will, leaving them to the British Library.

When I heard in the spring of 2010 that the Abbey Road studios, where the Beatles used to perform, might be taken over by the National Trust and part of it at least become a museum open to the public, I offered them the rest of my Beatles memorabilia. The National Trust said they would love it — if and when it ever comes to pass. Let's hope it does.

In the last few weeks I have also decided to offer something to the National Football Museum when it reopens. My football stuff is hardly unique, though I like to think I have got most of the classic books on football, dating back to the 1890s — and so has the football museum. But I have one book they don't have and might want, a modern one, a monster book, about the size of a small car, which is called the *Manchester United Opus*, signed by Sir Alex Ferguson and Sir Bobby Charlton.

So while I won't have my own museum, which was a really silly idea, I am going to have the quiet pleasure of knowing that two national museums — perhaps three — will have some of my stuff. My name will not be on them, and I won't even care if they shove things away in a storage room. I'll be *in* a museum, without all the faff of actually *having* a museum. I can die happy.

Hunter Davies, March 2010

Also available in ISIS Large Print:

Blood, Iron & Gold

Christian Wolmar

Blood, Iron and Gold reveals the huge impact of the railways as they spread rapidly across the world, linking cities that had hitherto been isolated, stimulating both economic growth and social change on an unprecedented scale.

From Panama to the Punjab, Christian Wolmar describes the vision and determination of the pioneers who developed railways that would one day span continents, as well as the labour of the navvies who built this global network.

Wolmar shows how cultures were enriched — and destroyed — by the unrelenting construction and how they had a vital role in civil conflict, as well as in two world wars. Indeed, the global expansion of the railways was key to the spread of modernity and the making of the modern world.

ISBN 978-0-7531-5249-2 (hb)
ISBN 978-0-7531-5250-8 (pb)

Out With Romany Again

G. Bramwell Evens

"Tired of holding back the weight of the vardo, or possibly indignant of my lack of appreciation of all her caution, Comma tossed her head and broke into a trot. The brakes squealed, the pots and pans rattled and bounced on to the floor behind me, and Raq in the neighbouring field set up a howl of mingled astonishment and fear, as he saw the vardo rapidly vanishing from sight."

Romany returns to Fletcher's farm in his caravan with spaniel Raq in tow. Once again he and Tim, the farmer's son, will venture out into the countryside to discover new friends such as Sleek, the Otter, Billy the Squirrel and Humphry the Mole. Through fictional tales told about these animals, and many more, learn the facts and real-life habits of some of Britain's best loved wildlife.

ISBN 978-0-7531-5253-9 (hb)
ISBN 978-0-7531-5254-6 (pb)

Journey to the Edge of the World

Billy Connolly

From the Atlantic to the Pacific via the fabled Northwest Passage; with idiosyncratic humour, Billy Connolly searches for the beauty of ordinariness and bumps into all manner of weird and wonderful people along the way, from the fiddle-playing scarecrow-maker to the septuagenarian pioneer who still lives as her ancestors did. He learns how not to be intimate with bears and how to pan for gold. He herds cattle, attempts the finer complexities of the Inuit language, jams with fellow musicians and kisses a cod.

At this pivotal moment in history when this once isolated wilderness is about to be invaded by hordes of modern-day speculators, the inimitable Billy retraces the steps of romantics and nutters, the broken-hearted, those looking for love or just hoping to get rich. He leads us through this land's incredible past and shares his optimism about its future.

ISBN 978-0-7531-5695-7 (hb)
ISBN 978-0-7531-5696-4 (pb)

The Lost Village

Richard Askwith

The idea of the unspoilt and unchanging village is one of the most potent in the English imagination. We have waxed lyrical on the theme for centuries, while tens of thousands now leave the city each year in search of the rural idyll.

Yet the English village is plainly dying. The unaltered rhythms of village life, as experienced with little variation by generations past, have all but vanished. But not without a trace . . . they exist in living memory, in the voices of men and women for whom the old ways were life-shaping realities.

Richard Askwith describes a journey in search of the true country dwellers. He captures the voices of poachers and gamekeepers, farmers and huntsmen, publicans and clergymen, thatchers and blacksmiths, and demonstrates that, while the landscape is more changed than we thought, the past is never so simple as we imagine.

ISBN 978-0-7531-5685-8 (hb)
ISBN 978-0-7531-5686-5 (pb)